About the authors

Julie Flint is a journalist and film-maker. She divides her time between London and the Middle East. She has worked in countries ranging from Colombia to China and has won several awards. She has been writing about Sudan since 1992, initially as Horn of Africa correspondent for the *Guardian* and later as a freelance jounalist with a special interest in human rights. Her work includes the BBC film *Sudan's Secret War* (1995), *The Scorched Earth* (2000) and *Darfur Destroyed* (2004).

Alex de Waal is a programme director at the Social Science Research Council, a fellow of the Harvard Humanitarian Initiative and a director of Justice Africa. His books include *Famine that Kills: Darfur, Sudan* (1989), *Famine Crimes: Politics and the Disaster Relief Industry in Africa* (1997), *Islamism and Its Enemies in the Horn of Africa* (2004) and *AIDS and Power: Why There is No Political Crisis – Yet* (2006).

African Arguments

African Arguments is a series of short books about Africa today. Aimed at the growing number of students and general readers who want to know more about the continent, these books highlight many of the longer-term strategic as well as immediate political issues confronting the African continent. They get to the heart of why Africa is the way it is and how it is changing. The books are scholarly but engaged, substantive as well as topical.

Series editors

Titles already published

Julie Flint and Alex de Waal, *Darfur: A Short History of a Long War*
Tim Allen, *Trial Justice: The International Criminal Court and the Lord's Resistance Army*
Alex de Waal, *AIDS and Power: Why There is No Political Crisis – Yet*
Raymond W. Copson, *The United States in Africa: Bush Policy and Beyond*
Chris Alden, *China in Africa*
Tom Porteous, *Britain in Africa*

Forthcoming

Jonathan Glennie, *Aid and Africa: Getting it Right*
Peter Uvin, *Life after Violence: A People's Story of Burundi*

Published by Zed Books and the IAI with the support of the following organizations:

InterAfrica Group The InterAfrica Group is the regional centre for dialogue on issues of development, democracy, conflict resolution and humanitarianism in the Horn of Africa. It was founded in 1988 and is based in Addis Ababa, with programmes supporting democracy in Ethiopia and partnership with the African Union and IGAD. <www.sas.upenn.edu/African_Studies/ Hornet/menu_Intr_Afr.html>

International African Institute The International African Institute's principal aim is to promote scholarly understanding of Africa, notably its changing societies, cultures and languages. Founded in 1926 and based in London, it supports a range of seminars and publications including the journal *Africa*. <www.internationalafricaninstitute.org>

Justice Africa Justice Africa initiates and supports African civil society activities in support of peace, justice and democracy in Africa. Founded in 1999, it has a range of activities relating to peace in the Horn of Africa, HIV/AIDS and democracy, and the African Union. <www.justiceafrica.org>

Royal African Society Now more than a hundred years old, the Royal African Society today is Britain's leading organization promoting Africa's cause. Through its journal, *African Affairs*, and by organizing meetings, discussions and other activities, the society strengthens links between Africa and Britain and encourages understanding of Africa and its relations with the rest of the world. <www.royalafricansociety.org>

Social Science Research Council The Social Science Research Council brings much-needed expert knowledge to public issues. Founded in 1923 and based in New York, it brings together researchers, practitioners and policymakers in every continent. <www.ssrc.org>

JULIE FLINT & ALEX DE WAAL

Darfur: a new history of a long war

revised and updated edition

Zed Books
LONDON | NEW YORK

in association with

International African Institute
Royal African Society
Social Science Research Council

Darfur: a new history of a long war was first published in association
with the International African Institute, the Royal African Society
and the Social Science Research Council in 2008 by Zed Books Ltd,
7 Cynthia Street, London N1 9JF, UK and Room 400, 175 Fifth Avenue,
New York, NY 10010, USA

www.zedbooks.co.uk
www.internationalafricaninstitute.org
www.royalafricansociety.org
www.ssrc.org

Cover designed by Rogue Four Design
Set in OurType Arnhem and Futura Bold by Ewan Smith, London
index: <ed.emery@thefreeuniversity.net>
Printed and bound in the United States by RR Donnelley,
Harrisonburg, VA and in Malta by Gutenberg Ltd.

Distributed in the USA exclusively by Palgrave Macmillan, a division
of St Martin's Press, LLC, 175 Fifth Avenue, New York, NY 10010.

A catalogue record for this book is available from the British Library
US CIP data are available from the Library of Congress

ISBN 978 1 84277 949 1 hb
ISBN 978 1 84277 950 7 pb

Contents

Acknowledgements

This book was possible because of the extensive co-operation and sharing of insights by a large number of people from Darfur and elsewhere in Sudan. Many of these must remain unnamed, at least for now. We extend special gratitude to many individuals in all parts of Darfur who extended hospitality despite their own hardships.

Hafiz Ismail and Sid Ahmed Bilal translated documents and interviews. Airserv provided many kindnesses in Chad. Phil Cox, Olivier Jobard and Jérôme Tubiana graciously let us use some of their photographs. Lars Bromley made superb maps.

The first edition of this book was funded by a grant from the Ford Foundation to Justice Africa. The second edition benefited from support from the UK Department for International Development, IDEA and several NGOs, all with long traditions of standing in solidarity with suffering people, which prefer to remain anonymous. Their assistance is gratefully acknowledged.

Preface to the second edition

This is a new history of Darfur's war. Since the publication of the 2005 edition of this book, the war has been continuous, and we recount three additional years of conflict, suffering and attempts to bring peace. This new edition is also an expanded history of the origins of the war, and we have revised chapters 3, 4 and 5 to include fresh perspectives and important new detail about how the war was fought during the years of fire and carnage of 2003–04. New information comes from original research, including investigations by the authors on both sides of the battle lines in 2007, and personal engagement in key episodes including the Abuja peace negotiations, efforts to press the rebels towards unity, and activism in support of human rights.

Many aspects of Darfur's crisis were only summarily dealt with in the first edition. Some of those gaps have been remedied. Among them are a greater examination of the plight of the Arabs, whose war-affected civilians are the forgotten victims of the conflict; a fuller account of the conduct of the rebels, especially the forces of Minni Minawi; and more detail on the SPLA's role in the early stages of the war. Much has happened in the years since the first edition was completed. The rebel groups have disintegrated. Darfur's Arabs have begun to assert their independence from the government. A peace agreement was born, and died, in Abuja. The African Union Mission in Sudan failed to fulfil the hopes invested in it and a sustained activist campaign has brought a 'protection force' of UN troops to Darfur in place of AMIS. Each of these developments is examined in this second edition.

Many people, episodes and even words in the recent history of Darfur are controversial. The roles played by many of the protagonists of the current crisis – men such as Abdel Wahid al

Nur, Minni Minawi, Khalil Ibrahim and Ali Osman Taha – are fiercely debated. Others, such as Musa Hilal and Majzoub al Khalifa, have been widely condemned for the roles they played. We explore more deeply their motivations and actions. We have listened to civilians, fighters, politicians and supporters of all the warring parties and where possible we quote them directly, allowing the reader to judge them from their own words. Episodes such as the attack on al Fasher airport, the attempts to unify the Sudan Liberation Army and the conclusion of the Abuja peace talks are also debated, often acrimoniously. We present the facts as we know them, after extensive research. Words such as 'genocide' and 'Janjawiid' are fiercely contested too, and again we provide the evidence that we have and draw our own conclusions.

Responses to the first edition ranged from admiration to condemnation. There is some consolation in the fact that the criticism came from both sides of the conflict, suggesting, we hope, that we achieved a balance of sorts. The most outspoken critics included the Sudan government and some Arab leaders in Darfur. Nafie Ali Nafie, Assistant President, complained of being identified as the mastermind of evil. ('Evil' is not a word we use. It implies absolute knowledge, but explains nothing.) In November 2007, a number of prominent Darfurian Arabs who felt that they had been misrepresented in the first edition – collectively and individually – called a meeting in Khartoum to complain. One of the main points they made was that the word 'Janjawiid' has demonized all Arabs and, since it has no agreed definition, is meaningless. Another point was that the Arabs of Darfur are also victims of violence, but have been overlooked in the near-exclusive focus on non-Arabs. We have always acknowledged this and examine the issue in more detail in this edition. But one basic fact remains: non-Arabs have been killed in their hundreds of thousands and driven from their homes in millions; Arabs have not been.

On the rebel side, the most critical was Minni Minawi, some of whose associates accused us of being hostile to the Zaghawa as a tribe. But the most despairing critics of Minawi we encountered were themselves Zaghawa. They, more than anyone else, know that Minawi has cast a dark shadow over the extraordinary accomplishments of their tribe, transformed in a little more than a generation from camel nomads on the fringes of the Saharan desert to a dynamic trans-national community that includes some of the most eminent businessmen, scientists and scholars in Sudan. We quoted one young Zaghawa graduate with the rebels as saying: 'Be careful, the SLA does not like criticism.' It does not indeed.

Abdel Wahid and his supporters have been critical of our position on the Darfur Peace Agreement. That position – echoing Alija Izetbegovic after Dayton – was and remains that a peace that is not completely just is better than a continuation of war. Had the DPA brought all the armed movements into Sudan's Government of National Unity, there might have been a chance of addressing the root causes of Darfur's war and bringing democratic government to all of Sudan – by challenging the National Congress Party politically, at elections in 2009. But the DPA failed and its failure warrants proper scrutiny, which we try to give.

With the exception of those who work in relief, no one involved in Darfur – Sudanese or international, politician, peacemaker, peacekeeper or activist – can claim much success for what has transpired since the outbreak of the war. There are no prizes for Darfur. What we try to do is to examine what has happened so that we can do better in future. Abdel Wahid himself told each of the authors separately, as the rebels splintered and fought each other and an agreement slipped out of reach, that 'If I had known what would happen, I would not have started this revolution.'

Darfur has been the focus of an extraordinary activist campaign. Perhaps inevitably, much complexity and fact are lost in high-profile celebrity messages and a sudden rush of 'experts'. In this book, we try to give voice to those, Sudanese and international, who have grappled with the complicated realities in Darfur, bringing real help to the victims of war and seeking practical solutions to the crisis. Their considered views from the front line of suffering have often been drowned out by high-decibel activism. No objective account of Darfur's crisis can avoid critical scrutiny of the role of the activist movement.

The first edition of this book was completed at a time of modest optimism for Darfur, inasmuch as there can be any hope in such wreckage. A Government of National Unity had been inaugurated with John Garang, chairman of the SPLM, as first vice-president. Khartoum and rebels had just signed a 'Declaration of Principles', which aroused the first, faint hopes at the Darfur peace talks in Abuja, Nigeria. Violence in Darfur itself was markedly down in the first half of 2005, and the humanitarian operation was making good progress.

Three years later, the prospects are much bleaker. Opportunities for peace existed but were not seized. Chapter 8 explores the many reasons why this was so. Without a political agreement between the government and what, just two years ago, were only three rebel factions, the possibilities of real peace and security in Darfur are remote. The chances of peace and democracy in Sudan as a whole are also fading, and it is becoming ever more likely that South Sudan will secede in 2011.

The centre of gravity of Sudanese politics remains the question of national unity – a North–South axis that was eclipsed by Darfur in 2004 but that was back at centre-stage within Sudan by 2007. This question, and the closely related question of elections, will dominate Sudan's political life for the foreseeable future. The prospects for an amicable settlement of these issues are not good, making it improbable that there can be a political settlement in Darfur either. The 2005 edition ended sombrely, with the words of a Darfurian elder lamenting the destruction of everything he had known. Our ending today is the same, but with darker prospects for restoring what has been lost.

Julie Flint and Alex de Waal, London, February 2008

Sudan

Darfur

1 | The people of Darfur

Northern Darfur is a forbidding place. It has landscapes of elemental simplicity: vast sandy plains, jutting mountains and jagged ridges, and occasional ribbons of green along the all-too-rare seasonal watercourses. A village, sometimes comprising no more than a cluster of huts made from straw and branches, may be a day's ride from its neighbour. Every place, however humble, counts. A hand-dug well in a dry river bed can be the difference between life and death for a camel herd trekking from the valleys of central Darfur to the desert-edge pastures.

Darfur's people are resourceful and resilient. Extracting a living from this land requires unrelenting hard work and detailed knowledge of every crevice from which food or livelihood can be scratched. A woman living on the desert edge will know how to gather a dozen varieties of wild grasses and berries to supplement a meagre diet of cultivated millet and vegetables, along with goat's or camel's milk. She will know the farms and village markets within a hundred miles or more, and will not hesitate to walk or ride such distances to buy, sell or work.

Nomads move three hundred miles or more twice a year, ranging even further in exceptionally wet or unusually dry years. 'Settled' people move also, migrating to open up new areas of farmland. In the dry sandy areas of eastern Darfur especially, villages grow and die along with their water supplies and the fertility of their soils; in the far south, along the forest edge, the frontier of cultivation creeps southwards every year. Mobility and distance make it difficult to maintain authority: those in power must always contemplate their subjects' option of simply moving beyond reach.

In the centre of Darfur, the extinct volcano of Jebel Marra rises 8,000 feet above the surrounding savanna. The green mountain can be climbed in a day, an arduous trek through orchards, terraced fields and pastures that reach nearly to the lip of the crater. There are wonderful myths about the fertility of the soils on the crater floor and the monstrous creatures that live in the deep waters of the crater lakes. Jebel Marra is the greenest mountain of Sahelian Africa, the only major watershed between the Ethiopian escarpment and the headwaters of the Niger close to the Atlantic Ocean. For many Darfurians this mountain possesses an almost mythical quality. It was when the Fur suspected a government plan to turn Jebel Marra over to the Arabs that Darfur's rebellion reached its point of no return, and the mountain became the rebels' sanctuary and first headquarters.

Yet the historic centre of Darfur is not the highest peak, which lies at the southern end of the massif, but the drier, broken mountains further north. Five centuries ago, in the mountainous triangle between Kutum, Kebkabiya and Korma, centralized states were created. The first was the Tunjur empire, named for a people who still inhabit the region, and whose rulers' castles still stand abandoned on hilltops, ringed by long-dry terraces. Tunjur origins remain an enigma: closely related in myth and language to the Fur, their history and ethnography has yet to be fully written. The successor to their empire was the Fur sultanate, the first Muslim state in Darfur, which emerged in the middle of the seventeenth century. The region takes its name from the homeland (*dar*) of the Fur.

By 1800, the Fur sultanate was the most powerful state within the borders of modern-day Sudan. In adopting Islam as the official state religion, the Fur sultans also embraced Arabic as a language of religious faith, scholarship and jurisprudence. Both Arabic and Fur were spoken at court. Darfurians – like most Africans – were comfortable with multiple identities. Dar Fur was an African kingdom that embraced Arabs as valued equals.

Dor village

The village of Dor lies north of Kutum, amid lumpy granite hills. It is drier and poorer than most parts of Darfur, but typical in the complicated allegiances of its people. In the middle of the eighteenth century, Dor was governed by a land grant from the ruler of Dar Fur, Sultan Mohamed Teyrab. Throughout this part of Darfur, even today, the chiefly families possess land titles in the form of documents, written on thick paper with a huge seal or stamp the size of a camel's hoof. This document is a *hakura*, or land grant. The term refers both to the grant and to the land itself.[1]

The *hakura* of Dor is known as Dar Sueini. Many inhabitants refer to themselves as 'Koraberi', which means 'Fur-Zaghawa' in both those languages. Most of the inhabitants of Dor speak three languages: Fur, Zaghawa and Arabic, the lingua franca of Darfur.[2] The Fur are the largest group in Darfur and Dor lies at their northern extremity; the Zaghawa are a Saharan people, whose homeland lies on the Sudan–Chad border at the edge of the desert. In the millennium-long dessication of the Sahara, the Zaghawa have slowly moved southwards.

Like all Darfur villages, Dor is ethnically mixed. Thirty years ago the village was dominated by four ethnic groups: Zaghawa, Fur, Tunjur and Kaitinga – this last a Fur clan that migrated north and adoped Zaghawa as its language. Some argue that Fur and Tunjur are parts of the same ancient group, and that Kaitinga embraces both Fur and Zaghawa. How could a person's identity be pinned down? It depended on the context. For political allegiance, blood-money payment and marriage considerations, ancestry was most important. But that didn't stop almost half the marriages in Dor crossing ethnic lines. In the marketplace, what mattered most was which language was spoken. A smart merchant would learn as many dialects as possible to gain the confidence of his customers. When dealing with the district tax collector and magistrate, or using the wells to water your animals, what counted was where you lived. If a Fur or Tunjur villager accumulated a lot of animals and chose to move with them seasonally, he might well prefer to call himself 'Zaghawa' or even 'Arab', in line with his livelihood.[3]

A minority of Dor's residents were drawn from a host of

other ethnic groups: Seinga, Berti, Jawamaa and Masalit, plus two categories of Arabs: Jellaba and Rizeigat. The Jellaba were traders from the Nile. The Rizeigat of Dor were Darfur Bedouins, members of the powerful Mahamid section. It was an impressive but not untypical array of ethnic groups in one remote village.

Darfur is home to more than 6 million people. There is just one rainy season, lasting approximately from June to September, which brings occasional storms to the arid north and regular showers across the well-watered south. The best cultivation is in the central belt, especially where big seasonal rivers, or wadis, run down from Jebel Marra. But even in the semi-desert, there are hollows that collect rainwater where millet can be grown. There is a span of rural livelihoods, from the poorest farmers who have no livestock, through farmers with sheep, goats and maybe a cow or two (the majority), to purely nomadic herders. Camels do well in the dry north while cattle prefer the wetter south. There is a regular cycle of boom and bust in the livestock economy, as herders acquire and lose animals and rely less or more on cultivation. It was ever thus: the historical records are full of references to settled Arab villages, and Arab sheikhs were granted land for farming by the sultans as far back as records exist.

Dor lies close to one of just three all-season livestock routes[4] to the desert – known as *masars* – used by camel herders on their annual north–south migrations. Six hours' walk to the east is Wadi Fokhma, one of those rare seasonal watercourses that run northwards from Darfur's central plateau into the desert. Traditionally, the nomads spent the rains and the following three months, October to December, in the desert, grazing their camels on the pastures along Wadi Howar, the last seasonal watercourse before the desert, and further north, where the grasses known as *jizu* are so succulent that camels can go without water for more than thirty days. Until just a few years ago, this rich grazing land was shared among Darfur's camelmen: Arabs, Zaghawa and Meidob. In January, the herds moved south, spending the winter and dry season in the valleys south of Kutum or travelling into the well-watered districts of south-west Darfur, along the major migration routes that everyone shared.

The people of Dor pay bridewealth and blood money in livestock. With no banks, animals are the store of wealth. At this latitude, keeping a cow, a thirsty animal that needs lots of grass, is little more than a vanity; most of Dor's animals are sheep, goats and camels, the latter traditionally entrusted to Arabs and Zaghawa herders for the northern migration. Not forgetting the ubiquitous donkeys, essential for travel to market and carrying firewood and water.

A few days' travel north, along the seasonal watercourse that serves as the route to the autumn pastures, is Rahad – or Lake – Gineik, a vast reservoir, several metres deep in the rainy season, created by an earthen dam. In 1968, a fight began at Rahad Gineik between Zaghawa and Arab herders from the powerful Um Jalul clan of the Mahamid camel-herders.[5] It was provoked by an attempt by Um Jalul herders to disarm a Zaghawa, Mohamed Omar Diko, who was watering his camels. It continued for three days before government troops and the police finally intervened.

'There were many Arabs, but few Zaghawa,' Diko recalled more than forty years after the event. 'The Arabs were well-armed; the Zaghawa had sticks and spears and old guns.'

In 1969, a tribal conference presided over by the sultan of the Masalit and the paramount chief of the Mahamid, Sheikh Hilal Mohamed Abdalla, sentenced twelve Zaghawa and twelve Arabs to ten years' imprisonment each. Mohamed Omar Diko was one of the Zaghawa – even though he fled after he lost his weapon. Looking back almost half a century later, he harboured no grudge at this rough justice. 'There was equal treatment then,' he said. 'Not like now. But after the conference, we lived like snakes and mice. And we were the mice.' The Arabs saw it differently. From that time, they said, the Zaghawa harboured plans to dominate Darfur by acquiring education, money, land and guns.[6]

After the Rahad Gineik trouble, the Zaghawa, Kaitinga and Tunjur ended their practice of entrusting their camels to the Arabs. Zaghawa herders began taking care of the camels from Dor.

5

This showed a pattern which became more and more marked over the next generation: conflict divided groups along ethnic-ancestry lines. As the people of Dor say, 'Conflict defines origins.'[7] Was this because people instinctively clung to their ancestral tribes in times of insecurity? Or was it because, when disputes came to be settled and compensation paid, corporate lineage groups were responsible for paying blood money? The Gineik fight levered open a tribal divide.

Although the two sides at Gineik were Zaghawa and Rizeigat Arabs, the Rizeigat themselves were not united. There was a long-standing dispute between the Mahamid and Mahariya sections. In our analysis of the origins of the Janjawiid, we will examine how this conflict played out over three generations, stoking the fires of violent conflict.

A history of statehood and ethnicity

A host of ethnic groups or tribes – between forty and ninety depending on one's definition – have emerged from Darfur's history. Dar Fur was an independent state for three centuries until 1916. It was one of the most powerful kingdoms in a string of such states positioned on the southern edge of the Sahara desert, trading with the Mediterranean and raiding its southern neighbours. When Napoleon occupied Egypt in 1798, he exchanged letters with the sultan of Dar Fur, which at that time had a trade with Egypt five times the value of that with the kingdom of Sennar, Dar Fur's rival on the Nile. The sultan was wealthy – the greatest merchant in the kingdom – and in theory possessed absolute power. At its zenith in the nineteenth century, Dar Fur's towns were prosperous: a visiting merchant, Mohamed al Tunisi, compared Kebkabiya favourably with country towns in Egypt.

The Dar Fur state was centred in the northern mountains, just south of Dor. The ruling clan here was the Keira dynasty, which gradually expanded its domain southwards. As the state spread its authority, it absorbed farming communities which adopted the Fur language, converted to Islam, and came under the political and administrative suzerainty of the state. They 'became' Fur. During the eighteenth century, the system of *hakura* land grants was formalized and expanded. The *hakura* system is commonly described today as 'tribal land ownership', but this is a misnomer in two respects. First, the system was not directly 'tribal'. The *hakura*-holders were court appointees, entitled to collect dues from the people living in their domain. Often, the *hakura* head became a local potentate, building a base independent from the sultan, usually by collecting his kinsmen in the area. By these means the office became hereditary and the dominant group the tribe of the *hakura* chief. Hence the 'tribe' consolidated around the *hakura* as often as the other way around. In other cases, tribal groups controlled territorial domains regardless of the sovereign's writ: 'The *hakura* system preceded the sultans,' says Saeed Madibu, head of the southern Rizeigat. 'It is a tradition from the people.' Second, the rights of the *hakura* owner started off as feudal jurisdiction, and never became freehold title. These subtleties are of more than historical importance: they influenced the political strategies of the land-hungry at the turn of the twenty-first century and can help determine workable solutions for Darfur's crisis.

Only a minority of people within Dar Fur's dominions were, or became, Fur. There were also the Tunjur, Meidob and Zaghawa in the north, the Berti and Birgid in the east, the Masalit in the west and many other smaller groups – all today labelled as 'African' tribes. The Masalit are especially significant. For centuries their villages were in the political no-man's land between Dar Fur and the Wadai sultanate to the west, based in Abeche in today's Chad. Only in the late nineteenth century, as both these powerful states were plunged into crisis, was Dar Masalit able to emerge briefly as an independent polity.[8]

The Arab presence in Darfur dates from the fourteenth century. Darfur's original Arabs fall into two groups: scholars and traders who arrived from the east and the west – the Nile and Arabia, the Maghreb and West Africa – and Juhayna Bedouins who arrived from the north west over several centuries in search of grass and water. The Juhayna Arabs trace their lineage back to the Qoreish tribe of the Prophet Mohamed. Their numbers increased through marriage with Darfurians and through assimilation as indigenous groups claimed Arab descent – partly because adopting an Arab-Muslim identity was a means of protection against enslavement. South of Jebel Marra, the Arabs took to herding cattle – becoming known as Baggara, or cattle-people – while those in the north remained as Abbala, or camelmen. In the sparsely settled south, the Fur sultans recognized the authority of each of the four main Baggara chiefs – Ta'aisha, Beni Halba, Habbaniya and Rizeigat – and in time their administrative jurisdiction became recognized as a *hakura* or *dar* (tribal homeland). Their Abbala cousins, moving as nomads in the northern provinces, where all land was already allocated to others, occasionally received small estates, but had no jurisdiction over any sizeable territories. To this day, many Abbala Arabs explain their involvement in the current conflict in terms of this 250-year-old search for land, granted to the Baggara but denied to them. An Arab *omda* (administrative chief) from North Darfur explained, 'the system of *hakura* is old and outdated like the feudal system in Europe. The right to [Sudanese] citizenship guarantees a right to a place to live.'[9]

The Rizeigat are the largest and most powerful of the Arab tribes of Darfur. Most live in south-east Darfur, under the tribal authority of the Madibu family. The Rizeigat in northern Darfur and Chad trace the same lineage but have no enduring political connections. They have three sections – Mahariya, Mahamid and Eteifat – and close political connections with two other Arab tribes, Awlad Rashid and Ereigat. Their camels made them rich and influential: the northern Rizeigat were among Darfur's specialist export hauliers across the desert.

On its southern periphery, Dar Fur showed a different and more violent face. It was a slaving machine, hunting the forest peoples for slaves, both for its own domestic and agricultural economy and for export along the 'Forty Days' Road' to Egypt and beyond.

In the middle of the nineteenth century, Zubeir Rahma Pasha, the greatest of the Khartoum traders, marched north from the slaving domain he had carved out in Southern Sudan and encroached deep into Darfur's own slaving hinterlands. Well financed and organized, Zubeir decided to invade the sultanate itself. The Rizeigat of southern Darfur, recently centralized under Sheikh Musa Madibu, lay in his path. Correctly calculating that Zubeir would win, Madibu allowed him through. Zubeir succeeded in defeating Sultan Ibrahim Garad's army at Menawashei, south of al Fasher, but was then cheated out of his victory by the Khedive of Egypt, who summoned him to Cairo to discuss his triumph and kept him there. Darfur was annexed to the Ottoman Empire, Zubeir languished in Cairo, and his lieutenant Rabih Fadlalla cut loose with the freebooting remnants to begin a quarter-century of pillage across central Africa – a rampage that was ended only by his defeat by the French near Lake Chad in 1900.

Islam in Darfur

All Darfurians are Muslims, and the majority are followers either of the *Tijaniyya* Sufi sect, which originates in Morocco, or the *Ansar* of the Mahdi, or both. Islam was a state cult in imperial Dar Fur.

A particularly powerful Islamic influence came from West Africa: Mahdism. In the 1880s, Sudan was convulsed by a messianic revolution led by Mohamed Ahmed 'al Mahdi', the Expected One. The Mahdi was a holy man from Dongola on the Nile, a mystic and scholar who sought to bring about a new caliphate. Frustrated by the riverain sophisticates, the Mahdi turned to the west of Sudan. In Kordofan, he met Abdullahi Mohamed Torshein, a mendicant of West African ancestry known as 'al Ta'aishi' because his family had settled among the Ta'aisha Arabs of Darfur. Abdullahi recognized Mohamed Ahmed as the Mahdi, and in turn became his deputy and successor. The two jointly defeated the Turko-Egyptian regime and its mercenary generals (most famously, Charles Gordon) and established a Mahdist state at Omdurman, across the river from Khartoum. When the Mahdi died, Khalifa Abdullahi ruled Sudan for fifteen years as an efficient despot. His chief lieutenants and many of his Ansar foot-soldiers hailed from Darfur – especially from the Baggara, whom he moved en masse to Omdurman and the White Nile to bolster his power. But Khalifa Abdullahi's enforced Mahdism generated strong opposition from many Darfurians, especially the Fur and others loyal to the old sultanate.

Khalifa Abdullahi was defeated by Kitchener's Maxim guns on the plains of Kerari in 1898. One of his prisoners, a Fur of royal blood, Ali Dinar, escaped to Dar Fur and restored the sultanate, describing his homeland as 'a heap of ruins'. The decimated Arab tribes trickled back. While sultanic authority was quickly asserted in the central areas, the peripheries remained trouble-some throughout Ali Dinar's eighteen-year reign. In 1913–14, his attempts to consolidate his rule were set back by a serious drought and famine which gained the popular name *julu*, mean-ing 'wandering', with reference to people's desperate migrations in search of food.

The downfall of the sultanate came in the First World War when ambitious British officials set a trap for Ali Dinar. Desir-ous of military glory and 'forgotten in an imperial backwater, [Governor General] Wingate devised his own western front'.[10] Wingate fabricated intelligence that Ali Dinar was conspiring with the Ottomans, provoked him with military deployments on his frontier, and finally dispatched an expeditionary force which defeated the Fur armies outside al Fasher in May 1916. The fugitive sultan was hunted down and killed soon after, and in January 1917 Darfur was absorbed into the British Empire.

Thus ended four decades which, even by the sanguinary stand-ards of Sudanese and Sahelian history, stand out, in Sultan Ali's own words, as an age of 'turmoil and bloodshed'. It was a period of exceptional dislocation and hunger, forced migration and des-truction. The only authority that survived was that which was able to wield unremitting force. The forced displacement of that era leaves many land claims disputed to this day, notably from Arab groups (including the Mahamid) who were relocated to Omdurman or fled to Chad. Much is missing from the written and oral histories. The social historian Lidwien Kapteijns describes how one army marauding across western Darfur 'ate, drank, wore or stole' everything in its path.[11] One assumes that gender-based violence – rape – is absent from the record only because of the sensibilities of the (male) transmitters of oral archive.

Becoming Sudanese

Britain's only interest in Darfur was keeping order. It administered the province with absolute economy. The core of this was the 'Native Administration' system, by which chiefs administered their tribes on behalf of the government. Darfur's subtle ethnic politics and panoply of leaders needed considerable tidying up if a uniform hierarchy of chiefly authority were to be imposed. British administrators sought to re-create a mythical age of tribal purity that included an array of chiefly titles (*sultan*, *malik*, *dimangawi*, *magdum*, *shartai* and *fursha*, to name but the upper ranks) and a racial hierarchy in which Arabs were considered superior to non-Arabs. The doyen of these reactionary orientalists was Harold MacMichael, intelligence secretary for the imperial administration, whose 1922 book on the Arabs of Sudan both documented and legitimized a host of lineage claims.[12] British district officers tolerated the idiosyncrasies of local potentates provided that their abuses were not too egregious and they kept the peace. A new rank of *omda* or sub-district administrative chief (and magistrate and tax collector) was introduced. The title *nazir* was bestowed on Arab paramount chiefs – four in the south, two in the north,[13] but none on the Abbala Rizeigat, to their lasting chagrin. With each paramount chieftaincy came an associated *dar* or homeland. This shift in the jurisdiction over land to tribal authorities began to cement both the idea and the system of tribal land rights in Darfur. The Masalit sultan, who had acceded to Sudan by treaty in 1922, retained his title and many of his judicial and administrative privileges. Along with the nazir of the (southern) Rizeigat, Ibrahim Musa Madibu, Sultan Bahr al Din

11

Andoka of the Masalit was the most powerful tribal potentate in British-governed Darfur. The Fur were politically decapitated, their landowning class reduced to penury, and – perhaps their greatest frustration – their contribution to Sudanese civilization reduced to a footnote in official histories that focused on the Egypt–Khartoum–South Sudan axis of politics and identity.

Only in 1945 did the colonial governor begin to consider possibilities for development in Darfur.[14] The file, 'Economic Development, Darfur Province' in the Khartoum national archives, contains just five entries for the entire period 1917–50. Most bemoan the impossibility of doing anything except encouraging modest exports of cattle and gum. In 1935, Darfur had just one elementary school, one 'tribal' elementary school and two 'sub-grade' schools. This was worse than neglect: British policy was deliberately to restrict education to the sons of chiefs, so that their authority would not be challenged by better-schooled Sudanese administrators or merchants. In the health sector, things were no better. There was no maternity clinic before the 1940s, and at independence in 1956 Darfur had the lowest number of hospital beds of any Sudanese province – 0.57 per 1,000 population (the next lowest was Bahr el Ghazal in the south).[15] The railway reached Nyala during the rule of General Ibrahim Abboud (1958–64). The first metalled road outside a major town was begun in the late 1970s. It was heralded as the Nyala–Geneina highway, but its construction halted halfway, at Zalingei. When the first agro-economic studies were done in the 1960s, in preparation for two immense rural development schemes (the Western Savanna Development Corporation, based in Nyala, and the Jebel Marra Rural Development Project, based in Zalingei), the first researchers and planners found themselves in virgin developmental territory.

Villagers in central and eastern Sudan complained that their land was taken over by commercial farmers armed with land titles and tractors. But they at least had a modicum of development. In Darfur, so distant from any sizeable markets, there was no investment at all. Most Darfurians who participated in the national economy did so as migrant labourers, following the old pilgrimage route across Sudan to seek work in the irrigated farms along the Nile or the sorghum prairie farms of eastern Sudan. Darfur's main export was its livestock and the Arabs, who owned two-thirds of the province's cattle and camels, repeatedly complained that the local taxes they paid were not matched by commensurate spending on schools and clinics in their areas.

Over the three generations from 1917, the people of Darfur 'became Sudanese'. They assimilated, almost entirely peacefully and voluntarily, to a Sudanese political, economic and cultural entity based on the River Nile. An insight into how this process operated, deeply sympathetic to local people, is provided by Paul Doornbos, a Dutch anthropologist who lived in Foro Baranga on the Masalit–Chad border in the early 1980s.[16] Foro Baranga is a small town with a vast market that lies at the confluence of the three great watercourses that drain West Darfur: Wadi Azum, which originates in Jebel Marra; Wadi Kaja, which flows through Geneina; and Wadi Saleh, which crosses the district of the same name. For eight months of each year, the three wadis flow into Chad, where they become the Salamat River, finally emptying their waters into Lake Chad. Foro Baranga is green, fertile and wet, and is the southern terminus of the livestock migration route that begins at Rahad Gineik, more than 400 miles to the north.

Doornbos observed a process of cultural change that involved partial abandonment of Masalit culture, notably the independent status of women, tribal dancing, drinking *marissa* (millet beer), barter and traditional ways of dressing. All this was replaced by a new orthodoxy that included speaking Arabic, restricting the public role of women, using cash, dressing in the characteristic northern Sudanese manner, with *jellabiya* for men and *taub* for women, and shunning alcohol. Doornbos preferred to call this 'Sudanization' and not 'Arabization', for two reasons. First, the indigenous Arabs – both local Salamat and itinerant Rizeigat camelmen – were themselves changing their Bedouin culture to 'become Sudanese'. Second, the villagers did not aspire to

13

become part of international Arab culture, but rather to be re-garded as citizens of standing – and creditworthiness – by the dominant stratum of traders and officials. Doornbos identified several agents of 'Sudanization', including traders, administra-tors, schoolteachers and itinerant fundamentalist preachers. The pedantry of this sermonizing, and its hostility to the tolerant Sufism of Darfur's older religious order, is captured in the edict of the preacher who denounced as 'hypocrites' 'those who use a plastic toothbrush and toothpaste rather than the seven kinds of twig claimed to be sanctioned by Islam'. Another thundered against drinking and sundry other evils even as market-goers in tea shops turned up cassette-recorded music to drown him out. As so often, many conversions were short-lived. A well-known alcoholic stayed on the wagon for just three days, missing the companionship of his 'un-Sudanized' drinking companions too much. Poor farmers simply could not afford to cultivate without the hard labour of their wives in the fields. But the traders who had subsidized the preacher were content: those who had given up home-brewed *marissa* would now buy tea as well as expensive *jellabiyas* and *taubs*. The next day they raised the price of sugar to cover their outlay.

In Foro Baranga, thousands of Chadians mingled with Darfuri-ans. They too were a mixture – Baggara Arabs from the Salamat tribe, Daju, Bornu and others. Many were becoming Sudanese in their own way, by the mere fact of settling on vacant land on the edge of Fur and Masalit villages.

In the 1980s, the complaint of most Darfurians was not that the process of 'becoming Sudanese' denied them their own, unique cultural heritage, but that the government in Khartoum was not treating them as full citizens of the Sudanese state. Services in Darfur's towns and villages were scarcely better than in the days of the British. 'We are surviving here thanks to the grace of God and diesel engines,' the sheikh of Legediba, a remote village in South Darfur, said in 1986.[17] Diesel lorries brought Legediba food supplies and fuel for its water pump. The sheikh knew that as economic crisis deepened and the price of fuel rose, traders would leave this small weekly market off their lorry routes. Sugar, tea and matches would run out and diesel for the pump would have to be rationed – pushing villagers one step closer to the edge. Darfur was a backwater, a prisoner of geography.

2 | The Sudan government

Emerging from the mosque on a Friday in May 2000, the faithful were met by young men quietly distributing copies of an ordinary-looking A4 typescript, its pages photocopied and stapled together. In tightly censored Khartoum, this was already surprising. But the contents of *The Black Book*: *Imbalance of Power and Wealth in Sudan* were more than surprising: they were revolutionary. They gave a detailed breakdown of where political and economic power in Sudan lay and documented how the state apparatus had been dominated, ever since independence, by a small group from three tribes who live along the Nile north of Khartoum: the Ja'aliyiin of President Omar al Bashir, the Shaygiyya of Vice-president Ali Osman Mohamed Taha and the Danagla of Defence Minister Bakri Hassan Saleh. The book showed that all other regions of Sudan had been grossly marginalized. Not just the South, which had been fighting for decades for a better deal – or failing that, for the right to separate – but also Sudan's eastern and western regions.

In three days, 1,600 copies were distributed: 800 in Khartoum, 500 in other parts of Sudan (excepting the South) and 300 abroad. President Bashir and other top government officials reportedly found copies on their desks after prayers. The contents of the book were further spread by government newspapers, which denounced it on their front pages, reiterating government charges that the authors were 'tribalists'. Photocopies proliferated after the governor of Khartoum, Majzoub al Khalifa, ordered the security services to buy up every copy they could lay their hands on.

The *Black Book* was the work of a group calling itself 'The Seekers of Truth and Justice'. Their meticulous statistics proved what everyone knew but never articulated: that the vast majority of government positions in Khartoum, from cabinet ministers to their drivers and all the bureaucracy in between, were held by members of three tribes which represented only 5.4 per cent of Sudan's population. Demanding 'justice and equality', time and again, the *Black Book* showed that northerners were overwhelmingly dominant in the police and military hierarchy, the judiciary, provincial administrations, banks and developmental schemes. Every president had come from this region and most senior ministers and generals too. The *Black Book* echoed the criticism of Sudanese leftists, who had presented facts of their own: three-quarters of the nation's industry and two-thirds of its doctors were located in Khartoum; Sudanese businessmen traded in the provinces but invested their profits in the metropolis, and regional governors could secure their budgets only by relocating to Khartoum and pestering the ministry of finance day in and day out.[1]

The *Black Book* roundly criticized the National Islamic Front (NIF) government, which had seized power in a coup eleven years earlier. The NIF, the authors said, had 'demonstrated its inability to depart from established patterns of injustice, despite the slogans which it raised in its early days'. It had even portrayed jihad as a northern enterprise, disregarding the fact that the vast majority of martyrs were from Darfur and Kordofan. 'Examine with us the documentary films on Mujahidiin which are produced by the Popular Defence Forces and charity corporations,' they wrote. 'Look at the pictures and scrutinize the names. Wouldn't you be certain that all the Mujahidiin in the Sudan are from the Northern Region?'

Sudan's Islamic revolution

The *Black Book* was the obituary of the Islamic revolution of Hassan al Turabi and his acolyte-turned-arch-rival, Ali Osman Taha. Just a few months previously, Ali Osman had sided with President Bashir in a power struggle in the leadership, enabling Bashir to dismiss Turabi and impose a state of emergency. But criticizing Bashir's government did not imply supporting Turabi. The *Black Book* was compiled, in large part, by men who had joined the Islamic movement in their youth, convinced that political Islam offered a solution to Sudan's seemingly intractable political crises and failures of economic development. Just a decade earlier, the Muslim Brothers – the Islamists' vanguard – seemed to offer a new formula: they promised honesty, hard work and a commitment to equal rights for all Muslims. They also promised an end to the instability that had plagued parliamentary and military regimes alike, as contending parties and factions, all drawn from the same northern elite, bickered over who was to rule Sudan. The incessant turbulence within the ranks of the ruling establishment had resulted in a state that was too weak to provide services – including policing – to its far-flung provinces.

Taj al Din Bashir Nyam is one of many Darfurians who joined the Muslim Brothers as a student in the early 1980s. He supported their call for Islamic law but, more importantly, he felt the Islamists overrode ethnic, tribal and class divisions. He felt respected.[2] Darfurians were furious because President Jaafar Nimeiri had imposed on them, and only them, a governor not native to the region – a decision Nimeiri was forced to reverse after thousands of protesters took to the streets threatening 'a million martyrs or a new governor'. The decision convinced young men like Taj al Din that most northern politicians had a 'very bad image' of Darfur. He felt Turabi was different. 'Even though most educated people in Darfur don't go to the mosque, Turabi had a close relationship with the people, a kind of respect for them.'

The Muslim Brothers won many Darfur youths over by the intensity of their involvement with them and their seeming lack of corruption. Darfurians were no longer being treated like hicks from the sticks – with contempt. Taj al Din:

They sent people from Khartoum to speak to us, something other parties were not doing. Many of them were teachers. We found they were honest, very straightforward and with great morality. That was an important thing for us. They organized meetings once a week between people from the towns and the villages, people who had never met before. No one asked about your tribe. They said: 'Islam is our mother and father.' They organized football teams and debates, and gave us books to read. We would read them, and then pass them on. This was the opposite of what was happening at the time: everyone was taking everything for themselves. They gave us confidence and we were well-respected by the community.

Sudan's traditional parties depended, above all, on the rural aristocracy. The Communists focused on the more educated youth of the towns. But Islamist activists focused their recruitment on all youth, especially students, irrespective of their background. Their favourite targets were young men and women from rural areas who were bewildered and intimidated by the secular, impersonal culture they encountered on first arriving in the city. Just as the Mahdi had forged his Ansar movement from the ranks of devout if unsophisticated western Sudanese Muslims, so Turabi saw that his Islamist party needed the votes of Darfur and Kordofan if it was to win an election. 'Hassan al Turabi had a prescient vision of Darfur,' explained one of the most senior Islamists, now a presidential adviser, Ghazi Salah al Din Attabani. 'He learned from history. The Mahdi had faced the elite of northern Sudan who rejected and ridiculed Mahdism. So he turned to the west and stormed the Nile from Kordofan and Darfur.'[3]

Turabi's 'western strategy' meant that he needed to break with the Muslim Brothers' exclusive orientation towards the Arab world. Along with their Egyptian parent movement, Sudan's founding Islamists had instinctively equated Islamism with Arabism. In western Sudan, however, they found Muslims who were not Arab. Ali al Haj Mohamed was one. Born in a village near Nyala, from the Bornu tribe which originates in West Africa, Ali al Haj became an influential Muslim Brother. His presence among the leaders held out the promise that the Islamic movement would be colour-blind.

For a while, the hope seemed to be justified. In 1973, the

Islamists fielded a Fur activist as their candidate for the presidency of the Khartoum University Students' Union. Daud Yahya Bolad became the first KUSU leader who was not from the riverine elite. All previous KUSU presidents had followed an accelerated track to national political leadership, and it seemed as though Ali al Haj and Bolad together would win Darfur round to the Islamists.

Bolad's deputy and bodyguard was a medical student called Tayeb Ibrahim, nicknamed 'al Sikha' after the heavy iron rods with which he threatened opponents during demonstrations. After leaving university, Tayeb 'Sikha' rose while his former boss did not. Bolad had no patron, no family ties to the rich and influential. Embittered by how the insidious racial discrimination of the Sudanese elite worked against him, Bolad returned to Darfur and tried to enter local politics. He flirted with Nimeiri's single party, the Sudan Socialist Union, and accused the Muslim Brothers of racism, a charge that the more thoughtful of his peers concede. 'The majority of the Islamists are from the Nile,' Ghazi Salah al Din later reflected, explaining that treating non-Arab Muslims as equal 'is not ingrained in their thinking. It is just a casual way of doing business.'

As Bolad lost his way, Ali al Haj remained a linchpin of the Islamist movement, and later the regime. When the Darfur protests forced Nimeiri to hold an election for the governorship, Ali al Haj stood for election. He was soundly defeated by the secularist Ahmad Diraige, a Fur, in a ballot in which ideology mattered less than ethnic base. Diraige's base was large, Ali al Haj's narrow. An internal memorandum commissioned by the Islamists after the election described the Fur as pious but introverted, a weak base for the Islamic movement. Thirteen years later, when Ali al Haj was minister of federal affairs, he divided Darfur into three states, splitting the Fur constituency in hope of creating openings for Islamist candidates.

Daud Bolad, meanwhile, drifted further to the left. Former friends describe him as obsessive and driven, meticulously and energetically building up his political network. His frustrated ambition drew him to the Sudan People's Liberation Army (SPLA), which, under the leadership of John Garang, had been fighting for a 'New Sudan' since 1983. Although Garang's base was in the South, he was a strong advocate for national unity, arguing that the marginalized minorities of Sudan formed a majority, and so should be entitled to rule. Garang attracted a loyal following among some northern Sudanese. The most impressive of these was the Nuba leader Yousif Kuwa Mekki, under whose charismatic leadership thousands of Nuba from southern Kordofan flocked to the SPLA. Kuwa was more than a guerrilla; he was the leader of a cultural renaissance in which the Nuba asserted their 'Africanness' with new-found confidence. Bolad saw himself in the same mould. Garang, for his part, saw Bolad as the SPLA's opening to Darfur, another region with an oppressed and neglected 'African' majority. Other left-leaning Darfurian politicians, including Diraige, suspected that the SPLA would swallow them up, and kept their distance.

Letting Bolad slip away was not the only fateful decision the Khartoum Islamists made in this period. When they first formed a political party in 1964, the Sudanese Muslim Brothers resolved that theirs should be a wholly civilian movement. They had seen the débâcle that overtook their Egyptian brethren in the 1940s after their leader, Hassan al Banna, created a 'Special Branch' within the movement which carried out a series of assassinations. Not only did this arouse the wrath of the Egyptian security forces – which shot al Banna dead – but the Special Branch then hijacked the Muslim Brotherhood itself and ousted its civilian leaders.

Yet in the bloody aftermath of the 1969 coup that brought Colonel Nimeiri to power, Sudan's Islamists turned to violence. The Ansar led the way by establishing an armed stronghold at Abba Island on the Nile, and many Muslim Brothers joined them there. In March 1970, Nimeiri moved forcibly to crush the incipient uprising. Hundreds were killed in an air and ground assault, and the surviving leaders fled abroad and set up training camps in Libya. While Tayeb 'Sikha' was wielding his iron rod at university demonstrations, his comrades were undergoing military training in the Libyan desert. Their plan: an armed invasion of Sudan from bases in Libya, crossing Darfur and Kordofan to storm the capital. In July 1976, the Ansar–Islamist alliance very nearly succeeded, occupying much of Omdurman for several hours. Bona Malwal, the minister for information, rallied support for Nimeiri in a broadcast from Omdurman radio station. The army counterattacked, and the rebels were defeated.

Libya's Colonel Muammar Gaddafi had his own plans for the region. He dreamed of annexing Chad as a prelude to establishing a vast Sahelian empire and spoke of an 'Arab belt' or corridor into central Africa. He established an 'Islamic Legion' to serve as the vanguard of his military adventures, and recruited militiamen from Sahelian lands as far apart as Mauritania and Sudan. (His expansive definition of 'Arabs' included Tuaregs from Mali and Niger as well as Zaghawa and Bideyat from Darfur and Chad.) Gaddafi's rhetoric often far exceeded his capacity: his announcement of 'unity' between Libya and Chad in 1981 was not followed by practical actions to cement the merger. But his resounding statements and generosity with weaponry were enough to ignite new supremacist ambitions among the Bedouins of the Sahara.

Turabi, ever the opportunist, accepted Gaddafi's military assistance. He didn't trust Sudan's national army, with its tradition of secularism and hard drinking, and sought an Islamic counterweight. Numerous, devout and heir to a warrior tradition, the Ansar seemed the ideal foot-soldiers for his Islamic revolution.

Turabi was impressively flexible. For him the means always justified the end: an Islamic state. In 1977, after the failed invasion, he performed a volte-face and made peace with Nimeiri. Back in Khartoum, he infiltrated Islamist cadres into the armed forces, including elite units such as the air force. (One such cadre was Mukhtar Mohamadein, an air-force pilot who was the nominated leader for a coup, should it be necessary. In March 1989, the Islamists' coup plans were thrown into momentary confusion when Mohamadein was shot down and killed over

Nasir in Southern Sudan.) Tayeb 'Sikha', now a qualified physician, joined the medical corps. And, in what was possibly the most disastrous decision of the entire Sudanese civil war, the Islamists backed the 'militia strategy' – the use of tribal militias as frontline counter-insurgency forces. Instead of helping to forge unified institutions of central government, they continued the established practice of divide-and-rule, turning tribes into military formations.

Counter-insurgency on the cheap

The militia strategy was unleashed in July 1985, two months after the overthrow of Nimeiri. Alarmed at an SPLA incursion into Kordofan, and fearing that Garang would deliver on a threat to bring the war to the North, the transitional president, General Abdel Rahman Suwar al Dahab, an Islamist sympathizer, resolved to step up the war against the SPLA. He dispatched his minister of defence, General Fadlalla Burma Nasir, to Kordofan and Darfur to mobilize Arab tribes against the SPLA. The minister selected former army officers and Ansar commanders to lead Baggara militias, and provided them with arms and military support. In return the Baggara were promised a free hand to seize cattle and other possessions from Dinka and Nuba suspected of supporting the rebels. Known in official parlance as 'friendly forces' and locally as *Murahaliin* (nomads) or *Fursan* (horsemen), these militias became synonymous with atrocity. They sprang into the public eye in April 1987, when more than one thousand displaced Dinka were shot and burned to death in the town of al Da'ien in south-eastern Darfur in retaliation for a series of battles in which the SPLA killed 150 Rizeigat militiamen.[4]

In Bahr el Ghazal in 1986–88, the Nuba mountains in 1992–95, Upper Nile in 1998–2003, and elsewhere on just a slightly smaller scale, militias supported by military intelligence and aerial bombardment attacked with relentless brutality. Scorched earth, massacre, pillage and rape were the norm.[5]

Khartoum, meanwhile, did a deal with Tripoli: in return for weapons, the Sudan government turned a blind eye to Gaddafi using Darfur as a rear base for his wars in Chad. Thousands of Islamic Legion troops and Chadian Arabs crossed the desert to Darfur. Given the increasing local tensions, this sparked a conflagration in Darfur: an Arab–Fur war between 1987 and 1989 in which thousands were killed and hundreds of villages burned. An inter-tribal conference reached a peace deal in the same week that Omar al Bashir seized power. But Darfur's respite was short-lived. It soon became clear that Bashir was strengthening the alliance with Libya and had no intention of enforcing the peace agreement. Anger grew, compounded by official indifference to a major drought in 1990. The government's slogan 'We eat what we grow!' glossed over disasters: economic policies that were causing hyperinflation and panic buying of food stocks, and a foreign policy that was alienating the Arab world and the West, cutting off foreign aid.

Fur politicians such as Diraige had long predicted that Darfurians' patience would run out. Daud Bolad gambled that Darfur just needed the right leader to ignite a rebellion. In December 1991, a well-armed band of SPLA troops entered Darfur, with Bolad as its political commissar and Abdel Aziz Adam al Hilu, who was born in the Nuba Mountains but has a Masalit father, as its military commander. It was a fiasco. The force had to cross an expanse of territory inhabited by Baggara Arabs who controlled every water source. The SPLA presence was immediately noted and reported to the military governor, Doctor – and now Colonel – Tayeb Ibrahim 'Sikha'. Before Bolad and his force could reach Jebel Marra, a combined force of regular army and a Fursan militia drawn from the Beni Halba Arabs hunted them down and defeated them. The Beni Halba district town, Idd al Ghanam ('Wells of the Goats'), was renamed Idd al Fursan in honour of this victory. Dozens of Fur villages were burned in reprisal. Bolad was captured alive, along with a notebook that contained detailed records of every member of his underground cells. He was interrogated by his former comrades and never seen again; his network was quietly and ruthlessly dismantled. The attempted rebellion and final débâcle fired young activists who would burst into the limelight a decade later, but it politically neutralized Bolad's generation. The Darfurian resistance was set back by ten years.

In a note of contrition, the *Black Book* honours Daud Bolad as a 'martyr'. His political journey from the Muslim Brothers towards armed struggle for his people prefigured the same conversion by a later generation. In the late 1990s, disillusioned Darfurians began to abandon the Islamist movement in droves as the movement itself began to fragment. Beneath this power struggle was an ethnic-regional split: the chiefs of the Islamist security apparatus joined with the riverine military elite to create a cabal at the heart of the Sudanese state. There were no Darfurians in the inner circle.

Ali Osman Mohamed Taha, 'hero of Sudan'

By 2000, Ali Osman Mohamed Taha was the pivotal figure in the regime. This is a man whose career encapsulates the entire history of Sudanese Islamism. He was born in 1948, the year Sudan's Islamists set up their first clandestine cells in Khartoum University, and is a Shaygiyya, one of the three controlling riverine tribes. He is from a poor family – his father was a zoo keeper – but climbed to the top because of his talent, tribal connections and clarity of goals, plus patronage from Turabi. He was leader of the NIF's parliamentary delegation during the democratic government of Sadiq al Mahdi from 1986–89, but conspired to bring the government down when his agenda was blocked. For Musa Hilal, the strongest government-backed militia leader during the most terrible years of the Darfur war, Ali Osman was 'the hero of Sudan'.[6]

In order for the coup against Sadiq to succeed, it was essential for the putschists to obtain the support, or at least the acquiescence, of Egypt and Saudi Arabia. If Turabi and Ali Osman were seen to be involved, that would be impossible. So Bashir portrayed himself as a nationalist army officer and created a Revolutionary Command Council, the sine qua non of a non-sectarian coup since Gamal Abdel Nasser. The NIF was dissolved, and Turabi and Ali Osman were sent to prison along with other members of the deposed government and parliament. Egypt and Saudi Arabia were fooled, but their fellow detainees were not. In Cooper Prison, the formerly feuding MPs reviewed their errors, and their feuds, and formed the opposition National Democratic Alliance. Ali Osman and Turabi were shunned. While the prisoners played football – parliamentarians versus trade unionists, with Sadiq al Mahdi, a fit fifty-five-year-old, at centre forward – Turabi paced the touchline reading the Quran.

The pretence continued for months, even after the two Islamists were released into house arrest. The RCC met in daylight, considered its decrees and dispatched the relevant papers at nightfall to the private residences of Turabi and Ali Osman for scrutiny and strategizing. The charismatic Turabi was the sheikh: aloof from the details, organizing the grand sweep of strategy. The introverted Ali Osman was the chief executive, scrutinizing the implementation of policy. The plan was for these two to remain in the shadows until the new regime was consolidated.

Because of Turabi's ambitious impatience, the plan failed. In August 1990, Saddam Hussein invaded Kuwait. Turabi was no supporter of Saddam, but he saw this as the historic moment in which the Gulf monarchies would totter and Islamic revolution would sweep the Arab world. Brushing aside the more pragmatic policies of President Bashir, he declared for Saddam. In so doing, he not only revealed where real power lay, but opened the doors of Sudan to every militant in the Arab and Islamic worlds and condemned Sudan to a decade of isolation.

Turabi had revealed his pre-eminence in the regime, but still held no formal post in it. Ali Osman took the job of minister for social affairs. This was an interesting and surprisingly powerful position that revealed the regime's priorities. In the early 1990s, the Sudanese Islamists had embarked upon a project of social transformation even more ambitious than Nimeiri's leftist developmentalism. Under the rubric of the 'civilization project' (*al mashru' al hadhari*) and 'the comprehensive call to God' (*al da'awa al shamla*), Ali Osman set about a far-reaching project of creating a new Islamist constituency. Islamist cadres were dispatched to foment a new Islamist consciousness in every village. Islamist philanthropic agencies were mobilized to open schools and clinics, and to support the Popular Defence Forces, an Islamist militia set up by government decree. A raft of programmes aimed at building an Islamic republic was launched.[7]

In 1995, Ali Osman was promoted to foreign minister, tasked with picking up the pieces of an ambitious foreign policy that had backfired. Turabi's gamble on an Iraqi victory in August 1990 was the mother of all miscalculations. After America and its allies triumphed in Operation Desert Storm, and drove Saddam Hussein's invading army out of Kuwait, Sudan was shunned by Arab governments and embraced only by the militant fringe – most notoriously, by Osama bin Laden, who was welcomed in Khartoum after being stripped of his Saudi citizenship. Sudanese foreign policy accordingly turned towards its African neighbours, in hope of exporting its Islamist revolution there. At first, everything seemed to go Khartoum's way. The first opening, which scarcely registered on the international radar, was the overthrow of Hissène Habré in Chad. The endgame of the Chadian civil war began with an attempted coup against Habré in February 1990. One of the three putschists, and the only one who escaped, was Idriss Deby, a military commander expert in desert warfare. Deby regrouped his forces in Darfur, but was routed, for a second time, by Habré's forces attacking across the border. Libya rearmed Deby, Khartoum assisted him by remobilizing 1,200 Chadian Arab militiamen, and France, already well aware of Habré's unspeakable human rights record, decided to look the other way. In December, Deby counterattacked and swiftly occupied N'Djamena.

Khartoum had several motives in backing Deby. One was to cut off a potential source of support for insurrection in Darfur. During the Fur–Arab war of 1987–89, Fur militants had made contact with the SPLA and opened an office in N'Djamena, where Habré was presenting himself as the African victor over Libya's Arab territorial aggrandizement. A second was the opportunity presented to remove armed Chadians from Sudan – both those in Darfur, who were running wild, and fighters of the radical Arab

Conseil Démocratique Révolutionnaire (CDR), restive in a training camp near Khartoum. Third, Sudan now had a friendly and indebted government on its vulnerable western border. Khartoum expected Deby to share power with the CDR, and its Arab fighters to return to Chad and stay there. In the event, the Deby–CDR coalition was short-lived and the Arabs returned to Darfur, where their alliance with Khartoum endures to this day.

The other two regime changes that favoured Turabi's strategy were the fall of Siad Barre in Somalia in January 1991, which ushered in anarchy the Islamists could exploit, and the overthrow of Mengistu Haile Mariam in Ethiopia in May 1991. Guerrillas who had been extensively aided by Sudan in their long wars were now in power in Eritrea and Ethiopia – and they were favourably disposed towards Khartoum.

After this, Turabi and Ali Osman overreached. Their Popular Arab and Islamic Conference – a militant rival to the Arab League and Organization of the Islamic Conference – met several times, and the parallel Arab and Islamic Bureau sponsored a range of radical jihadist organizations across Africa. Having backed victorious rebel movements in 1990–91, they planned to repeat the exercise, only this time with ideological fellow-travellers. They aimed at regime changes from Cairo to Kampala, with the result that by 1994 they were engaged in wars of destabilization with Egypt, Eritrea, Ethiopia and Uganda.[8] In June 1995, Sudanese-backed militants ambushed Egyptian President Hosni Mubarak's limousine as it drove down an Addis Ababa boulevard to a summit meeting of the Organization of African Unity. The Egyptian leader had insisted that his special bullet-proof car be flown in for the fifteen-minute drive from airport to conference centre and escaped unharmed. But the shock waves of the assassination attempt reverberated throughout the region. Sudan was sanctioned at the UN Security Council, its support for international terrorism exposed to all. A dozen foreign militants were named, including Osama bin Laden. All were expelled over the following twelve months.

The line of responsibility for the assassination reached right into the heart of Khartoum's security cabal. Bashir was furious and summoned his lieutenants, including Ali Osman and the chief of external intelligence Nafie Ali Nafie, accusing them of running a state within a state. The division of power between Bashir and the NIF was based on an agreement that the president kept the government together while the civilians ran the executive. But a small, clandestine group including Ali Osman and Nafie had run training camps for international jihadists, hosted Osama bin Laden, and hatched a series of terrorist plots using off-budget security agencies accountable only to themselves. One of these agencies – known as *Amn al Ijabi*, or 'Constructive Security' – was using Islamic humanitarian agencies as cover for the militants' activities inside and outside the country. The jihadist security officers had not only violated their agreement with the president; they had endangered the very survival of the regime. Bashir called in a relative and confidant, Qutbi al Mahdi, to clean up the security services, but renewed the old survival pact. In return for pledges of loyalty, no Sudanese was thrown to the wolves. Ali Osman was retained as foreign minister until 1998, when he was promoted – to the post of vice-president.

Khartoum's foreign overreach was mirrored in the rise and fall of Turabi's and Ali Osman's plans for titanic social transformation. By the late 1990s, the Islamist project was imploding in military reversal, anger at the wastage of human life, and cynicism over the flagrant corruption of its leading cadres. But Turabi was undaunted. He succeeded in having his new constitution adopted in 1998 and became Speaker of the House. He formed a new single party, the National Congress Party (NCP). Apparently oblivious to the wreckage of his project, and ready to blame everyone except himself, he embarked upon a campaign of finally taking power for himself. By the end of 1999, it seemed that he had won every round and that President Bashir was what he had been a decade earlier – a figurehead. But Turabi miscalculated in two areas. As he had feared in the 1960s, the movement's security organs were loyal only to themselves. Also, his lieutenant and chief implementing officer, Ali Osman, had had enough of his recklessness. In December 1999, Bashir declared a state of emergency and stripped Turabi of all his power.

The Bashir–Turabi split lost Darfur for the government, but created the new dynamics that made peace in the South possible. Bashir and Ali Osman were much weakened by the split among the Islamists and needed allies. The option they chose was reaching out to the SPLA and seeking international respectability – not least, to attract investment and find a way of paying Sudan's $22 billion debt. In 2001, a serious peace process began at last, seeking a negotiated settlement to the civil war with the South. The first step was taken by the US, which changed policy in the first eight months of the Bush presidency to support the peace process run by the north-east African inter-state organization, the Inter-Governmental Authority on Development (IGAD). The plan was to revive this almost moribund process under Kenyan leadership, with substantial financial, technical and diplomatic support from western powers. Then fate intervened: no sooner had the framework been agreed than the attacks of September 11 – organized by some of Khartoum's one-time protégés – made Bashir fall into line with American proposals.

For eighteen long months, government and SPLA delegates met, argued and broke up. A month after a framework agreement was signed in the town of Machakos in July 2002, the SPLA overran two government garrisons in the South and the government broke off the talks while it mobilized for a counterattack. Militia attacks continued, especially in the oilfields, and the two sides backed different sides in the on-off civil war in the Central African Republic. Both talked peace while they waged war, but gradually did more of the former than the latter. The negotiations were lifted to a different plane after Ali Osman went to the Kenyan lakeside resort of Naivasha in September 2003 to talk directly with John Garang. The two men met in private, without even note-takers, and over fifteen months hammered out a meticulously detailed set of protocols and unwritten bargains whose contents they kept to themselves. Negotiations continued right up to the last minute before a final Comprehensive Peace

Agreement was initialled on New Year's Eve 2004. The signing ceremony in Nairobi on 9 January 2005 was disorganized, behind schedule and, because of Darfur, anticlimactic. Suspecting that Ali Osman had made a secret pact with Garang to marginalize him, President Bashir did not attend, clearly signalling that this peace deal was his deputy's, not his. Yet it was a historic moment. A generation of Southern Sudanese who had known nothing but war believed they had peace within their grasp at last. Bashir heralded it with a rare flash of humour, crying out at a rally, 'La illahi illa Allah – Halleluyah!'

The Comprehensive Peace Agreement provided for the sharing of power between the NCP and the SPLM for a period of six years, with a referendum on self-determination for the South to follow. John Garang was to be first vice-president, Ali Osman to be second. Posts in central and state governments were allocated according to complex formulae. Blue Nile and South Kordofan, the site of substantial SPLA insurrections along the North–South divide, were granted lesser regional autonomy. National elections were to be held by July 2009. Revenues from the oilfields in the South were to be divided equally between Khartoum and Southern Sudan. The national army was to withdraw almost wholly from the South and hand over to the SPLA. 'Joint integrated units' consisting of the Sudan armed forces and SPLA were to be formed for the national capital.

The Naivasha agreement was a remarkably good deal for South Sudan. It was an attractive deal for retaining unity, if implemented, yet had an opt-out clause. John Garang had every reason to be satisfied. But why did Ali Osman sign? The government was not defeated on the battlefield, and was gaining substantial revenue from oil – which it didn't have to share. Ali Osman told his party that Naivasha was the best chance for unity, and preserved the gains of the Islamic revolution: Shari'a law remained in the North, and the NCP kept a 52 per cent majority of seats in the National Assembly. President George W. Bush had signalled that when peace was achieved, the US would start to normalize relations with Sudan. There was even talk of a signing ceremony on the White House lawn. Ali Osman promised a feat of political escapism: a pariah regime would become an accepted member of the international community. The security cabal in government was sceptical, convinced that America would never honour its promises. But for the moment it stayed its hand.

Ali Osman did not count on the war in Darfur. Whatever legitimacy Khartoum was set to gain from the North–South peace deal was soon vitiated by the horrors it unleashed in Darfur.

3 | The Janjawiid

The nomad encampment lay in the middle of a stony, trackless waste, two hours' drive from the district town of Kutum. Broad black tents were spread among the few thorn trees and in the distance was the great sweep of Wadi Kutum, its pale red sand ringed by date palms and vegetable gardens. Visitors waited on a fine Persian carpet while the sheikh was informed. 'Actually he is Nazir,' a paramount chief, one of his retinue explained, 'but Sheikh Hilal insists that he is called just Sheikh. Sheikhdom is from God, but its degrees are man-made.'[1]

Even in his eighties, bedridden and almost blind, Sheikh Hilal Abdalla was a commanding figure. As the visitors entered his tent, he swung his tall frame upright and ordered his retainer to slaughter a sheep for dinner. He was courteous and imperious in equal measure. 'Who are you?' he demanded. 'You can't be British. All the British speak Quranic Arabic!' It was Hilal who controlled the discussion that followed, reminiscing about Guy Moore and Wilfred Thesiger, British colonial officers who spoke fluent Arabic, and praising Thesiger's skill in hunting lions – animals which had long since vanished from North Darfur. Then a servant served sweet tea on a silver platter while Hilal explained that the world was coming to an end.

Although settled in Aamo for more than a decade, Hilal kept to the old nomadic ways. Hung on the sides of his tent were only those things that could be packed on the back of a camel in an afternoon – water jars, saddles, spears, swords, an old Remington rifle, his silver tea-set and well-worn rugs. 'All the Um Jalul possess camels,' he said. 'You see that small boy?' He gestured at his grandson. 'Even he has camels!' He spoke about the traditions of mutual support among the Um Jalul, the subsection of the Mahamid which is the most traditional of Darfur's Rizeigat Arab nomads. During the famine which had devastated the region over the previous eighteen months, one of his nephews had donated more than a hundred camels to support hungry kinsmen. He himself had loaned many animals, from a herd that was shrinking faster than he knew. 'None of us will need to cultivate,' he said. 'None of us even need to collect wild foods like the Zaghawa. Camel nomadism is our way of life.'

Yet just an hour's walk away was a small encampment of destitute nomads whose animals were dead and who were scraping away at infertile, sandy soils in a desperate attempt to grow enough millet to support their families. They pointed bitterly at the distant wadi and its fertile alluvium. 'There's enough land here,' said one, 'but the Tunjur have registered every inch.' Their cooking pots were filled not with millet but with wild foods, especially the *mukheit* berries, bitter and scarcely palatable, that had been the staple diet of most Darfurians during the famine months.

The proud old sheikh refused to talk about his people's poverty. Instead he spoke darkly of how the cosmic order was changing. In the old days, the nomads had been welcome guests of the Fur and Tunjur farmers. He himself had travelled south every year to Kargula on the slopes of Jebel Marra, where the Fur senior chief, Shartai Ibrahim Diraige, would welcome him with a feast and the nomads would assist the farmers by buying their grain, taking their goods to market and grazing their camels on the stubble of the harvest. On leaving, the sheikh would present the *shartai* with two young camels. But now all this was changing: Fur farmers were barring the Arabs' migratory routes and forcing the camel-herders to range further south in search of pastures. The *masar* (livestock migration route) that began at Rahad Gineik now passed through Foro Baranga into the lawless domains of southern Chad and the Central African Republic.

Aamo was a *damra* – a settlement allocated to nomads within land under the jurisdiction of other tribes, in this case the Tunjur. In the far north, in Wadi Howar, the Rizeigat shared the pastures with other herders, the Zaghawa and Meidob. But this, too, was changing. The famous *jizu* desert pastures had bloomed that season – 1985 – for the first time in seven years. Hilal brooded on the ecological changes that were disturbing the region. But he would rather die than change. For him, the old ways were the only ways. Contemptuous of police procedures, he presided over swift customary justice at his tribal court in Aamo. He had no hesitation in tying a witness or a suspect to a tree in the midday sun, or smearing him with grease to attract biting insects, to extract a confession. Punishment – payment of blood money, or whipping – was immediate. But people from many different tribes, in Chad as well as Darfur, trekked to Aamo's court. There was no appeal, but the sheikh was famously just. The fame of his son Musa has spread even further: his name is first on a list of suspected genocidal criminals compiled by the US State Department.

Musa Hilal, a big sheikh

On 27 February 2004, hundreds of armed men mounted on camels and horses attacked the town of Tawila on the eastern slope of Jebel Marra. By the time the attack was over three days later, 75 people had been killed, 350 women and children abducted and more than 100 raped,[2] including 41 teachers and girls from Tawila boarding school. Six of the women were raped in front of their fathers, who were then killed; some of the schoolgirls were gang-raped. Overseeing this mayhem, moving between a temporary headquarters in a large canvas tent and a convoy of land cruisers protected by mounted men, was forty-four-year-old Musa Hilal, the most powerful leader of the government-supported militias that have come to be known as 'Janjawiid'. In the days before the attack, more than 500 militiamen had converged on Tawila from different directions and congregated, without interference from any of the government forces in the area, in a makeshift camp on a nearby hill. This was more than Arab raiders settling old scores. These militiamen had light and medium weapons, communication, internal structure and impunity. The state capital, al Fasher, is just forty miles away from Tawila, and Governor Osman Yousif Kibir was fully informed of the attack while it was happening. But it was only on the third day, after the militia withdrew, that the governor sent representatives to Tawila. Video footage shows fly-covered corpses, charred and smoking ruins, and weeping women cradling terrified children.

Musa Hilal has denied being present in Tawila. But the attack was witnessed by hundreds of people and many later said they recognized him, dressed in the uniform of an army colonel. One, a retired teacher, hid in the bushes when the attack began and took notes, feeling it was his duty as an educated man to record what was happening.[3] He saw military helicopters bringing food and weapons in and taking wounded out. 'Hilal moved and gave instructions, with men unloading guns off the helicopter … If you said you were Arab he would say, "Come fight with me."'

Confident of the impunity afforded him by the government, Hilal amused himself by playing word games while his men burned Darfur. He never convincingly denied the crimes of which he stands accused, nor showed any regret over the destruction of Darfur, its people and its multi-ethnic society. He only protested at being called 'Janjawiid' – a word customarily used to refer to gangs of outlaws from Chad. 'The Janjawiid are bandits, like the mutineers. It is we who are fighting the Janjawiid.'[4] What Hilal does not deny, indeed emphasizes, is being a government man. 'A big sheikh … not a little sheikh.'[5] As the father in his desert tent took pride in his independence, so did the son in his lavish, scented villa in Khartoum, hundreds of miles away from Darfur, take pride in being the government's man, 'appointed' by the government to fight the rebels. 'I answered my government's appeal, and I called my people to arms. I didn't take up arms personally. A tribal leader doesn't take up arms. I am a sheikh. I am not a soldier. I am *soldiers*!'

And not only 'soldiers'. Documents obtained by the authors refer to Hilal as leader – *amid* – of an Arab supremacist organization called the *Tajamu al Arabi*, usually translated as the 'Arab

Gathering'. Since it first appeared in Colonel Muammar Gaddafi's Libya, the Arab Gathering has taken on different identities and agendas. More a gathering of the like-minded than a formal organization, it never possessed military forces of its own, but opportunistically claimed the loyalty of Arab militia leaders – some of whom, such as Hilal, were happy to comply. In August 2004, at the peak of the confluence of interests between urban politicians and field commanders, Hilal spelled out his objective in a directive from his headquarters in Misteriha, twenty-five miles south west of the garrison town of Kebkabiya: 'Change the demography of Darfur and empty it of African tribes.' The directive was addressed to no fewer than three intelligence services: the Intelligence and Security Department, Military Intelligence and National Security, and the ultra-secret 'Constructive Security' or *Amn al Ijabi*.

In the figure of Musa Hilal, criminal impunity converged with Arab supremacism and counter-insurgency, and left in its wake a trail of devastation. Hilal's justification is that, at the request of the government, he raised a tribal militia to fight the rebellion in Darfur. This is true, as far as it goes. In December 2003, President Bashir vowed publicly to 'use the army, the police, the Mujahidiin, the Fursan to get rid of the rebellion'. But there was more to Hilal's war than he acknowledged publicly. In the documents obtained by the authors, Hilal made clear that he was doing more than merely combating a rebellion. He was waging 'jihad', 'cleaning our land of ... agents, mercenaries, cowards and outlaws'. He urged resolve despite the spotlight focused on the violence perpetrated by his militiamen. 'We promise you that we are lions, we are the Swift and Fearsome Forces. We fear neither the media and the newspapers nor the foreign interlopers.' He sent greetings to his supporters, a roll call of some of the most important men in national and regional government: 'General Omar al Bashir ... *Ustaz* [learned man] Ali Osman Mohamed Taha, Vice-president and the hero of Sudan ... Brother Major General Adam Hamid Musa, Governor of South Darfur ... Air Force General [Abdalla] Safi al Nur ... Brother *Ustaz* Osman Mohamed Yousif

37

Kibir, Governor of North Darfur' – and the man who turned a blind eye to the rape of Tawila. Hilal signed himself 'The Mujahid and Sheikh Musa Hilal, Amir of the Swift and Fearsome Forces'. He was a holy warrior, tribal leader and military commander. Even before the rebellion in Darfur began, Musa Hilal had a direct link to Khartoum. In 2000, a city councillor in Geneina, Mohamed Basher, challenged a group of Arab civilians he found carrying weapons. They told him the weapons were legal. On being asked who had authorized them, they showed him permits signed by Musa Hilal. Basher complained to the governor of West Darfur, Omar Haroun, and was told: 'We can't do anything. We will send your complaint to Khartoum.'[6]

Ambition

Without friends in high places in the capital, Musa Hilal's recruitment and training centre at Misteriha could not have expanded as it did after he left Aamo in 1996. Over a decade, the little hamlet grew into a sprawling military base, in theory under Salah Gosh's National Intelligence Service, with a helicopter pad, luxurious (for Darfur) officers' quarters, a mosque, a guest house and electricity. The 20,000 men Hilal could reportedly muster at the height of the war were distinguishable from regular troops only by their sandals, turbans and the emblem they wore on their jackets – an armed man on camel-back. The government denied any responsibility for militia abuses, but Musa Hilal claimed Khartoum had command responsibility. 'All the people in the field are led by top army commanders … These people get their orders from the Western command center and from Khartoum.'[7]

At the height of the atrocities in 2004, a senior officer in the national army, Lieutenant Colonel Abdel Wahid Saeed Ali Saeed, was in charge of military operations in Misteriha. He confirmed Musa Hilal's claim, telling a visiting US official he himself 'got his instructions from Khartoum'.[8] In the course of a few months early on in the war, Misteriha was transformed into a major military centre fully equipped with heavy weaponry and supplied by helicopter every few days. The camp had as many as eighty vehicles, a huge number in this remote region.[9] The link was not weakened, far less severed, as international condemnation of the war grew. In 2006, Colonel Saeed was replaced by another military intelligence officer, Colonel Salah Mustafa, whose chief of operations was Lieutenant Colonel Abdel Rahim Abdalla Mohamed. These two took their orders from a military intelligence officer in Khartoum, Major General Ali Hadi Adam Hamid.[10] Many of the border intelligence officers came from Hilal's own Um Jalul clan of the Mahamid.

The Misteriha barracks was only one of many camps across Darfur where regular officers worked closely with militias. Hassan Ahmad Mohamed, a member of the Mahariya section of the Abbala Rizeigat, visited an Arab settlement called Dawa, west of Kutum, on several occasions while serving as a security officer in al Fasher in 2003–05. It was no longer a traditional *damra* settlement but, like many after the rebellion began, a militia camp. 'Soldiers sent the civilians of the *damra* away,' Hassan said.

> The head of the camp was from the Um Jalul. He was called Mohamed Salih Kayom 'Silmi', which means peaceful! Helicopters brought weapons – Kalashnikovs and magazines. General [Awad] Ibn Auf [head of military intelligence] and high-ranking members of the Ittihad al Merkazi [the Central Reserve Police] came from Khartoum every month. The orders they gave the trainers [of the militia] were: 'Destroy everything. If possible, catch the rebels alive.'[11]

Hilal's message to recruits in Misteriha was that civilians from the same tribes as the rebels were the enemy. '*Zurga* [blacks] always support the rebels. We should defeat the rebels.' A young Zaghawa who ran away from the camp was told that non-Arabs like him would be sent to fight the rebel soldiers – their ethnic kin – while Arabs would attack villages. 'We are the lords of this land,' the young Arabs in Misteriha told him. 'You blacks don't have any rights here ... We are the original people of this area.'[12]

In reality, it is the Fur who claim the *hakuras* of Misteriha and the middle reaches of the Wadi Barei valley in which it lies, and who have always been the dominant tribe there, outnumbering a host of other tribes including Tama, Masalit and Arabs. Nomads from the Mahamid and Ereigat began settling in Wadi Barei in the 1950s and their numbers were augmented by drought migrants in the 1980s.[13] Local pacts protected many of the Fur villages from destruction during the conflict, but at the cost of extortionate 'protection' arrangements whereby the area became a supply centre for Musa Hilal's army. In one village, the arrangement involved monthly payments of 5,000 Sudanese pounds per family plus contributions of food and labour. Villagers' travel was controlled: when they left the area, they were not permitted to carry anything and were usually obliged to leave members of their families behind as a guarantee that they would be back.[14]

How did Musa Hilal get from the tents of Aamo, where his father inspired such respect, to the paramilitary base that is Misteriha, where he commands such fear? The answer lies in desperation, lawlessness and a militarized ideology.

Roots of the northern Janjawiid

From the time of the sultans, the camel-herding Abbala Rizeigat had been a headache to the rulers of Darfur. They refused to stay in the places allotted to them, and had no paramount chief to keep them in order. The British authorities tried to tidy up the tribal hierarchies, but never succeeded. Since the Abbala were too few to qualify for their own nazir, the first plan was to put them under the authority of one of Britain's staunchest allies – Ibrahim Musa Madibu, nazir of the cattle-herding Baggara. But the Abbala were too far away from the nazir's headquarters in south-eastern Darfur for that to be feasible. So the district officer proposed that the sheikhs of the Abbala elect their own deputy nazir.

The election, held at the annual horse fair in al Surfaya in December 1925, was anti-climactic. The most influential clans of the Mahamid section of the Abbala Rizeigat boycotted the conference to protest against British support for Abdel Nabi Abdel Bagi Kiheil, a rival candidate. Abdel Nabi, elected in their absence,

40

turned out to be ill-suited for the post: he didn't have the wealth to provide the continual generosity expected of a leader, quarrelled with Ibrahim Madibu, and preferred town life. A few years after the conference, he left his headquarters and court at Ghreir, a *damra* north of Kutum given to the Mahariya section in colonial times, and a sheikh of the Mahariya, Mahdi Hassaballa Ajina, became the most senior chief. But Mahdi never became nazir. His claim was disputed by the sheikh of the Mahamid, Issa Jalul, whose Um Jalul clan was the richest and most numerous of the Abbala Rizeigat in North Darfur. No decision on the nazirate was possible without Jalul's consent.[15] Had the Rizeigat camel-herders won their nazirate, a vast area of pastureland north of Kutum could have been allocated to them as a tribal homeland, ending their search for land to call their own.[16] Wells and reservoirs could have been dug to assist the herders in their annual trek northwards to the desert, minimizing the risks of clashes with other nomads. But the status of the Abbala Rizeigat in Darfur's tribal hierarchy was never resolved, fuelling a cycle of tribal conflicts and economic grievances that culminated in the emergence of the Janjawiid.

In 1948, Issa Jalul died. None of his sons was considered worthy of succeeding him as sheikh of the Mahamid, and the clan leaders met to decide a successor. Hilal Mohamed Abdalla, then in his forties, came from a humble background: he had most recently been a guard in Jalul's court. But Jalul on his deathbed endorsed him as his successor and he was elected by acclaim. Hilal spent the following forty years striving to become the first nazir of all the Abbala Rizeigat sections.

Sheikh Hilal and his Mahariya rival, Sheikh Mohamed Hassaballa – son of Mahdi, and known as 'al Dud', the lion, on account of his size – shared a court for fifteen years. But in 1963 the courts divided – Hilal moved to an encampment called Zeleita – and the two began competing for the allegiance of the smaller Rizeigat sections.[17] Neither did well: the Ereigat and Eteifat established separate courts, and some subsections went their own way entirely, relocating south to Wadi Saleh. The rivalry between Hilal and al Dud took on party political dimensions during Sudan's second democratic period in 1965–69, when the two men aligned with different parties. But what most effectively stalled Hilal's ambition was the fighting between Rizeigat and Zaghawa at Rahad Gineik in 1968. A sheikh who could not control the violent proclivities of his followers stood no chance of becoming nazir.

The Abbala Rizeigat were disadvantaged even by Darfur standards. The only ones with fertile farmland were their Ereigat cousins. Historically poor, owning few camels, this tribe had been given small land grants by the Fur sultans. Although small in number and traditionally looked down on by the camel-owning clans, the Ereigat now found themselves hosting their kin from other sections and gaining new influence. Few nomads were educated – families rich in camels did not send their sons to school – but the Ereigat had an advantage here too. In the 1930s, District Commissioner Guy Moore had employed them in the police stables at Kutum, and several of their sons subsequently became policemen. One such was Ali Safi al Nur, whose son Abdalla became an air force general, friend of President Bashir and the most powerful member of the tribe in Khartoum. But if the rural Abbala hoped that their cousins in the halls of government in Khartoum would bring them schools, clinics and deep boreholes for watering their camels, they were disappointed. Abdalla Safi al Nur and the son of the Ereigat sheikh, Hussein Abdalla Jibreel – who rose to the rank of general, before becoming an MP – did not deliver development to their impoverished people.

Nimeiri's 1969 coup, and his abolition of nazirates two years later, stalled Hilal's aspirations. Thereafter, Hilal's career focused on his court as a means of building a following. In 1973, he moved to Aamo, much closer to Kutum. It was a chance to build an alliance with the up-and-coming Ereigat, and to put Mahamid boys into the only two elementary schools in Arab villages, in Um Sayala and Misrih. The school in the Ereigat village at Misrih was a very basic structure – two lines of box-like classrooms facing each other across a stony assembly ground where the boys lined up every morning to salute the Sudanese flag – but it was the first school built in a North Darfur Arab village. Hilal also sought to expand his numerical constituency by drawing into Darfur Mahamid clans from Chad. He provided protection and assistance to the small Awlad Rashid clans that had settled in Darfur in the late 1980s, winning the support of their much more powerful kinsmen in Chad. To compete with him, Sheikh al Dud encouraged immigration by Chadian Mahariya. Twenty years later, in March 1995, each of these immigrant groups was awarded a chieftaincy to reflect their new strength in Darfur and to swing the balance of tribal power in the favour of Arabs.

Recurring drought in Chad gave additional impetus to immigration into Darfur. In the 1970s a drought-stricken immigrant was asked by the head of Sudan's refugee commission when he expected to return home. He replied, 'Wherever there is land and rain will be my homeland!'[18] In the 1980s, not just Abbala Rizeigat but whole clans of Beni Halba, Missiriya and Mahadi moved eastwards to join their kinsmen in a swathe of territory reaching from the border at Geneina as far as Kebkabiya and Kutum. Further south, the Salamat nomads – cattle-herders – were drifting eastwards too, seeking land and security. Small groups moved up the Salamat river and crossed into Darfur at Foro Baranga. They set up camps on the edges of Fur, Ta'aisha and Beni Halba villages, joining brethren who had already settled there. They clashed with the Ta'aisha in 1982 over land claims, and lost. In Wadi Debarei, near Garsila, Arawala and Deleig – the site of a series of massacres in early 2004 – the Salamat had no sheikh and selected a young man, Abdel Aziz Ali, as their spokesman, but he and his people were dismissed as *umshishi* – 'savages' – by the local Fur. The Abbala Rizeigat who transited through the area didn't treat with them either. Yet the numbers of Salamat grew slowly, and by the 1990s they had thirteen omdas, but still neither nazirate nor *dar*. Tensions were building.

Sheikh Hilal stayed at Aamo until his incapacitation in 1986. In his last years at Aamo, he witnessed one momentous event beyond his control and was caught up in another for which he shared responsibility. The first event was the great drought and famine of 1984–85; the second, the arming of his tribe. By the time of his death in 1990 in Kutum, where he had been house-bound, Darfur had irrevocably changed.

The death of the old order

Seeing the northern desert dying, and drawn increasingly to the savanna to the south, the Zaghawa say that 'the world finishes south'.[19] The drying of the Sahara is an integral part of their cosmos. The same is true for the camel-herding Rizeigat. They, too, have drifted southwards across the desert over the centuries. Speaking at the time of the great drought of 1984–85, Sheikh Hilal recounted this historic migration, and how it had been driven by drought, war and political rivalries: whenever two cousins disagreed, one could always move somewhere else. Unlike other Darfurian Arabs who claimed that their forefathers had come across an empty land, Hilal didn't dispute that Darfur was always inhabited. Taking his stick, he drew a chessboard in the sand. One set of squares he allocated to the Fur and Tunjur farmers; the second set he labelled as pastureland, available for the use of the nomads. But Hilal brooded on how the drought was disrupting the age-old order: wind was blowing sand on to cultivated farms and huge rainstorms were carving gullies out of the wadis. Farmers were now barring the nomads' way by erecting fences or burning off the grass.

Even worse, although the old sheikh was too proud to admit it, the Mahamid were losing their beloved camels. Many were becoming farmers or labourers in towns like Kebkabiya and Birka Saira, and villages in between like Misteriha. In 1985, a food security assessment noted that the main problem faced by the Rizeigat settled close to Kutum was the quality and quantity of the land they had been allocated by the Tunjur, who controlled the land, and the shrinking demand for daily labour on farms.

The settled Rizeigat claim that they now have so few resources that they cannot outmigrate because they cannot afford the costs of transport and setting up new farms ... There are some Rizeigat farms in goz [sandy soil] areas close to Birka Saira. Many of these have been abandoned due to declining yields, but there is currently an influx of impoverished Rizeigat ex-nomads into the area looking for work.[20]

The failed nomads of Aamo and Birka Saira, seeking a route out of poverty, were ready conscripts to rapacious militias and bandit gangs. Along with the other peoples of Darfur, the Mahamid were eating or selling their precious assets in order to stay alive. Darfurians were astonishingly resilient in the face of the worst threat to their lives and livelihoods since the famine of 1913. Thanks to their hardiness and skill, and especially to their ability to gather wild foods, far fewer died than aid agencies predicted. But survival came at a price which was only apparent later: they exhausted their land, their assets and their hospitality. The fabric of rural life never fully recovered.

Sheikh Hilal was less innocent of the second change that killed the old order: guns. Just as the rains failed, semi-automatic firearms began to flood Darfur. Nimeiri had allowed Sudan's famine to develop unchecked and in April 1985 popular protests brought him down. Relief aid at last began to reach Darfur and, with a new regime in Khartoum ready to deal with Libya, the trans-Saharan road to the Kufra oasis in Libya was opened, transforming Darfur. The desert road allowed impoverished Darfurians to migrate to oil-rich Libya and send money back to their families. It also allowed Ansar and Islamist exiles to return to Sudan. Having trained in Gaddafi's camps, alongside the Islamic Legion or as part of the Arab Gathering, they arrived infused with a supremacist agenda. They also came with weapons: huge convoys of military trucks rolled across the desert to set up rear bases in Darfur for Libya's war in Chad.

Gaddafi's designs on Chad needed an intermediary in North Darfur. He chose the Mahamid. Sheikh Hilal, endeavouring to boost his clan's power, had long been in close touch with his brethren in Chad, and Um Jalul camps had been used for storing Libyan arms destined for Chadian Arabs. But Hilal never saw the

45

automatic weapons that changed the face of Darfur. Incapacitated from early 1986, the old sheikh lost his sight, rarely rose from his bed, and withdrew from worldly affairs. Musa Hilal, the only one of Sheikh Hilal's seven sons who had attended secondary school, took over the leadership of the Mahamid before his father's death. As clashes with the Fur grew more frequent, it was he who organized the Mahamid's new arms supplies – from the market and from the Libyans.[21]

The Mahamid disagree among themselves over whether Sheikh Hilal wanted Musa to succeed him as head of the tribe. The young Musa was known to everyone as a difficult boy who was violent 'even with his own people'. Mohamed Matar Mukhtar, a Fur schoolteacher who taught Musa Hilal in primary school, found the Um Jalul children 'so rough – always quarrelling with everyone' – but held Musa to be especially troublesome. 'He fought with other boys and called them "Nuba".' Mohamed Matar knew Sheikh Hilal well, and observed that his favourite son was Musa's elder brother – Hassan 'Gerji' Hilal. His younger son he considered 'disobedient'.[22] But friends of the family say the wise old sheikh knew that the placid Gerji could not succeed him; it had to be Musa. As a child, al Sanosi Badr sat at Sheikh Hilal's knee and to this day refers to him as 'jiddo' – grandfather. He says,

> It is true that jiddo liked Hassan, not Musa. Once Musa came in very drunk. Jiddo got a very thick rope and tied him to his [punishment] tree, Um Kulaka,[23] for twenty-four hours.[24] Hassan was different. He was very peaceful. But a peaceful man cannot lead the Arabs. Jiddo knew the chieftaincy needed Musa. He gave him a one-year trial period. Musa did well. He was very good when Hilal was alive.

The Kalashnikov rifle changed the moral order of Darfur. The Abbala had lived by an honour code that included loyalty, hospitality, strenuous self-discipline when herding camels and communal responsibility for homicide. The principle of paying *diya*, or blood money, to the kin of an individual killed in a feud ensured that violence was a collective responsibility. In the era of spears and swords, and even the early rifles, a killing was a deliberate and individual act readily traceable to the man responsible. Fights rarely had more than a handful of fatalities. The AK-47 – capable of slaughtering an entire platoon, truckload of people, or family – swept this aside. Blood money for a single massacre could exceed the camel wealth of a whole lineage. The sheer number of bullets fired made it impossible to ascertain who had shot whom. Young men with guns were not only able to terrify the population at large, but were free of the control of their elders.

By the time Sheikh Hilal Abdalla died in 1990, a Kalashnikov could be bought for $40 in a Darfur market. A jingle of the time ran: 'The Kalash brings cash; without a Kalash you're trash.' Armed robbery was rife. The regional government in al Fasher had neither the resources nor the will to control the crime epidemic: its camel-mounted police with their colonial-era rifles were massively outgunned by well-organized gangs of outlaws. The government tried to compensate for the rarity with which it caught criminals by the savagery of the punishments it meted out, including amputation and the public display of corpses on gallows – a practice known as 'crucifixion' in Islamic law.

The Arab Gathering

As significant as lack of rain and an abundance of guns was a new political trend in Darfur: Arab supremacism. Sheikh Hilal, for all his stature and ambition, was a parochial and traditional man; neither he nor his courtiers were educated or had ideological sophistication. But by the end of the 1980s, the old Bedouin intrigues became caught up in national and international currents far stronger than they. The origins of those currents lay in the Libya of Colonel Gaddafi in the 1970s. The roots of Arab supremacism in Darfur do not lie in the Arabized elite ruling in Khartoum. They lie in the politics of the Sahara.

In Sudan in the 1960s, the Umma Party and the Muslim Brothers had supported the Arab factions that led the Chadian opposition with arms, money and rear bases, believing that they were fighting for the rights of Muslims against the Chadian government's Christian, 'African' agenda. But Nimeiri normalized relations with Chad in 1969 and the axis of Sahelian Arabism shifted to Libya, where Colonel Gaddafi was dreaming of an Arab state straddling the desert and where, thanks to oil money, he was busy fashioning his instruments. These included the *Failaq al Islamiya* (Islamic Legion), which recruited Bedouins from Mauritania to Sudan; the *Munazamat Da'awa al Islamiya* (Organization of the Islamic Call), which fostered Islamic philanthropy and evangelization; and sponsorship of the Sudanese opposition National Front including the Muslim Brothers and the Ansar, the Umma Party's military wing. In addition, Gaddafi hosted a raft of Arab opposition movements, known popularly as the 'Arab Gathering', and gave them military training in the Kufra oasis in the south east of the country, near the border with Darfur.

Gaddafi's own immediate interest was Chad, a first step in his plan to establish an Arab 'belt' across Africa. In 1975, he formally annexed the Aozou Strip in northern Chad. The following year he sponsored a National Front invasion of Sudan across the desert, which failed. By 1979, Libyan troops were fighting in N'Djamena. In 1981, Gaddafi proclaimed the unity of Libya and Chad.

Libya was vigorously opposed by the United States and France, which backed not only the Chadian leader Hissène Habré but also President Nimeiri in Khartoum. When Habré was briefly out of power in 1981–83, he retreated to Darfur, from where, rearmed with Sudanese support, he marched to N'Djamena and reclaimed power. Determined to get rid of Habré, Gaddafi poured ever more arms and money into Chad and when his antagonist Nimeiri was overthrown in 1985 quickly cut a deal with the successor government. In return for oil and weapons for Khartoum's war in the South, Libya was allowed to use Darfur as the back door to Chad. Gaddafi's leading Chadian protégé was Acheikh Ibn Omar, who had taken over the opposition Conseil Démocratique Révolutionnaire (CDR) in 1982 after its founder

Ahmat Acyl Aghbash stepped backwards into the propeller blades of his Cessna aeroplane. Acyl had already forged a military alliance between his own Salamat tribe and the Abbala Mahamid, based mainly on their common opposition to Habré's rule. Ibn Omar was not a simple warlord; he had imbibed Gaddafi's Arab supremacist philosophy.

In Darfur, the first signs of an Arab racist political platform emerged in the early 1980s. Candidatures had taken on ethnic dimensions during regional elections in 1981 and the Arabs had been hopelessly split, allowing the Fur politician Ahmad Diraige – the son of the *shartai* who had hosted Sheikh Hilal many years before – to sweep to power as governor of Darfur. Many Fur celebrated: for the first time since the sultanate, one of their own was ruling Darfur. Two underground Fur revanchist movements over the preceding decades, Red Flame and Suni (the latter named after a famously green valley high in Jebel Marra), had vowed to restore Fur rule across the land. Earlier in his political career, Diraige had founded the Darfur Development Front (DDF) which, while mainly secular and modernist, also gained support from Fur tribalists. Darfurian Arabs were alarmed at Diraige's election and the Fur assertiveness that followed. They argued that if they were united, and drew into their constituency the Fellata, Sudanese of West African origin, they could command an absolute majority. All that was needed was an 'Arab Alliance'. Around this time, leaflets and cassette recordings purporting to come from a group calling itself the 'Arab Gathering' began to be distributed anonymously, proclaiming that the *zurga* had ruled Darfur long enough and it was time for Arabs to have their turn. The speakers claimed that Arabs constituted a majority in Darfur. They called upon them to prepare themselves to take over the regional government – by force if necessary – and to change the name of Darfur, the 'homeland of the Fur', to reflect the new reality, which would be Arab.

The notion of Arab superiority had been a feature of northern Sudanese society for centuries, but this was something new. This was militant and inflammatory. With Darfur generally calm and

49

inter-tribal relations generally good, most officials dismissed the Arab Gathering as a lunatic fringe. But in February 1982 an attack took place that forced a reassessment. Armed men cordoned off the weekly market in Awal, near Kebkabiya, ordered everyone to lie on the ground and then ordered their victims to declare their tribe. Arabs were allowed to take their belongings and leave; non-Arabs were robbed, beaten and kicked. Security reports on the incident said the bandits wore army uniforms and carried modern firearms.[25] Similar events, although on a smaller scale, occurred in other villages around Jebel Marra.

On 5 October 1987, the Arab Gathering emerged from the shadows with an open letter to Prime Minister Sadiq al Mahdi written by twenty-three prominent Darfur Arabs – three of whom later claimed that their names had been used without their consent. One of the leading authors was a Rizeigat from al Da'ien, resident in Khartoum, Abdalla Ali Masar, who became President Bashir's adviser for Darfur affairs in the mid-1990s. Published in the independent Al Ayam newspaper, and signed in the name of the 'Committee of the Arab Gathering', the letter was a disturbing mixture of familiar political demands and supremacist claims. It claimed that Arab tribes represented more than 70 per cent of Darfur's total population and were politically, economically and socially 'predominant'. Despite this, they had been 'deprived of true representation in the leadership of Darfur region'. The signatories called for decentralization and regional administrative reform, and 'requested' 50 per cent of all government posts in the region. They called upon al Mahdi to assist them, as 'one of their own'. It was a demand for an Arab governor next time around. This much was the standard fare of competitive politics. But the letter ended in more sinister fashion:

> Should the neglect of the Arab race continue, and the Arabs be denied their share in government, we are afraid that things may escape the control of wise men and revert to ignorant people and the mob. Then there could be catastrophe, with dire consequences.

The following year, in response to Sadiq's choice of Tijani Sese Ateem as the second Fur governor of Darfur, an unsigned directive from the Executive Committee of the Arab Gathering, a committee not heard of before, enjoined Darfur's Arabs to 'cripple' Sese's administration. Marked 'Top Secret', the directive said 'volunteers' should be infiltrated into *zurga* areas 'to stop production in these areas, to eliminate their leaders' and to create conflicts among *zurga* tribes 'to ensure their disunity'. 'All possible means' should be used to disrupt *zurga* schools. This document, which came to be known as 'Qoreish 1', was a war cry.

A decade later, a second directive laid out the aims and strategies of the Arab Gathering in greater detail, and set a 'target date' of 2020 for completion of its project. The directive is undated, but from internal references was written in 1998 or 1999 – a period it described as the 'critical stage'. Invoking, for the first time, the name of the tribe of the Prophet Mohamed, the document was entitled 'Qoreish 2'. The crux of Qoreishi ideology, a convergence of Arab supremacy and Islamic extremism, is that those who trace their lineage to the Prophet Mohamed are the true custodians of Islam and therefore entitled to rule Muslim lands. Adherents regard Sudan's riverine elite as 'half-caste' Nubian-Egyptians and believe the country's only authentic Arabs are the Juhayna, the direct descendants of the Qoreish, who crossed the Sahara from Libya in the Middle Ages. They claim that these immigrants found an empty land stretching from the Nile to Lake Chad, and say this land should now be governed by their descendants – the present-day Abbala and Baggara Arabs.

Qoreish 2 laid out an agenda for taking power. At national level, it proposed feigning 'collaboration' while secretly infiltrating the National Congress Party, government and all the institutions – political, economic, security and military – of the 'hybrid' riverine tribes that 'have been an obstacle for us for more than a century'. It also set out a plan for dominating Darfur and Kordofan by cooperating tactically with non-Arab tribes, including the Dinka of Southern Sudan. It proposed securing 'sufficient pastures for nomads in Sudan, Chad, and the Central African Republic' and stressed the importance of 'strategic understanding with Libya' and the 'brothers in Gulf States'.

A jumble of ambitions and racist claims devoid of intellectual sophistication, Qoreish 2 never reflected an organized agenda for Darfur's Arabs and its authorship has never been established. Some blame educated Darfurian Arabs in Khartoum; others ascribe it to Libyan-trained Arabs from West Africa. Some argue that it is a fabrication. Abdalla Safi al Nur, who became governor of North Darfur in 2000, ascribes it to Zaghawas associated with Turabi, then at the height of his power struggle with President Bashir.[26] Whatever its origin, Qoreish 2 resonated with the strange and desperate worldviews of the young men who would soon be flocking to Darfur's Arab militias. Abdullahi al Tom, a Darfurian academic who later joined the Justice and Equality Movement (JEM), noted the unresolved question of the authenticity of the Qoreish manifestos, but also 'the conspicuous absence of their public condemnation among Arab groups'.[27]

> Racist principles contained in most of these documents seemed to have enjoyed wide support in the current Darfur conflict and are well in tune with the perception of black people in the Arab culture of northern Sudan ... In examining these documents, one must avoid the temptation of treating them as work of a lunatic fringe that has little impact on what has happened and [is] still happening in Darfur.

There is no evidence that the Arab Gathering ever existed as a coherent organization.[28] But the cause of Arab domination of Darfur had supporters in Khartoum from the start. Its true ideological bedfellows – specifically mentioned in Qoreish 2 – were certain Chadian Arab leaders and in particular Acheikh Ibn Omar. In the 1980s, Ibn Omar's CDR, an explosive cocktail of Libyan-trained soldiers and undisciplined, untrained Bedouins, was already better armed and more mobile than any Sudanese force.

Darfur's conflict began as a sideshow of the Chadian war. In March 1987, Chadian forces armed by France and the CIA, and using high-speed guerrilla tactics, smashed a much larger

Libyan army in the battle of Wadi Doum in the Chadian Sahara. It was the beginning of the end for Gaddafi's Saharan ambitions, but the Libyan leader fought on for another eighteen months using the CDR as his proxy and Darfur as his battleground. Forced to retreat from Chad two months after the Wadi Doum fiasco, the CDR leader Ibn Omar's first base in Darfur was a refugee camp at Anjikoti, adjacent to the teeming border market of Foro Baranga. More than three-quarters of the 27,000 refugees in Anjikoti had started farming, alongside some 10,000 kinsmen already settled in the area. The Chadians, almost all of whom were illiterate, had few opportunities in Sudan but even worse prospects back home, where they felt that Habré's Goraan tribe, a Saharan people with close ties to the Zaghawa, nursed a visceral hatred of Arabs. For these refugees, neglect by Khartoum was infinitely preferable to N'Djamena's regime of institutionalized robbery and arbitrary violence. As a result, parts of Wadi Saleh were becoming Chadian enclaves. A 1983 survey by UNHCR found that only 3 per cent were prepared to go back to Chad.[29] But these simple rural people, seeking security and a modest livelihood, were denied the chance to live in peace. Anjikoti was also a magnet for Chadian dissidents who recognized its strategic location – close to the biggest mercantile centre in the border zone, on the Abbala migration route, and the water source for eastern Chad – and set up an armed camp. The first violent displacement of Fur villagers occurred here. Twenty years later, they are still displaced around Nyala, and known as *jimjaabu* – 'the rifle brought them'. After Anjikoti was attacked by Chadian troops and French Foreign Legionnaires, Ibn Omar moved deeper into Darfur and set up camp with the Islamic Legion in the mountains near Kutum. Fighting intensified as the CDR and its local Darfurian Arab allies assaulted Jebel Marra in March 1988 at the beginning of what has come to be known as the first Fur–Arab war.[30]

The Chadian power struggle ignited new conflicts as it crossed the border into Darfur. In Wadi Saleh, the CDR armed their Salamat cousins; in Kutum, they sought an alliance with Musa Hilal and the Mahamid. Tijani Sese, governor of Darfur at the time, already regarded Sheikh Musa Hilal as a troublemaker, a hothead who 'was inciting tribal hatred and conflict'.[31] Military intelligence in al Fasher was also worried by Hilal's activities and alliances. When Hilal requested a meeting with representatives of Ibn Omar in al Fasher, military intelligence agreed – and taped the discussions. They heard Hilal thanking the Chadians for the weapons and ammunition with which they had provided him, and advising them not to trust Zaghawa and Masalit. The Fur, meanwhile, were making contacts with Habré's government, smuggling in weapons of their own and attacking the Arabs where they were most vulnerable – their animals. They blocked livestock routes, burned pastures and erected what the Arabs called 'wind fences' – enclosures that contained nothing but air and grass. The Arabs escalated the war. For eighteen months, the government simply denied the problem. It was common knowledge that Sadiq al Mahdi was turning a blind eye to Gaddafi's intrigues because he needed Libyan money. Darfurians organized large peaceful protests in Khartoum and three Fur MPs elected on the NIF ticket resigned their party whip in protest, claiming there was 'a conspiracy to reshape Darfur and open it up for foreign resettlement' by those seeking to overthrow the N'Djamena government.[32] Many Darfurian Arabs warned against the disastrous path that Darfur's politics were taking.

In 1988, the Chadian army, supported by French jets and attack helicopters, again defeated Ibn Omar near Kutum. The Libyan leader reconsidered – and recognized the Habré government, catching Ibn Omar by surprise. As the historians of the thirty-year Sahara conflict write: 'Ideology, principle and even honor were no substitute for self-preservation by the chieftains of the Sahara.'[33] Ibn Omar surrendered and took a post in Habré's government, though many of his troops refused to follow him. In Darfur, the Chadian war had mutated into coordinated banditry and land-grab. Musa Hilal was a prominent and effective leader, who contemporaries say was telling the Arabs of North Darfur: 'Fight – or lose your land and be destroyed.' Until his time, the word 'Janjawiid' had referred to outlaw bands of Bedouins, with echoes of the Arabic words *jim* (the letter 'G', referring to the G3 rifle), *jinn* (devil) and *jawad* (horse). Now, for the first time it was used to refer to an ethnic militia.

In May 1989, Governor Sese convened a peace conference in al Fasher with the Masalit sultan, Abdel Rahman Bahr al Din, as principal mediator. At the conference, the Fur claimed 2,500 of their people had been killed, 400 villages burned and 40,000 animals stolen. The Arab side claimed 500 deaths, 700 tents and houses destroyed and 3,000 livestock lost. Each side accused the other of being driven by ethnic exclusivism, of trying to establish, respectively, an 'Arab belt' and an 'African belt' in Darfur. The speeches and a reconciliation agreement signed on 8 July 1989, a week and a day after the 30 June coup that brought Brigadier Omar al Bashir to power, all stressed the local dimensions of the conflict.[34] The tribal leaders stuck to the local issues that fell within their remit and glossed over the political dimensions of the war. Their agreement called for restitution and compensation, mutual disarmament, the deportation of illegal aliens – Chadians – and a host of measures concerning pasture, water, local land rights and return of displaced people. A second agreement in Zalingei in December 1989 identified the collapse of local government and policing as a major problem and called for the disarming of Fur self-defence groups and Arab Janjawiid – the first and last use of the name 'Janjawiid' in a Sudanese government document. The word 'militia' – Arabized simply as *milisha* – was used for the Fur armed groups. In that same month, the regional Security Committee in al Fasher decided unanimously to suspend Hilal from the sheikhdom of the Mahamid.[35]

But the peace deal was not implemented, and politics in Darfur continued to polarize. Gaddafi and the Sudanese Islamists had common agendas – not least a $250 million weapons deal. Shortly after the NIF's takeover, the two leaders announced ambitious plans for cooperation, including free movement of people between their countries. There was free flow of ideas too. In a statement with distinct echoes of Qoreishi beliefs, Gaddafi emphasized the unity of Arabism and Islamism, saying, 'We [the

Arabs] are the Imams. We are responsible for Islam, which was revealed in our language. It is our book and our prophet alone. We do not accept a foreigner to come to us with his ideas ...'[36]

The Masalit war: 'the beginning of the organization of the Janjawiid'

Drought and destitution embittered the Darfur Arabs. Weapons and a self-asserting ideology gave them new aggression and confidence. They were ripe for picking by the government, which began to harness them as a proxy instrument of military control. In the beginning, Khartoum's use of tribal militias was purely opportunistic: they were there, they had fighting skills and they allowed the government to conserve its own, overstretched resources. But as time went on, the militias also gave the government the cover of 'tribal conflict' between nomads and farmers, enabling it to deny there was a war at all.

The militia strategy was well entrenched by the time Daud Bolad led SPLA forces into South Darfur in 1991. With few regular troops in the region, it was predictable that the government would turn to militias for help. The Beni Halba Fursan obliged and played the leading role in routing Bolad's force. Army and Fursan burned entire villages on suspicion of having helped Bolad's men. The military governor of Darfur, Colonel Tayeb Ibrahim 'Sikha', was anxious to ensure that the reprisals did not spark a wider war; he had learned the lesson of South Kordofan, where government over-reaction had driven the Nuba into the arms of the SPLA. For two years, he tried to keep Darfurians within the Islamist movement, publicly complimenting the Fur on their piety and telling them that loyalty would have its rewards. But the governor's overtures to the Fur and Masalit were purely tactical. Behind them he was playing divide-and-rule – promoting the Arab tribes of West Darfur.

In 1994, the logic of the central government strategy became clearer when the minister for federal affairs, Ali al Haj, redrew the administrative boundaries of Darfur as part of a constitutional reform that created a pseudo-federal system of administration across Sudan. Darfur's historic single region was divided into three states: North Darfur, with its capital in al Fasher; West Darfur, headquartered in Geneina; and South Darfur, administered from Nyala. The reform divided the Fur, the largest tribe in Darfur, among the three new states and made them minorities in each, significantly reducing their influence.

A second administrative reform – within West Darfur – revolutionized the tribal hierarchy there and unleashed a war. Previously, Dar Masalit had a sultan – a hereditary post in the family of Ismail Abdel Nabi, who established the sultanate and ruled from 1884–88 – and five *furshas*, administrative chiefs with land jurisdiction.[37] In the 1980s, the founder's great-great-grandson, Sultan Abdel Rahman Bahr al Din, hung maps of Dar Masalit and French West Africa – pointedly, not of Sudan or even Darfur – on the wall of his reception hall in Geneina and would tell visitors, only half joking, that his father had joined Sudan by voluntary treaty in 1922 and retained the right to secede. 'I am sovereign here,' he insisted with an imperious manner that brooked no dissent.[38] Successive attempts to reform local government in the 1960s and 1970s had left Dar Masalit largely untouched, as the last remaining bastion of old-style Native Administration – a domain where the sultan's word was law. The Arabs, who had grown to make up approximately a quarter of the population because of immigration from Chad – they claimed one-third – were under-represented and frustrated by their exclusion from local authority. Unlike in other parts of Darfur, they did not even have their own courts. During the drought of 1984–85, local government officers and some NGO staff not only denied Arabs relief rations; they blamed them for worsening the famine. These Arabs were not citizens of Darfur, the Masalit said; they were Chadians, and it was their uninvited presence in Dar Masalit that had depleted local food resources. 'By feeding the nomads you are starving us,' a local government official told relief workers in 1985 – meaning that if the herders got relief rations, they would no longer need to sell their animals in the market to buy foodgrains.[39]

57

The Arabs' fears of political exclusion increased during the parliamentary period of 1986–89 – in part because the Masalit voted overwhelmingly for the victorious Umma Party and swept the seats reserved for the district. Not only that, but the sultan's cousin, Ali Hassan Taj el Din, was elevated to be one of the five members of Sudan's collective presidency, the Council of State.[40] By contrast, Dar Masalit's Arabs did not have a single representative to speak for them in the National Assembly in Khartoum. Most were uneducated and many hadn't even voted. They became fearful that Masalit leaders would keep their grip on local councils and parliamentary seats, and perhaps even disenfranchise them altogether by labelling them as foreigners.

Local government reform was overdue, but when it came in 1995 it was disproportionate and inflammatory. The governor of West Darfur, Mohamed al Fadul, created eight new administrative chieftaincies – and gave all but one to Arabs. The new chiefs were given the title *amir* – prince. Since the NIF had seized power, the tables had been turned and it was the Masalit who were now becoming worried about being disenfranchised. From its earliest days, the NIF wanted to break the Umma Party's grip on Darfur, and set to work undermining its stronghold among the Masalit. Governor Tayeb 'Sikha' transferred Masalit administrators out of the area and tilted towards the Arabs – a policy that intensified in the wake of the 1991 SPLA incursion. The most prominent Masalit leader in Khartoum, Ali Hassan Taj el Din, disappointed his people with his conspicuous silence – some even accused him of competing with the Arabs for government favour. In the 1994 national elections, the first under the military regime and with no political parties allowed, the Arabs of Dar Masalit won two seats for the first time, causing consternation among the Masalit, who had never lost an electoral contest. In that same year, the ageing sultan became incapacitated and confined to his bed, leaving a power vacuum in which his sons, Saad and Tariq, contested the direction of their political inheritance. Saad had an Arab mother, from central Sudan, and was generally seen as pro-government; Tariq had a Masalit mother and was fiercely partisan towards his tribe. Faced with the challenge posed by the administrative reform, the Masalit centre didn't hold.

When the governor proposed a ceremony to inaugurate the new Arab amirs, the Masalit refused to participate. Rather than seek a compromise, the governor asked the Arabs to organize a festival for the dignitaries from Khartoum.[41] Ibrahim Yahya, who became governor two years later, recalled that 'Omar al Bashir came to Geneina and personally gave flags to Arab amirs.'[42] The title 'amir' implied parity with the Masalit sultan and many Arabs believed that they were now entitled to a *hakura* or *dar*. A further reform was also mooted – and adopted four years later – stipulating that the sultan would be 'elected by the electoral college that consists of all the furshas and amirs subject to the sultanate'.[43] His term would be seven years, but the state government could extend it, without limit. The implication was clear: the Masalit sultan would in due course be replaced by an Arab.

Dar Masalit was polarizing along racial lines. On the Masalit side, some militants espoused a radical anti-Arab agenda. Adam Mohamed Musa 'Bazooka', a Masalit from Chad who had been a colonel in the Chadian army, was one. His reputation spread among Darfur's Arabs, one of whom recalled that he used to incite Masalit to spear the camels of Chadian Arabs as they passed through Dar Masalit – 'especially the pregnant females.'[44] The sultan's son Tariq pushed hard for the Masalit to keep their paramount position. According to al Sanosi Badr, 'When Arab chiefs went to the sultan and said "We must sit together as tribes and solve this problem," Tariq said: "No, you Arabs must be under our shoes."'[45]

On the Arab side, an agenda of domination was assertively promoted by Mohamed Salih al Amin Baraka, a 'nomad MP' in the national parliament and subsequently a commissioner in West Darfur. Voluble and restless, Mohamed Baraka looks more like a political pundit than a politician. And indeed he was editor-in-chief of *Al Bouhaira* newspaper in N'Djamena in 1990, when the CDR was briefly part of Chad's ruling coalition. After coming back to Sudan in 1994 – where his brother Bashir was appointed as amir of the Awlad Ali section of the Mahariya in the administrative reform of 1995 – Mohamed Baraka became treasurer of the Herders' Union, an influential lobby dominated by Arabs, and then MP, helped by the backing of powerful friends in Khartoum. Mohamed al Amin Baraka ignores Masalit sensibilities over the *hakura* system. 'The *government* owns all the land,' he insists. 'Much of it is empty and not used, and things have changed since the *hakura* system was set up. The *hakura* is not a Bible, and it should be replaced by a new law to organize the land.'[46]

Another influential Arab leader was al Hadi Mohamed Rifa of the Awlad Zeid section of the Mahamid. A former Masalit classmate, Mohamed Yahya, remembers him as 'a nice guy, a good man'.[47] The two lived in the same neighbourhood of Ardamata, formerly the colonial administrative centre on the edge of Geneina, where al Hadi was a schoolteacher – one of the few Arabs to obtain an education – and coach of the local football team. There was no hint of racial animosity at that time. 'We didn't think who is an Arab and who is a Masalit, we just thought we were the same people.' But, after being appointed amir in 1995, al Hadi became a controversial figure. For some, he retained the reputation of an impartial peacemaker. 'He was famous for his kindness and loyal to all tribes,' said Abdalla Adam Khatir, a Tunjur journalist who wrote about his case at the time.[48] 'He was a special leader, educated and refined, with good connections to other tribes,' said Yousif Takana, who served in government and tried to promote conflict resolution across Darfur.[49] But Mohamed Yahya said that his former friend changed. 'Al Hadi became very aggressive against other tribes. He declared, "I am the God of the Masalit, I can destroy the Masalit." He even beat people in the street. People who had respected him were very surprised.'[50]

No sooner had the administrative reform been promulgated than Dar Masalit exploded in violence. In August 1995, a cluster of Masalit villages around Mejmeri, east of Geneina, was destroyed by Arab raiders and 75 people killed. A further 170 were injured and 650 cows stolen. The government did nothing. Darfurians on both sides of the racial divide concur that the reason was 'Arab aggression' and 'the government was not impartial'.[51] Both sides were armed, and the voices of moderation were drowned out. A reconciliation meeting was convened in 1996 but failed to stop the violence.

As unrest grew, the government began arming the Arabs. A military man, Major General Hassan Suleiman, replaced the civilian governor, Mohamed al Fadul, and began giving weapons to the Arab amirs – several of whom, like Hamid Dawai and Abdalla Abu Shineibat, later commanded attacks on Masalit villages in 2003–04. Soldiers trained Arab irregulars – among them Mahariya, Um Jalul, Beni Halba and Misseriya – at Jebel Endia, north of Geneina. Prominent members of the Masalit community were arrested, imprisoned and tortured; Masalit civilians were disarmed, placed under curfew and restricted in their movements. Masalit and Zaghawa had dominated the Popular Defence Forces (PDF); now they were sent to South Sudan to fight. Masalit self-defence groups were disorganized, despite the sympathy of the Native Administration and the active support of the local PDF. In a series of attacks and counterattacks over three years, 686 civilians were killed, 50 villages were burned and 8,803 animals looted.[52]

What Darfurian leaders recognized as the 'turning point' came on 17 January 1999.[53] It began as a relatively minor incident. Al Haj Ismail Izhaq Omar, an elderly Masalit farmer from the village of Tabarik, found animals belonging to Arab herders trampling his fields. When he attempted to chase the animals away, the herders shot and killed him. They then shot at three more villagers, killing two and wounding the third. It was the first day of Eid al Fitr, a Muslim feast of thanksgiving and forgiveness that marks the end of Ramadan, and a delegation of Arab tribal leaders headed by Amir al Hadi Mohamed Rifa sped to Tabarik, just thirty minutes' drive from Geneina. Angry Masalit farmers opened fire on the chiefs in their car, killing al Hadi, three omdas and their guard.[54] Arabs and Masalit disagree about what exactly happened, and why. Arabs accuse the Masalit of unprovoked aggression, and even conspiracy.[55] But Masalit believe al Hadi was leading an operation to arrest Masalit suspected to be in possession of weapons for rebellion. Mohamed Yahya, a native of Tabarik, said the Arab chiefs refused to get out of their vehicle when villagers invited them to share their Eid meal. He said the first shots were fired from al Hadi's vehicle.[56]

Arab fury exploded. Armed Arabs rampaged through villages east and south of Geneina, killing people and burning villages and unharvested fields. They refused to speak to the governor, Ibrahim Yahya, accusing him of siding with his Masalit kinsmen. Masalit activists used the word 'genocide' to describe militia attacks that they say killed 2,000 people:

> Most attacks took place late at night, when villagers were sleeping. Upon reaching a village, the attackers typically began by setting fire to all the houses. Villagers who managed to escape the flames were then shot by the Arab militias as they fled their homes. By burning the fields just before they were ready to be harvested, or while the crop lay on the ground after first being cut, the militias destroyed the year's crop and exposed Masalit farmers to starvation ... The atrocities were well planned, and directed by the Sudanese military governor of the area.[57]

Two senior ministers flew to Geneina and announced that the situation was out of control and that outlaws were in charge, assassinating Arab leaders. President Bashir dispatched his deputy chief of staff for operations, a retired general named Mohamed Ahmad al Dabi, to 'restore calm'. Putting on his khaki uniform again, al Dabi arrived on 9 February with full personal authority from the president, two helicopter gunships and a company of 120 soldiers. He demanded an immediate end to the violence. 'If anyone fires a shot, my reaction will be very hard against the man who fired the bullet and the leader of the group.'[58] He ordered the gunship pilots to put on a display of firepower in front of tribal leaders – 'to show them what the helicopters could do'.

General al Dabi stayed four and a half months in Geneina. Accounts of what happened during his tenure diverge sharply. Governor Ibrahim Yahya describes the period as 'the beginning of the organization of the Janjawiid', with militia leaders like Hamid Dawai and Shineibat receiving money from the government for the first time. 'The army would search and disarm villages, and two days later the Janjawiid would go in. They would attack and loot from 6 a.m. to 2 p.m., only ten minutes away from the army. By this process all of Dar Masalit was burned.'[59] Yahya said he challenged an army officer and was told: 'They are only doing their duty.' He went to Khartoum, where he asked Bashir and Ali Osman why the army was taking its orders from Khartoum's representative and not from him. Their answer, he says, was: 'You Africans are not reliable.' Five years later, the SLA commander of Dar Masalit would say that 'things changed in 1999: the PDF ended and the Janjawiid came; the Janjawiid occupied all PDF places'.

General al Dabi tells a very different story.[60] He says he arrived to find Dar Masalit in chaos, with the Arabs angry at the killing of their leaders and what they saw as the governor's bias. The state government lacked resources and could not tackle the root causes of the crisis, which he identified as lack of water for the nomads' herds. With a firm hand, undisputed authority, and money from Khartoum to pay expenses for the leaders on both sides, al Dabi insists that he brought the crisis under control. He gave fuel for the state government's cars, dug wells and repaired reservoirs. He pressed both Arabs and Masalit for a ceasefire and then a full tribal reconciliation conference – threatening them with live ammunition when they dragged their feet. Conference documents enumerated 292 Masalit and 7 Arabs killed – all of them in January and early February.[61] Before leaving at the end of June, al Dabi instituted a council of advisers for the sultan, with equal representation of Masalit and Arabs. 'I was very proud of the time I spent in Geneina', he said.

From Aamo to Misteriha

Colonel Gaddafi had been mentor of the Arab Gathering. When relations with the Arab League soured in the 1990s, he turned his attention towards building strategic alliances in Africa, and opened Libya's borders to African workers. But an estimated one-third of Libya's youth were unemployed, and race riots in 2000 killed an estimated 250 black migrants. Thousands more were expelled from the country. Many African Arabs who had been in Libya under the umbrella of the Arab Gathering moved across the border to North Darfur, where they were divided among six camps.[62] A visitor to the camps in 2000 found military trainers from Yasser Arafat's Palestine Liberation Organization. He also found Musa Hilal controlling two of the camps, south of Keb-kabiya.[63]

Musa Hilal's links with Arab supremacists date from his co-operation with Acheikh Ibn Omar in 1988. His removal from the chieftaincy of the Mahamid in 1989 did not last long. In November 1992, he represented the Mahamid at a meeting of the Arab Gathering called to establish a permanent Arab settlement at Rahad Gineik, where his father's kinsmen had fought the Zaghawa in the 1960s. The meeting, provocatively held at Rahad Gineik itself, was a failure: the Zaghawa got wind of it and forced the regional government, under threat of attack, to agree 'not to violate any traditional rights or to establish new rights' in the area.[64] In challenging the government, the Zaghawa were better placed than the Masalit. They were well represented in the upper echelons of the NIF and the security services. Their kinsman Idriss Deby was in power in Chad, and they could draw on Chadian quartermasters for weaponry and off-duty Chadian army officers for military advice (and more). An arms race was underway.

The next flashpoint for Rizeigat–Zaghawa conflict was the Abu Gamra area – a place of good grazing and deep wells in the southern reaches of Dar Zaghawa. Abubaker Hamid Nur, an NIF supporter, who later joined the rebel Justice and Equality Movement, was there.

I saw many Arabs from Chad. They had travelled more than 250 miles. I asked why, and they said, 'We are from Chad, but our roots are here.' What was very strange was that they had weapons and government soldiers were near. I told the government, 'Foreigners have weapons.' The reply was, 'These are orders from Khartoum. Do not intervene.'[65]

For their part, the Arabs stressed how Zaghawa control of Chad was making it increasingly difficult for Arab herders to take their herds to the desert-edge pastures, and how Zaghawa outlaws – whom they in their turn sometimes called 'Janjawiid' – intercepted and robbed camel caravans crossing the desert to Libya.[66] Retaliating, Musa Hilal's men set up checkpoints between Aamo and Kutum. In 1994, two trucks carrying Zaghawa were attacked at night and seventeen Zaghawa were killed.[67] Hilal became well known for responding to any theft by raiding the closest Zaghawa settlement and seizing its animals. His clansmen argue that when they pursued Zaghawa raiders they invariably fell into ambushes, so the better retribution was to attack elsewhere.[68] A cycle of escalation and collective punishment set in. In 1996, a feud between the Um Jalul and Zaghawa of Donky al Hosh, a water point on the Gineik route, took dozens of lives.[69]

In that same year, with the viability of his father's *damra* at Aamo eroded by years of drought and desertification, Musa Hilal moved his tribal headquarters to Misteriha. For some years it remained a village with little to distinguish it from its neighbours. Hilal himself didn't trust the government and throughout the 1990s flirted with opposition parties. But in January 2000, Hilal's friend Safi al Nur was made governor of North Darfur. Safi al Nur's former schoolmate and colleague in regional government, Ibrahim Yahya, said the new governor believed the Arabs' survival in Darfur depended on close relations with the government and quoted him as saying, 'I am in this government because we Arabs cannot live in Darfur if we are not with this regime.'[70] Safi al Nur, he said, played a big role in convincing the government the Arabs could achieve great things in Darfur.

Reports that the government recruited some 20,000 Janjawiid from other African countries are wildly exaggerated. But militia recruits from Chad and other West African countries arrived for training in Misteriha. Hassan Ahmad Mohamed, the Mahariya Arab who worked in Security in al Fasher, met Arabs from Cameroon, Niger and Nigeria among young recruits to whom the government was giving weapons and salaries – 300,000 to 400,000 Sudanese pounds per person, he said. 'In al Fasher they had separate barracks, but in Misteriha, Jebel Juk and Jebel Si they mixed with the Janjawiid. They were promised land and loot.'[71] The government also mobilized the remnants of the *Um Bakha* militia – named '*bakha*' after the plastic water containers that they beat and rattled to terrify the villages they raided – and others who went by the names *Um Kwak*[72] and, generically, Janjawiid. These volunteers were initially spread among four main centres equipped and trained by the government. Misteriha, in North Darfur, was for the Abbala Rizeigat. South Darfur had two camps – Jebel Adola for southern Rizeigat and Ma'aliya, and Gardud for Sa'ada and Beni Halba. West Darfur had one – Jebel Kargo in Wadi Saleh for Terjem, Ta'aisha and Salamat.[73]

Arming the South Darfur Arabs

Like the Masalit of West Darfur, the people of South Darfur trace their troubles back to the arrival of Arabs from Chad – most importantly, the Sa'ada, whose first eleven families are said to have crossed the border in 1938, and the Awlad Mansour clan of the Mahariya, who settled on the southern side of Jebel Marra in the 1980s.[74] Suleiman Hassaballa Suleiman is the longest-serving *shartai* of the Fur. He took the position in 1966 after serving in the Sudan army for fourteen years and, when rebellion began, elected to remain in rebel-controlled territory in his home village, Kidingeer. He remembers the arrival of the Awlad Mansour as 'the beginning of the process of occupying Fur land'.

I heard the word 'Janjawiid' for the first time in 1987 – from the Arabs themselves. Beginning in 1986, under Sadiq al Mahdi, the government began arming and training Arab tribes against non-Arabs and making conferences with them. They were given small salaries, and food for themselves and their horses. They cut the roads and the police did nothing. Then, at the end of the 1980s, the government brought the Awlad Mansour to Dogi [a Fur village on the southern edge of Jebel Marra, some twenty miles south of Kidingeer]. They gave it an Arabic name – Um al Gura, which means 'the Mother of all Villages', one of the names Arabs use for Mecca. Their leader is [Omda] Juma Dogolo. At the beginning of the 1990s, Dogolo made many attacks against the Fur. There was much rape. Dogolo is an uneducated and immoral man. He was a nobody until the government gave him weapons.

In 1990, Shartai Suleiman sent a letter of complaint about the arming of Arabs to the commissioner of Nyala – one Arab commissioner was given sixty guns; he, as *shartai*, was allowed only three – and was detained for eight months. The following year, he was captured by the army on the road between Malam and Kidingeer, trussed like a chicken and tossed into a pickup truck. Bags of ammunition were put on top of him. He was tied, hanging, to a tree and cursed: 'Slave! Black monkey!' One of his tormentors jumped on his right foot, and broke it.

Chadians from the Sa'ada tribe settled initially in the Missiriya village of Kugi north west of Nyala, which they renamed 'Gardud' – 'Grazing Plains'. After the 1989 coup, the Sa'ada were given six omdaships, weapons and training. The authority of the most senior Fur chief, Magdum Ahmed Adam Rijal, over the new omdas was withdrawn. 'They were made Janjawiid.' All six omdas later became militia leaders, with the most senior of them, Mohamed Harin Yagoub, in charge of the Sa'ada militia and responsible for bringing weapons from the army in Nyala. Years later, as war spread to South Darfur, government troops brought Arabs from Anjikoti – Rizeigat, Missiriya and Fellata – to a camp at Gardud and armed them. In September 2004, the minister of state for the interior, Ahmed Mohamed Haroun, flew into Gardud by helicopter and oversaw the distribution of weapons and ammunition to the militia.[75]

The government policy of promoting smaller Arab tribes – indigenous tribes like the Terjem and immigrants like the Awlad Mansour and Sa'ada – set a time bomb ticking. 'When you give someone a post, he will next search for land,' said Ahmed Fadul, a Fur who during the rebellion became SLA representative in the Ceasefire Commission in Nyala. 'The Terjem were given a chieftaincy in 1992, but no land. The nazir of the Terjem, Mohamed Yagoub Ibrahim, became a big militia leader! The government uses these militias as mobile troops, with priority in their own areas, to protect Nyala [from the SLA] in Jebel Marra.'

Countdown to war

For Khartoum, the stakes in Darfur increased hugely in 2000, when the ruling NCP split – and for the first time a Darfurian Arab, Safi al Nur, occupied Sultan Ali Dinar's palace. Darfurian Islamists tended to align themselves with Turabi, raising fears in Khartoum that Darfur would be the springboard for dissident Islamists to launch a putsch. Turabi first commanded his followers to quit the NCP, and then to remain inside as secret cells. Bashir was as worried by this fifth column as by the many desertions.

With grassroots Darfurian opposition growing and Darfurian Islamists abandoning the ruling party in droves, senior figures in regional and central government accelerated the mobilization of Darfur's Abbala Arabs. The key players were Governor Abdalla Safi al Nur and General Hussein Abdalla Jibreel, an MP and chairman of the Parliamentary Security and Defence Committee. In South Darfur, among the most active were Lt. General Adam Hamid Musa, a Zayadiya Arab and future governor of South Darfur state, and three Baggara Rizeigat: Abdel Hamid Musa Kasha, minister of foreign trade in the Khartoum government; Abdalla Ali Masar, governor of River Nile state and a prime mover of the 1987 Arab Gathering letter to Sadiq al Mahdi; and Hasabo Abdel Rahman, a senior security officer.[76]

Relations between Arabs and non-Arabs deteriorated sharply

in North Darfur. 'Weapons were collected from non-Arabs – even from the police – and given to the government,' said a Zaghawa who sought refuge in Chad in 2003.[77] Safi al Nur denied arming the Janjawiid, saying, 'Not even a bullet was handed to the governor.' The Arabs, he said, had no need of weapons. 'You know the Arabs – everyone has weapons, so there was no need to give them weapons or ammunition. Any guy to protect himself and his camels had a gun.'[78] The Zaghawa said 'planes [helicopters] began coming to Misteriha' and it became a place to avoid: they no longer took their camels to market there. Safi al Nur said helicopters flew just once to Musa Hilal's headquarters during his tenure, after an armed clash in Kulbus more than 100 miles away.

Attacks on Arabs became more common, fuelling the cycle of violence. One incident that caused great consternation was the killing of Sheikh Jabura Adam Abdel Nabi of the powerful Awlad Zeid tribe. The sheikh was passing through a valley on his way back from market in Seraf Omra in 2001, carrying sugar for distribution in his village of Milleketa, when he was set upon by men wearing khaki. According to al Sanosi Musa,

> his assailants challenged him, saying, 'We don't want Arabs here.' The sheikh replied, 'Where do you want us to go?' They said, 'Go to Libya or Saudi Arabia' – and shot him dead. After this, they killed his eleven-year-old son Mohamed by hitting him with a stone and beat his nephew Dahab Ramadan unconscious. Dahab died forty-eight hours later, claiming his attackers were Masalit and Zaghawa.[79]

In October 2002, government-supported Arab militia from the camps in South Darfur launched a major offensive on Jebel Marra, the greatest offensive since the Fur–Arab war of the 1980s. The militia had attacked many villages around Mershing, Kindingeer and Malam over the previous eighteen months, killing and burning. The new attacks were larger and more systematic. The militia swept down on villages before dawn, killed and often mutilated men, raped women and abducted children. Villages were burnt, livestock seized, fields torched and all infrastructure methodically destroyed. The Awlad Mansour leader Juma Dogolo led the unit that entered Kidingeer on 10 October 2002, and killed thirty civilians including three of Shartai Suleiman Hassaballa's brothers. 'They came in thirty cars,' Shartai Suleiman recalled. 'An Antonov dropped eighteen bombs. After they withdrew, we buried their dead in three places: by the market, south of the school and on the hill.'[80]

Some villagers had already been displaced several times by late 2002. A displaced man in Nyala recounted the saga.[81]

> The problem started in Jebra in 2001. At that time we didn't know the Janjawiid, we just knew that the Arabs had attacked. They killed our doctor and his children and burned the village. The people of Jebra fled to Tegi. A commissioner from Nyala came and told them to return. But in 2002 Janjawiid on horses came and burned the village. This time they ran to Keila after two or three weeks and killed twenty-two people including five teachers. So we all moved to Malam. Then the Janjawiid attacked Siloh and killed four people so we moved to Mershing. There was a second attack on Keila and some people died there, others came to Mershing. They attacked Tegi and killed twenty-five. This time it was army and Janjawiid together. By January 2003 all the people were gathered in Mershing.

It was now clear that the Arab militia enjoyed complete impunity. In the words of a tribal leader in Dar Zaghawa who was once not unfriendly to the government: 'When the Janjawiid burned a village, our people went to the police, but the government didn't care about it. But if Zaghawa attacked Arabs, they went quickly to kill the Zaghawa.' Worse even than impunity, people suspected that powerful men in government in Khartoum were giving the orders. By the end of 2002, at least 160 civilians had been killed, hundreds more wounded and scores of villages burned.[82] Tens of thousands had fled the land, some seeking safety high in Jebel Marra, others congregating in the small towns at the foot of the mountain. It was a prelude to the firestorm that would soon sweep across all Darfur. Determination to resist was growing.

4 | The rebels

He was, at first acquaintance, an unlikely rebel – a security officer, briefly, in the Nimeiri regime, who had travelled across the Arab world for eight years, more concerned with making money than with the NIF's seizure of power back in Sudan. But on returning to Sudan in 1994, Khamis Abakir soon had a first brush with NIF law: angered by the state's refusal to release money he had made while working abroad, he demonstrated in the streets of Khartoum, and spent two days in jail.[1] A decade later, he was the Sudan Liberation Army's (SLA's) most prominent Masalit commander, surrounded by a vastly disparate of group of men like him – men who were not political animals, but who knew injustice when they saw it and who, after years of rising conflict with the government and government-backed militias, finally felt they had nothing left to lose. They, like him, were Muslims; most, unlike him, were devout Muslims who prayed five times a day – on the sand beside their horses if on patrol or, if camped, under the mango trees where they slept. They ranged from teenagers in second-hand T-shirts to fifty-year-old men with gnarled peasants' hands. Their courtesy was striking: without being asked, they fetched water for washing and drinking, offered the best bits of meat on the rare occasions that they had meat, and walked willingly for hours to gather information about this village or that.

These were not the 'armed bandits' the government insisted they were. They were farmers who had been driven from their smallholdings by men wearing army uniforms. Their attacks so far had been precise, against military and security targets. Some had served in the police or army, turning a blind eye to ethnic discrimination until the government they served began attacking their villages and killing their families.

Khamis Ahmad Osman had spent twenty-one years in the

army. He encountered discrimination from the outset. Arabs got two holidays a year; non-Arabs only one. Arab friends who had signed on with him became officers; he never rose above sergeant. He accepted this without protest, seeing no other route out of poverty, until his village, Kassieh, was burned and twenty-one people including his brother, the village imam, were killed. At this point, he asked himself: 'Why am I working for the government? I am not working for money. I am working for my community.'[2] He joined the SLA as soon as he heard of it, to fight 'for freedom and justice'. The Masalit had never had hospitals or schools, he said. Now they had been driven off their land. They had nothing.

Ali Yaqoub Idriss, always impeccable in a blue shirt with two pens in the pocket, had spent twelve years in the police force.

> Arabs pass examinations; Africans do not. My Arab friends
> became officers; I did not. Arab police are kept in the towns.
> African police are sent to villages, where salaries come late. If
> you go to the town to protest you are told: 'Who ordered you to
> come here? Go back!'

In 1999, Ali Yaqoub had been jailed for three months for criticizing the mistreatment of civilians. 'Arab police beat any African who is accused. They torture them by pulling them along with strips of rubber tyre around their necks. Investigations are always done by Arab police. You know the results ...' He joined the SLA after his village, Nouri Jebel, was attacked in December 2003. Almost fifty villagers were killed, and he named them all: Izhaq Idriss Adam, sixty; Ali Ibrahim Barra, sixty; Hussein Barra, four ... 'It is the Janjawiid who are criminals – not us,' he said on a journey through the burned villages of Dar Masalit. 'I was a policeman. I know them all. Many have been in jail, but bought their release.' He named the militia leaders, one by one: 'Ali Ibrahim, thief! Brema Labid, thief! Shineibat, thief! Hamid Dawai, thief!'

There was a smattering of professionals, too, among Khamis Abakir's men. Jamal Abdel Hamman gave up his job in a Khartoum law firm and returned to work as a teacher in his home village, Abun, after four relatives were killed when government planes bombed Habila town in August 2003. He joined the SLA after government and Janjawiid forces burned Abun to the ground in February 2004. Mohamed Dafalla had been a doctor, but joined the rebels, and put hand grenades in his pockets, after Janjawiid burned his clinic in Direisa.

Like most early rebel commanders, Khamis came to the SLA through the self-defence groups which first emerged in Jebel Marra in the late 1980s. When he returned to Darfur in 1995, a new round of communal hostilities was erupting. This started with the administrative reorganization of West Darfur, which Masalit saw as an attempt to usurp the authority of their sultan, and the appointment of a military governor who began a campaign of arrests, imprisonment and torture among prominent members of the Masalit community.[3] Within months, Dar Masalit was in flames. In August 1995, a cluster of villages near Mejmeri were burned to the ground, in a massacre without precedent. In June 1996, another threshold was passed when raiders burned seven villages – Shushta, Kassim Beli, Haraza, Awir Radu, Deeta, Sisi and Torre – in a single day. At least forty-five people were killed, most of them women and children. The Masalit accused the military governor of directing the attacks, which they said were 'well planned ... much more than a tribal or ethnic conflict'. Khamis began rallying Masalit youths to form self-defence groups, to protect their families and their farms. He told them this was not a little local trouble with Arab pastoralists, but a government plan to change the ethnic geography of the region.

Resistance was a local affair – but across Sudan at that time it seemed that the NIF's days in power were numbered. The war in South Sudan had turned against Khartoum and new fronts were opening in eastern Sudan, with more promised elsewhere. In June 1995, at a meeting in Asmara, Eritrea, the SPLA had taken the lead in forming a broader military coalition, the National Democratic Alliance (NDA), which busily recruited Darfurians – especially Masalit – in eastern Sudan and trained them in camps in Eritrea. Later that year an Eritrean mission visited N'Djamena

73

and while it made no progress in getting Idriss Deby's support, Khartoum was worried. In 1997, Arab militiamen based in Jebel Endia burned villages north and west of Geneina, meeting little resistance. Khamis moved to the offensive and in December 1997 led 130 men to Jebel Endia. Most were farmers who had to sell camels to buy weapons. But they attacked and defeated what he called 'the government' in a six-hour battle that ended when the Arab forces fled to Chad, ten miles away, leaving seven men dead. Khamis lost no one.

After this, he said, the burning became continuous.[4] 'They began burning villages twice. By the end of 1998, more than 100,000 Masalit had fled to Chad. We had no choice but to organize. We were fighting for our lives.' In January 1999, the arrival of General Mohamed al Dabi as President Bashir's personal representative heralded a tougher crackdown, and in May Khamis was captured in his home village of Fanganta, a stone's throw from the Chad border. His house was searched and a cache of weapons discovered. President Bashir had just announced a mandatory twenty-year prison sentence for anyone found possessing unauthorized weapons in Darfur, and Khamis was duly sentenced, imprisoned for six months in Geneina and then moved to Cooper prison in Khartoum. After his lawyer, Khamis Yousif Haroun, successfully challenged the legality of his transfer, he was transferred back – first to Geneina and then Zalingei. Khamis was kept shackled in Khartoum and Geneina. 'I spent four years in solitary confinement in tiny cells – one was only one metre by one-and-a-half, without a window. Geneina was the worst place. They tortured me badly.' Despite his ill-treatment, still evidenced by deep scarring almost a decade later, his vision was of a future where Arab and non-Arab would live together as before. 'Our problem is not with the Arabs,' he said. 'It is with the government.'

While in jail in Zalingei, early in 2002, Khamis was visited by a Fur lawyer called Abdel Wahid Mohamed al Nur – a local man who, under the cover of taking up his case, told him about an embryonic rebel movement that was uniting Fur and Zaghawa in Jebel Marra. Khamis determined to escape in order to organize the Masalit too. It was only after he won parole that he managed to slip out of Zalingei at night, in July 2003, and return to his former base in the Achamara mountains, between Mornei and Habila. By then, Abdel Wahid's clandestine resistance had grown into a full-scale rebellion.

The Fur resistance

As Khamis began to organize self-defence units in Dar Masalit in 1996, and presidential elections gave a veneer of respectability to the NIF's seizure of power, a meeting took place in Khartoum which contained the seeds of the future rebel movement in Darfur. The group included three young Fur activists – Abdel Wahid Mohamed al Nur, the SLA's first chairman; Ahmad Abdel Shafi, an education student and the SLA's first coordinator; and Abdu Abdalla Ismail, a modern languages graduate and much later the SLA's first representative in the Ceasefire Commission headquarters set up under the African Union in al Fasher. The three had little political experience, but they began a clandestine organization of remarkable effectiveness.

'We had heard about looting and burning and knew that the Arab Gathering was working very hard, arming Arab tribes and training them in the PDF,' Abdel Shafi recalled almost a decade later.[5]

> Its publications said: 'We are going to kill all *zurga*. Darfur is now Dar al Arab.' They were trying to force us to leave, to take over water and grazing. We said: 'The government is planning to crush our people. What can we do?' We spoke to members of parliament in Khartoum. They agreed on the threat, but said: 'What can we do about it?' We began talking about rebellion and started collecting money from our people in Khartoum.

With the money raised in Khartoum – more than a million Sudanese pounds, an unexpectedly large sum – the Fur bought ammunition from kinsmen in the army and distributed it among self-defence groups. Babikir Abdalla, a young lawyer working in Qatar, began fund-raising among expatriates.

Soon the Fur decided to try to organize the scattered resistance activities that were emerging all over Darfur, starting from the mountainous stronghold of Jebel Marra. Babikir returned from Qatar and Abdel Wahid from Syria, and in October 1997 they met Abdel Shafi in Jebel Marra, set on winning the support of the *aqa'id* (singular: *aqada*), the village commanders who led Fur self-defence groups. Their message to the *aqa'id* was that the real enemy was not the Arabs. It was the government. Young men should be encouraged not to leave Jebel Marra in search of work or education, but to stay in their villages, where they would be trained.

Training on this scale needed serious money, and Abdel Shafi and Babikir travelled to Chad to seek help from President Idriss Deby. They were, they admit, political innocents: Chad and Sudan had signed a mutual security agreement and Deby refused even to meet them. With only $100 between them, the pair soon found themselves without a penny in their pockets and were forced to sell clothes and blankets to pay their way back to Jebel Marra. But they were not discouraged and on their return to Darfur their message was unequivocal. 'The Arabs will not allow us to stay in our land unless we defend ourselves. It is a war of "to be or not to be".' Army veterans were brought in to train new recruits. Each household was asked to provide a little millet for the recruits and emergency food reserves were sold to buy ammunition. Sheikhs saw their powers whittled away as the activists argued that *aqa'id* carried greater authority in time of war. By December 1997, Jebel Marra was mobilized and Abdel Wahid began organizing outside the mountains, in Zalingei and Wadi Saleh. Abdel Shafi returned to Khartoum to mobilize students, political leaders and women. In the evenings, he toured the suburbs, asking for financial contributions to help defend Darfur.

In 2000, while Security's attention was distracted by the split in the ruling party, Fur in Khartoum set up 'cultural groups' that provided a front for political activity and fund-raising. The Ali Dinar Centre for Education and Culture was established, ostensibly to raise awareness about the history and culture of the Fur, in Khartoum's suburbs and shanty towns – Mayo, Haj Yousif and Soba – and soon after in the eastern Sudanese towns of Gedaref and New Halfa, where many Fur had migrated in search of work. A young law student, Tayeb Bashar, was mandated to mobilize students to return to Darfur and formed the Darfur Students' Union. In Jebel Marra, military camps were established outside villages for the first time. To support the new activities, Fur professionals and those in government service were asked to pay a small monthly tax.

Abdel Wahid and his group sought to situate the Fur struggle in a Darfur-wide context, believing that only unity could defeat the NIF. Their first overture, in 1999, was to the Masalit, a tribe with which they shared a common border and which, like them, was suffering at the hands of government-backed militias.[6] But the timing was bad – the Masalit were in the middle of a war and Khamis Abakir was in solitary confinement. The Fur decided to remain in contact with Masalit activists, but not to identify themselves as a political movement, even to their own people. Abdel Shafi attempted, but failed, to make contact with the SPLA underground cells in Khartoum.

The Zaghawa link

It was not until 2001 that the Fur forged their first alliance – not with the Masalit, with whom they had so much in common, but with the Zaghawa, in whom they had little trust. As with the Fur, the Zaghawa armed rebellion was late and reluctant, but for very different reasons. Because of their proximity to Chad and Libya, and the lawlessness of the desert, the Zaghawa had been armed since the 1980s. They clashed with Arabs over grazing and had come into disputes with Fur and other farming tribes over land for the resettlement of drought migrants, but had stayed out of the 1987–89 war. They were well represented in government and the security services in Khartoum and N'Djamena, and had strong links to Libya. Most importantly, Zaghawa merchants were coming to dominate Darfur's trade and commercial sectors. Zaghawa accounted for no more than 8 per cent of the population of Darfur, but, because of their energy, drive and capacity for strategic action, were acquiring wealth and influence disproportionate to their number. Zaghawa merchants dominated the marketplaces in many towns the length and breadth of the region, and Zaghawa farmers were opening up new frontiers of cultivation in South and East Darfur.

Clashes between herders were nothing new in Darfur, but guns and lack of rain made them more frequent and more deadly. 'There were no problems in the 1960s and 1970s,' said Mohamed Tijani, brother of Shartai Adam Sebi Tijani, the head of the Kaliba clan of Dar Gala, whose capital is Kornoi. 'But since the end of the 1970s there was constant fighting with Arabs. This was [Prime Minister] Sadiq al Mahdi's policy from 1987 on. People used to organize themselves in small camps. There was close coordination with the Native Administration.'

As competition for precious water sources increased during the 1983–84 drought, the Zaghawa began establishing small armed camps in the months when Arab herders moved north to water their animals. In 1987, the pattern was reversed: another drought in North Darfur drove Zaghawa south and they fought with Arab militias south of Kebkabiya. Dozens of Zaghawa were killed in the fighting and the survivors were chased back north. By the time the chase was over, almost 200 people were dead.[7] A peace meeting of tribal elders in Kutum reached agreement on compensation, but the agreement was not honoured and the symbiotic relationship of Arab and non-Arab was put under severe strain.

'The Arabs used to send an advance guard when they came to our areas, to tell us how many were coming,' recalled, early in 2004, Omda Bakhit Dabo Hashem of Furawiya, a refugee in Chad's sprawling Oure Cassoni camp.

They took our grass but took good care of the gardens and the people. There was no theft. We ate meat and in return gave the Arabs millet and salt. But we knew trouble was coming when we saw the letters of the Arab Gathering and heard of the burning of

Dar Fur. The attackers wrote *Tahrir Watan al Arabi* [A Liberated Arab Nation] in the ashes. The camels began eating our gardens.

Young Zaghawa activists began buying weapons. Intermittent clashes continued, with half-hearted efforts by the government and tribal leaders to mediate. In May 1991, Zaghawa elders sent a memorandum – the first Zaghawa complaint – to President Bashir, accusing the government of committing 'crimes against humanity' and creating an 'apartheid region' in Darfur by manipulating tribal hierarchies for political ends and attempting to turn 'black' tribes against each other.[8] In 1997, another conference in Kutum agreed that Arab herders would be permitted to move on specific routes, escorted by government forces. But once again the agreement was not enforced.

Survival on the Saharan frontiers of Sudan, Chad and Libya has made Zaghawa chiefs expert in judging political currents and hedging their bets. The arts of forestalling, prevaricating and playing off faraway governments against one another became second nature to desert-edge potentates, skilled at preserving their bailiwicks. The British administration even coined a word 'tagility' (from the Arabic *tajil*, to delay) in grudging admiration for Darfurian chiefs' ability to outmanoeuvre them.[9] As the Masalit wars convinced Darfurians that the government had fallen in with the Arab agenda, Zaghawa intellectuals and politicians looked more closely at the options for joining the opposition.

Sharif Harir, deputy chairman of the Sudan Federal Democratic Alliance and a Zaghawa, actively fomented armed rebellion from Eritrea, his base from 1995 onwards. In 1997, Mustafa Mahmoud Tijani, the elder brother of Shartai Adam Sebi, travelled to Chad to seek support for rebellion among Zaghawa officers from Dar Gala serving in the Chad army. Dar Gala had suffered more than most other Zaghawa areas from clashes with Arabs and Mustafa Mahmoud found considerable support – including from an artillery officer called Abdalla Abakir, who would emerge a few years later as the first military leader of the SLA. He also sought support from Sadiq al Mahdi, who, after being overthrown, had briefly set up an armed wing in Eritrea as part of the NDA. But by 1997 Sadiq was having second thoughts about armed insurrection, remembering the débâcle of 1976, and told the would-be rebels that he wanted peaceful removal of the NIF.[10] Abdalla Abakir and the others remained in Chad.

Escalating local clashes drove the militarization of the Zaghawa. In 1998, six of the seasonal camps that young Zaghawa herders had established more than a decade earlier became permanent armed camps. The following year, tribal leaders met with senior government officials in Khartoum, but in so doing only exacerbated tension. Young activists complained that 'the omdas took money from the government and didn't stop the war'.[11] Soon, Zaghawa began to refuse to pay taxes to a government that they said 'provided no security at all for human beings in Dar Zaghawa, no medical services and no education.'[12]

The Zaghawa's worst fears were realized when the Islamists split in 1999–2000. Many Zaghawa Islamists left the government and Security kept a close eye on them. The biggest crackdown on suspected insurgents took place in September 2000, as the authorities in al Obeid, Port Sudan and above all al Fasher detained dozens of Turabi's followers, suspecting a plan to mobilize the provinces against the centre. But the crackdown didn't stop the swelling resistance, and by 2001 Zaghawa outside Darfur – expatriates in Libya, merchants and students in Khartoum – were agreed there was a need to form an organized resistance group. Clashes with Arab nomads – most seriously the Awlad Zeid – were escalating in Dar Gala, especially around the Bir Taweel wells near Abu Gamra, the most important water source in the area for all tribes. In May 2001, Awlad Zeid killed more than seventy Zaghawa at the wells.[13] Among the dead was the brother of Abdalla Abakir. After the clash, the army deployed in the area and kept Zaghawa away.[14] Weapons captured at Bir Taweel included some that were made in government factories in Khartoum. 'After Bir Taweel we knew for sure that the government was against us,' says one of the first Zaghawa to join the SLA. 'All the people in the area knew they had to do something to respond.'

The first response came at a meeting in Dar Gala, in the Kornoi area, when a twelve-man committee was formed to support the Zaghawa camps. The committee was headed by Khater Tor al Khalla. His deputy was Abdalla Abakir. Just weeks later, a Zaghawa activist with close ties to Chad, Daud Taher Hariga, met Abdel Wahid in Khartoum and suggested a joint effort against the government. Hariga was the representative in Sudan of Chadian President Idriss Deby's ruling party, the Patriotic Salvation Movement, and his involvement seemed to promise Chadian help. The two men agreed to travel to Jebel Marra together to visit the camps the Fur were organizing. Daud Taher and Abdel Wahid set out from Khartoum on 1 July 2001, bound first for Geneina, where they hoped, but failed, to meet leaders of the Masalit resistance: Khamis Abakir was in jail and the second well-known rebel leader, Adam Bazooka, was with the SPLA in Southern Sudan. From Jebel Marra, they travelled to North Darfur. After a second attempt to meet Masalit in Kebkabiya, they arrived in the Kornoi area on 20 July and met immediately with the committee that had been formed to manage the Zaghawa camps.[15] The committee agreed to joint efforts with the Fur and gave Daud Taher a mandate to speak for the Zaghawa.

When did the insurrection begin?

It is usually said that the rebellion in Darfur began on 26 February 2003 when a group calling itself the Darfur Liberation Front (DLF) issued a statement claiming an attack on Golo, the district headquarters of Jebel Marra. But by the time of the attack on Golo, war was already raging in Darfur: the rebels were attacking police stations, army posts and convoys, and Jebel Marra was under heavy ground and air attack. The international community was slow to notice the rebellion in Darfur, focused as it was on efforts to end the war in South Sudan. But the existence of a rebel movement in Darfur had been known to the government since an attack on a police station in Golo in June 2002.[16]

Although it is difficult to identify a single date for the beginning of the rebellion, given the SLA's slow emergence from similar but separate tribally based movements, the most plausible is 21 July 2001, when an expanded Fur and Zaghawa group met in Abu Gamra and swore a solemn oath on the Quran to work together to foil Arab supremacist policies in Darfur. On the Fur side, the group included Abdel Wahid and Abdu Ismail. On the Zaghawa side, it included the first three military leaders of the future rebel movement – Khater Tor al Khalla, Abdalla Abakir and Juma Mohamed Hagar, all of whom came from Dar Gala. The Zaghawa of Darfur had supported Idriss Deby in his bid to overthrow Hissène Habré in 1990. Deby had used Darfur as his rear base, and had fought his way to N'Djamena with Sudanese Zaghawa at his side. On finding no payout in Chad – just like the Arabs who had enlisted to overthrow Habré – they had returned to Darfur, temporarily rebels without a cause.

The two groups decided to continue efforts to forge an alliance with Masalit activists, finally making contact with them in November 2001, and agreed not to declare themselves as a movement until they had political and logistical support to buttress them against the military reaction they knew would follow. Most importantly, they agreed that Khater Tor al Khalla would take 150 Zaghawa to Jebel Marra to train the Fur. A first group of seventeen left immediately, led by Khater. A second group of twenty-five left on 1 August, attacking on the way a police and army post in Abu Gamra.[17]

One of the Zaghawa was a young man called Minni Arkoi Minawi, whose older brother Hussein was married to the sister of Sherif Harir. Minawi, a secondary school graduate with no experience of either civil politics or combat, had been living in Nigeria with his uncle Bahr el Arabi. Harir says he gave Minawi $5,000 to fund rebellion.[18] Minawi denies it and says he never received any support from the SFDA. Whatever the truth of the matter, Minawi was not just on the road to Jebel Marra; he was on the way to claiming leadership of the rebel movement and personal transformation from 'a very, very good guy, very humble', in the words of Abdel Wahid, to a tyrant courted by US diplomats and welcomed in the White House.

The plan agreed in Abu Gamra called for the Zaghawa to stay in Jebel Marra for only three weeks. But many stayed on when training ended, and on 25 February 2002 the rebels mounted a first joint operation against a garrison in the south of the mountain, between Nyala and Tur.[19] Like the SPLA in its day, the SLA began its military activities before its political agenda was clarified. But the operation was a success: the garrison was burned, arms seized and the government troops routed.

The head of the National Security and Intelligence Service in Khartoum, Salah Abdalla 'Gosh', was disturbed. The Fur–Zaghawa alliance and the military proficiency of the rebels were cause for concern. In the National Assembly, an Ereigat Arab MP from North Darfur, Hussein Abdalla Jibreel, called for action. Jibreel complained 'the Fur are arming themselves! Instead of grow-ing mangoes they are growing hashish!' Mohamed Baraka, a Fur MP from Kebkabiya,[20] whose village of Shoba had already been attacked more than a dozen times, replied, 'Why do we not discuss the Janjawiid attacks on Jebel Marra?' He protested that the 300 army soldiers in Kebkabiya, just five miles from Shoba, had never moved to protect the village. Seventeen Fur MPs signed the petition demanding a debate. To their surprise, President Bashir invited them to present their case. The president – well-known among his inner circle for his meticulous grasp of detail – feared what was afoot. A year earlier he had appointed a new governor for North Darfur, General Ibrahim Suleiman, who he hoped would calm the tribal tensions and prevent those he saw as political agitators from escalating the conflict. General Suleiman told Shartai Adam Sebi it would take him six months to settle the situation, and promised to arrest the miscreants.

By the time the Fur MPs went to Bashir's home on 1 May, the war had widened. Their petition documented 181 attacks on eighty-three villages in the Kebkabiya, Jebel Marra, Zalingei and Kas areas. A total of 420 people had been killed and thousands of animals stolen. This was the first real publicity for the growing conflict in Darfur, and the security chiefs were angry. Bashir formed a committee, for the 'Restoration of State Authority and

Security in Darfur', chaired by Ibrahim Suleiman. The committee's first act, following the attack on Golo, was to detain activists on both sides, including two dozen Arab militants and sixty-six prominent Fur, including lawyers, teachers and elders. Some of the Fur were accused of belonging to a group called the Darfur Liberation Front.[21] One of these, arrested in Zalingei on 11 July, was Abdel Wahid Mohamed al Nur. 'Unlike the Zaghawa, the Fur had no experience of fighting a government,' Abdel Wahid said some years later. 'It was not acceptable to fight the government. I lied to them: I told them we needed area defence more than village defence. I did everything to convince [tribal leaders]. I paid, threatened, convinced. But I became their hero when I was captured – because I was defending the *area*!'[22]

Four weeks after his arrest, Abdel Wahid wrote a letter from jail that was smuggled out of Sudan. Signed by him, in an act of some courage, it brought the hidden conflict in Darfur to international attention for the first time. After detailing his own poor health and ill-treatment – 'I have only one lung and I am diabetic. When I was arrested I was suffering from malaria ... The security forces have refused to allow me to see a doctor' – Abdel Wahid wrote: 'In the area of Jebel Marra, Zalingei and Kebkabiya, the security forces act with virtual immunity, terrorizing the Fur people, raiding houses randomly, arresting people including the elderly and children, and detaining them without charge or trial. Many Fur men have fled to the mountains, to find a safe haven, and have left their lands ...' He spoke of the suffering of prisoners held under emergency legislation without charge or trial: 'The cell space is sixteen square metres and is overcrowded: there are twelve of us in this small room without ventilation or windows ... The detainees collected some money among themselves and asked the guards to buy insect spray to kill the mosquitoes, but the guards refused.'

Security's calculation was that, with the leadership decapitated, the embryonic rebel movement would wither and die. It was wrong. Attacks on government forces continued. After an army bus was ambushed on the road between Zalingei and Nyala, and three soldiers were killed, the government agreed to let Fur MPs and chiefs assemble in the small town of Nyertete, on the eastern flank of Jebel Marra, to 'solve the Fur problem', and released a number of Fur detainees to attend it – though not Abdel Wahid. The strategy was divide-and-rule – they wanted to avoid a Fur–Zaghawa alliance.

On 16 August 2002, the 'Fur Leadership Conference' opened in Nyertete, attended by 129 delegates and chaired by a prominent Fur elder, Sultan Hussein Ayoub Ali. The delegates' first act was not what the government wanted: they sent ten men up the mountain to find out the rebels' demands. Mohamed Baraka from Shoba was one of them.[23] A few miles outside Nyertete, in an area completely controlled by the rebels, Baraka found a large meeting in progress between the rebels and the local people, with banners in the Fur language and Abdalla Abakir, recently chosen as the rebels' military leader, presenting ambitious demands. The ten reported back to Nyertete, where the consensus was that the rebels were asking for too much. It would be better to meet alone with the leaders and discuss their real needs. So the ten men trekked back up the mountain and sat until the early hours of the morning with Abakir and his fellow commanders. There were just twenty-three armed men in Abakir's Zaghawa camp, and they said they were ready to withdraw from Jebel Marra. They wanted medicines for their wounded, and a month to prepare.

In a closing statement on 22 August, notable for its conciliatory tone and criticism of all armed actions, the Leadership Conference avoided pointing a finger at 'Arabs' and put the blame for the trouble in Jebel Marra squarely on the government's shoulders. It said Khartoum had failed to implement previous agreements. It had also failed, 'with all its instruments', to tackle injustices and grievances. The government's own forces had committed 'many wrong acts', including rape, and 'continuous humiliation' of Fur civilians. If there was support for rebels, it was because the people had lost all confidence in the security forces. The conference demanded that 'the state carry out its duties in a decisive and firm way to stop the repeated aggressions carried out by some Arab tribes (Janjawiid) against the land and possessions of the Fur'. But the conference also condemned attacks against the police and, stressing the need to maintain Fur unity, sent a thinly veiled warning to the rebels: 'No individual or group has the right to decide any affairs of the tribe without being delegated.' It called for the release of all detainees, the implementation of previous agreements and the withdrawal from Jebel Marra of all 'foreign forces'. Abdel Wahid later clarified that final demand: it was aimed at the Zaghawa forces encamped in Jebel Marra. The government had threatened to attack the mountain unless the Zaghawa left and the Fur put down their arms.[24]

The Nyertete Conference was a brave attempt, very late in the day, at compromise by the Fur leaders. But South Darfur's Arab militants killed it. Less than a month later, another conference was convened in Kas, thirty miles to the south, under the auspices of a well-known supporter of the Arab Gathering – Major General Salah Ali al Ghali, governor of South Darfur. Although billed as the 'Conference of Peaceful Co-existence for the Tribes in and around Jebel Marra', the Kas Conference blamed all the trouble in the region on Fur militias, supported, it alleged, by Fur serving in the Popular Police and Popular Defence Forces. It demanded a 'decisive step' against the Fur militias and, paving the way for the creation of the Arab paramilitary units that came to be known as Janjawiid, the 'liquidation' of the PDF. It called for the creation of new 'nomad constituencies' and development programmes for nomads, ignoring the devastation of Fur areas. It insisted on the release of tribal leaders arrested in North Darfur – among them, a month earlier, Musa Hilal.

Most Fur saw the Kas Conference as a slap in the face to the conciliators who had met in Nyertete, a 'declaration of war' on the Fur. And not without reason. Even as it was claiming to be seeking peace, Khartoum was attempting to win the active support of Arab tribes in the region. Government officials approached the nazir of the Beni Halba, al Hadi Issa Dabaka, and offered him a car, furniture, money and much-needed development projects if he would fight for the government. The nazir had dispatched his Fursan militia against the SPLA in 1991, but this time he refused, saying: 'If an enemy attacks me on my own land, I will defend myself.'[25] The omda of the Awlad Mansour section of the Mahariya, Juma Dogolo, was more ready to do Security's bidding. His militia attacked Jebel Marra in October 2002.

By the beginning of 2003, Jebel Marra was surrounded by government forces and under attack from government-supported militias supported by Antonov bombers and helicopter gunships. One exile group reported that more than 100 Fur civilians were killed between October and December 2002. It said 'government troops are ready to destroy Jebel Marra' and called on the international community to intervene 'before it is too late'.[26] The plea would not be heeded for more than a year.

Looking for friends

For political and logistical support, the Fur and Zaghawa rebels looked initially to the Sudan Federal Democratic Alliance (SFDA) of former governor Ahmad Diraige, a member of the National Democratic Alliance. They found sympathy from his deputy Sharif Harir, who had resigned his post as a lecturer in social anthropology in Norway in 1995 and gone to Eritrea to head the SFDA forces based there. Harir recruited Darfurians from eastern Sudan, some of whom had fought on Sudan's eastern front, and later went as far as to claim that the fighters in Jebel Marra were the military wing of the SFDA. But Diraige disagreed with him over the wisdom of armed rebellion and the Darfur rebels received little or no help from the SFDA. Some in the SLA say it was at this point that the SPLA leader, John Garang, offered Abdel Wahid support – on condition that he form a strategic alliance with the South.

The disastrous finale of Daud Bolad's adventure in 1991 had not discouraged the SPLA from seeking to draw Darfur into war against the government. Abdel Aziz Adam al Hilu, who had commanded that force and was now the SPLA's commander on the eastern front, was in charge of SPLA recruitment and training of northern Sudanese, including Darfurians. His prize catch was a Chadian Masalit, Adam Mohamed Musa, known as 'Adam Bazooka', who had helped Idriss Deby seize power in Chad in 1990 and then served as acting commander of the Abeche garrison. In 1994, Deby appointed a fellow Zaghawa to command Abeche and Bazooka crossed to Darfur with two burning aims: to collect and train young men to fight the Arabs, and then to depose Deby as president of Chad.[27] Bazooka's vision, which conflicted with Khamis Abakir's agenda of village self-defence, troubled Masalit leaders in Khartoum. They summoned Bazooka, contacted the SPLA and convinced Bazooka to join the SPLA's 'Eastern Front'. 'The Masalit wanted to get rid of Adam,' said the activist who hid Bazooka in his house in Khartoum. 'Adam wanted help to become president of Chad.' As militia attacks escalated in 1995, Adam Bazooka was smuggled to Gedaref, linked up with the SPLA there and crossed to Eritrea.

Hundreds of other Masalit, including former PDF members, joined him to form a Masalit unit within the SPLA's 'New Sudan Brigade' under the command of Abdel Aziz al Hilu.[28] Their plan was train the recruits, give them political orientation, and invade Darfur from South Sudan with the aim of linking up with Khamis Abakir in Dar Masalit. In 1999, Bazooka and his forces flew from Eritrea to South Sudan. But instead of beginning a new Darfur operation, they were redeployed in an attack on Torit, one of the government's most important garrisons in the South. Then Abdel Aziz al Hilu, who was to have commanded the Darfur mission, was sent to the Nuba mountains to replace the Nuba leader Yousif Kuwa after his death from cancer in March 2001. The Darfur operation didn't begin until three months later, when a combination of Southern and Darfurian troops, including Bazooka, captured Raja in Bahr al Ghazal and headed north towards Darfur. An army counterattack defeated and dispersed the SPLA troops and the government retook Raja in September. Bazooka would not return to Darfur until October 2003, at the head of a thirty-strong SPLA-trained unit of Masalit guerrillas.

Attempts to mobilize Darfur to the SPLA continued. The SPLA's point man for Darfur was Yasir Arman, a prominent northerner in the Southern-based rebel movement, with the SPLA's representative in Tripoli, Omar Abdel Rahman, known as Omar 'Fur' on account of his Fur ethnicity, in a supporting role. Before the emergence of the SLA, Omar Fur had held a meeting in Tripoli with thirty-eight 'of the blackest' Darfurian activists and told them: 'Collect one hundred people, and we will support you.'[29]

As Abdel Wahid's name gained currency, Garang made direct contact with him, sending two people from the SPLA-controlled Nuba mountains to meet him in Jebel Marra early in 2002 with a Thuraya satellite telephone hidden in a jerrycan. Abdel Wahid spoke first to Abdel Aziz al Hilu and then to Garang himself. He recalls a two-hour conversation in which Garang asked him 'Why are you fighting?' He replied: 'To liberate my country. This is a movement – not a militia.' The conversation concluded, according to Abdel Wahid, with Garang saying: 'You have vision and self-confidence. Do you have an airstrip? I want to send you weapons and bring you to Southern Sudan.'[30]

Abdel Wahid was an enthusiastic but not wholly uncritical admirer of John Garang. 'Dr John was sometimes very tough with his people,' he said. 'But he was a man of vision. I was very, very, very, very happy with his vision. The only problem was the call for self-determination. I was very tough with him. I told him: "Why accept something you are not fighting for? The problem is not the Sudanese; the problem is the system."'

On New Year's Day in 2003, two of Abdel Wahid's most trusted associates, Ahmad Abdel Shafi and Babikir Abdalla, met Garang at the small Hillcrest Hotel in Nairobi, an SPLA favourite. Garang wanted the Fur to declare for the SPLA, but they refused. They told him: 'We believe in the New Sudan as a concept, but we have our own problems in Darfur. If we declare ourselves as SPLA, the Arabs will not accept us. Let us have our own movement first. Then we can make arrangements.'[31] Garang agreed, but urged them to organize militarily and politically and to publish a manifesto.[32] 'Without strong political work,' he told them, 'the government will call you thieves and robbers.'

The two continued on to Rumbek in South Sudan where they

were joined by Abdalla Abakir and Minni Minawi, who had been dispatched to the South to receive the weapons promised by Garang. Abdel Wahid's decision to send only Zaghawa is criticized by some of his colleagues as a lapse of judgement that opened the door for the Zaghawa 'to steal the movement'. Abdel Wahid, however, defends his decision. 'Abdalla was a military man and knew weapons, but he was not even able to write his own name. Minni was a high school graduate; he was Abdalla's secretary. I thought it would give the Zaghawa confidence that they were a part of our movement.'

In February 2003, the SLA delegation flew back to Darfur together with twenty-two SPLA officers led by Paul Molong, the SPLA commander of Bahr al Ghazal and an expert in the use of artillery, anti-tank rifles and heavy machine guns. Abdalla Abakir's bodyguard, a seventeen-year-old Fur from Jebel Marra called Ahmad Nur, refused to return with them. He understood the Zaghawa language and had overheard conversations that led him to believe the Zaghawa were plotting against Abdel Wahid. 'If we go back, I am going to blow up the plane,' he warned the Fur in Rumbek. 'It is better we die here than have problems there. They are planning to destroy you.' A few days later, Nur refused to get on the plane when it prepared to depart from Akot in Bahr al Ghazal. The flight took off, without him, only after Commander Malong had called John Garang, who said: 'Leave him behind![33]

In the same month, the Darfur rebels attacked and briefly occupied the village of Golo and claimed to have set up a rebel civilian administration. The man chosen as administrator, Abdalla Korah, appealed to local people to support him to end the marginalization and injustice that he said was depriving Darfur of development.[34] It was the first political statement by the rebels to reach the outside world. Days later, Abdel Wahid announced, in telephone calls to Sudanese researchers in London, that the Darfur rebels were concerned with the rights of all marginalized Sudanese. To reflect this, he said, the DLF had been renamed the Sudan Liberation Movement/Army, or SLM/SLA.

On 16 March, two and a half months after the meeting with Garang in Nairobi, the SLM/SLA made public its 'political declaration', or manifesto. Senior SPLA officials claim that they wrote it, and the declaration certainly bears a striking resemblance to the SPLA's vision of a 'New Sudan that belongs equally to all its citizens'. Like the SPLA, the SLA deplored political and economic marginalization and demanded decentralization as a basis for 'viable' unity. Like the SPLA, it demanded secular government. Without specifically mentioning Shari'a law, it said, 'Religion belongs to the individual and the state belongs to all of us.' It appealed to Arabs to join it:

> The Arab tribes and groups are an integral and indivisible component of Darfur social fabric who have been equally marginalized and deprived of their rights to development and genuine political participation ... The real interests of the Arab tribes of Darfur are with the SLM/SLA and Darfur not with the various oppressive and transient governments of Khartoum.

Four days later, the SPLA issued a declaration of its own.[35] It denied any connection to the rebellion in Darfur, but expressed 'full political solidarity with the people of Darfur and their just cause'. It said the formula being discussed at the North–South peace talks on the status of the so-called 'Three Areas' – the Nuba mountains, Abyei and Blue Nile – could be the 'correct formula' for Darfur too. The SLA leaders were not happy with that; they wanted a much stronger deal for Darfur, with the North–South talks widened to include them.

The nature and extent of the relationship between the SLA and the SPLA was, from the very beginning, a matter of heated debate, both inside and outside the SLA. The Sudan government claimed that Abdel Wahid was being supplied by the SPLA and attempted to depict the rebels as tools of the southerners. Within the already fractious rebel movement, the issue of relations with the SPLA quickly became one of the most divisive issues. By late 2004, some Zaghawa commanders were threatening to go their own way entirely if the SLA allowed itself to be 'used' by the SPLA.

'John Garang is a very bad man,' said a Zaghawa commander who attended the peace talks in Abuja:[36]

> He sent weapons separately to the Fur, Masalit and Zaghawa in order to divide and rule. He wants us to belong to him like Abyei and the Nuba mountains. He wants us to join the Naivasha process [under the SPLA]. We are going to tell Abdel Wahid we don't want to belong to the SPLA. The fighters on the ground in Darfur are Zaghawa. They control all of North Darfur and half of South Darfur. Most SLA commanders are Zaghawa; most victories are Zaghawa victories. In the SLA there is no victory without our people.

The Sudan government accused Eritrea of organizing logistical support for the Darfurian rebels and it is likely that the first weapons sent to the SLA through the SPLA were Eritrean in origin.[37] Eritrean policy was run by Yemane Gebreab, the second most powerful man in Asmara next to President Isseyas Afewerki. The political and security side was implemented by Abdella Jaber and the military logistics were organized by Major General Teklay Mangoos, the army chief of staff. The Eritreans were both consistent and opportunistic, and had been trying since 1995 to open a western front against Khartoum. The SPLA was a willing partner in Eritrean designs, even after it signed the Machakos Protocol with the Sudan government on 20 July 2002 – a protocol which was the turning point in the negotiations to end the war in South Sudan. At Machakos, the government recognized the right of self-determination for the South. Sudanese, North and South, celebrated. But there was no ceasefire, and just a few weeks later the SPLA captured Torit, with substantial Eritrean military assistance. President Bashir, who had called Garang a patriot just a few days previously, was furious, and vowed to recapture Torit before resuming any peace talks. In the event, the Sudanese army retook Torit in October and the talks resumed. A ceasefire was agreed this time, but routinely violated as both sides continued to position themselves in case the talks fell apart.

Darfurians were aggrieved by their exclusion from the North–

South peace process. Sharif Harir of the SFDA visited Nairobi in July 2001 in the hope of getting a Darfurian voice heard by the mediators, but IGAD officials refused to meet with him unless the SPLA made a formal request. Garang consistently refused to do this, demanding instead that Harir join the SPLA. Garang was not only blocking the Darfurians – along with the Beja and other northern opposition groups – from the peace forum. He was encouraging rebellion in Darfur by providing crucial military support to the Darfur rebels. Throughout the peace talks, the SPLA commander-in-chief continued to follow parallel tracks to create a 'New Sudan'. Seeking a negotiated peace was one, a combination of military pressure and popular uprising to bring down the NIF regime was another, and a third was an outright military victory. The offensive in Torit and arms shipments to Darfur were elements of the third track.

Garang's confidence in the armed track reflected the support that his rebellion had always had from neighbouring governments, including (at that time) Uganda and Eritrea. Both these countries were actively engaged in supporting insurgents in the Democratic Republic of Congo and Sudan. In 1996 the governments of Eritrea, Ethiopia, Uganda and Rwanda hatched a master plan to enact regime change in Kinshasa and Khartoum, and won a green light from the Clinton administration's Africa team.[38] By 2002, the grand plan was in tatters, but the war it had unleashed in DRC was out of control. Across the rainforests of Equateur province, Chadian ground forces supported by Sudanese aircraft fought with Ugandan troops and the guerrillas of the Movement for the Liberation of Congo led by Jean-Pierre Bemba. Both sets of adversaries then extended their wars into the Central African Republic (CAR), where tens of thousands of Southern Sudanese refugees were living and the SPLA was exercising de facto control over the country's eastern hinterlands. The Sudanese army was briefly there too, ostensibly as part of a peacekeeping mission. After failed coup attempts in August 2001 and October 2002, Zaghawa mercenaries based in Chad finally overthrew the government of Ange-Félix Patassé in March 2003, in the process defeating and expelling Bemba's forces and their Ugandan and Libyan advisers.[39] With French support and Sudanese welcome, the Chadians installed François Bozizé in power in Bangui. The CAR operation united Zaghawa of all political affiliations. Even those opposed to Deby and involved in the SLA were keen to participate and celebrated its success. While Bemba rearmed, courtesy of Eritrea, the SPLA faced the threat of being outflanked by Sudanese forces based in CAR. In the context of this great game, played out from the Red Sea to the Congo estuary, Uganda and Eritrea took a renewed interest in Darfur as a strategic flank to their continental war, and sought to nurture a special relationship with the Zaghawa as the kingmakers in CAR.[40]

The SLA commanders who arrived in South Sudan in early 2003 were given not only weapons, but military training and extensive political advice. At least one of them – Ahmad Abdel Shafi – returned to Darfur as a member of the SPLM. Sudanese Security was well aware of what was going on, and accused the SPLA of negotiating the Naivasha accords in bad faith. Whatever Garang had in mind for the SLA, there is no doubt that he was playing the Darfur card to strengthen his hand vis-à-vis Khartoum, positioning himself for either the success or the failure of his negotiations with the North.

Search for a cohesive leadership

Despite the anxieties of many Zaghawa, time would prove that the SLA's contact with the SPLA was not the core problem facing the young rebel movement. Far more fundamental problems sprang from ethnic divisions, issues of personality, lack of leadership skills and the rapid growth of the movement, especially after the rebels launched a spectacularly successful attack on the government's main air base in Darfur, at al Fasher, in April 2003. In its earliest days, the SLA leadership was clandestine and relatively disciplined. But Darfur was already militarized and every community controlled its own means of waging war. The Fur had their *aqa'id,* the Zaghawa their armed camps and the Masalit their self-defence groups. All had men with experience in the Sudan army. The Zaghawa had experts in desert warfare from the Chadian campaigns who were becoming stronger as they seized government vehicles in attacks on police and army posts. There was no way the young SLA leaders could impose their command either on these seasoned warriors, or on the thousands of raw recruits who flooded the infant movement as a result of triumph but also defeat. From a few hundred recruits in 2001, the SLA was claiming, by 2005, to be fielding a force of almost 11,000 men organized in thirteen brigades.[41] Many had their own guns, and were driven by bitterness.

The SLA emerged into the political arena as a marriage of convenience rather than of conviction – a coming together of tribally organized armed groups on the basis of what united them, with very little discussion of what divided them. It was a recipe for disaster. In their first meetings with the Darfurian activists, SPLA leaders had urged them to learn from the mistakes they had made, and not to succumb to the tribal divisions that had so weakened the southern rebel movement. 'We told them: "Unity, unity, unity",' said Abdel Aziz al Hilu. 'They didn't listen.'[42]

The divisions were already apparent in a series of meetings held in Boodkay, on the western slopes of Jebel Marra, early in 2002. The Boodkay area had been deserted for several years because of militia attacks and it was here that the Zaghawa were taken when they arrived in Jebel Marra in August 2001. Feeling neglected by the Fur in this desolate place, Minawi says, the Zaghawa established their own leadership structure[43] and determined 'to bring the Fur inside the [Zaghawa-led] movement'. In a series of difficult, disorganized meetings between March and May 2002, the two sides attempted to unify their ranks and eventually agreed to distribute the key posts in the movement on a tribal basis. A Fur would be chairman, a Zaghawa military commander and a Masalit vice-chairman. In the following days, each tribe chose its man: the Fur chose Abdel Wahid and the Zaghawa Abdalla Abakir. The post of vice-chairman was left empty and filled, by Khamis Abakir, only in February 2005.[44] Although there were no Arabs in the leadership, several held, or would soon hold, the rank of commander – among them, in South Darfur, Ahmad Kubbur, a Rizeigat merchant who had been recruited by the SPLA some years earlier, and in Jebel Marra, Ismail Idriss Nawai, a Hawazma lawyer from Kordofan.

The Boodkay meetings were the first and only time that Fur and Zaghawa principals in the SLA sat down together to give the movement shape. As a result, the SLA was always structurally weak and prone to tribal splits. In the years that followed, it divided, sub-divided and then fragmented until more than half a dozen groups claimed the name SLA and many commanders represented little more than the environs of their own villages.

The ordinary people of Jebel Marra had never wanted the Zaghawa in their midst. They tolerated them for a while, reluctantly, because Abdel Wahid told them they were there to help defend the mountain against the Arabs. But when they realized that the rebels were fighting the government, with its planes and its artillery, they came to see the Zaghawa as a threat. Government agents stirred the pot, spreading word that the Zaghawa wanted to create a 'greater Dar Zaghawa' that reached as far as South Darfur and the Central African Republic. The Fur were soon accusing the Zaghawa of arrogant and abusive behaviour, including the murder of a number of chiefs, among them Shartai Yousif Yahya of Rokero.[45] The Zaghawa, for their part, felt disregarded by the Fur. Whenever there was a threat from the Arab militia, Minawi said, the Zaghawa were sent off to repel it. 'Soon after we arrived, we were told Janjawiid had attacked the Oseja area, and were killing and looting. Twenty of us moved. We arrived at 10 a.m., saw the bodies and buried them. I got an idea we were being used.'

Tensions increased sharply with the decision, which Abdel Wahid says was his, to send the SPLA weapons to North Darfur rather than to Jebel Marra, which was under close government scrutiny at the time. Abdel Wahid and his colleagues would later disagree on many things; but they remained united in their account of what happened at this stage of the rebellion. The Zaghawa collected weapons from the Fur in Jebel Marra, saying they were needed to protect the airstrip that was being built to receive the weapons shipments at Um Grud, north of Furawiya; SLA forces in Jebel Marra were ordered to Dar Zaghawa, ostensibly to prepare the airstrip; the SPLA officers sent by John Garang, whom the Fur believed were meant to train recruits in Jebel Marra, never got there and instead were retained in Dar Zaghawa to advise on military operations (and to participate in some of them). The SPLA men left after only a few months, concerned by indiscipline and tribal tensions, and warning one of the older Zaghawa activists: 'You will have trouble with these boys!'[46]

In February 2003, the government sent 4,000 troops from Nyertete to try to capture Jebel Marra. The Fur were driven high up the mountain before they managed to turn the offensive around. They captured more than a thousand weapons, but were short of ammunition. Abdel Wahid called Ahmad Abdel Shafi and Babikir Abdalla in North Darfur on their Thuraya telephones, but was unable to connect with them: Minawi had taken their phones away.[47] It was not until Abdel Wahid telephoned Minawi and accused him of killing his friends that he was finally able to make contact with them. They left North Darfur secretly and returned to Jebel Marra, agreed not to challenge the Zaghawa in North Darfur but rather to open a new front in the south of Jebel Marra. The tribal split was becoming military, and relations between Fur and Zaghawa were stretched to breaking point.

As the war spread to Dar Zaghawa, more and more SLA fighters were moved north from Jebel Marra. The Fur claim they were supposed to be rotated back, but never were. In April 2003, a Zaghawa commander in Jebel Marra, Mohamed Adam, told Abdel Wahid he had received orders to move all troops to Dar Zaghawa. When Abdel Wahid protested that Jebel Marra would be left undefended, Adam told him: 'These are orders!' Abdel Wahid claims his personal protection was reduced to 'fourteen people, twelve guns, four of which were not working, and 412 bullets'.

Following a string of rebel victories in the middle months of 2003, the government counterattacked, unleashing a new campaign of destruction in Wadi Saleh in August and sending its troops on a massive operation into North Darfur in December. In February 2004, thousands of government troops and militia attacked the Sindu area, an SLA stronghold in Wadi Saleh. A number of Fur villages in the area were completely destroyed: Zari, Arwala, Furgo, Kerti, Sogna, Gaba, Kaskildo, Dege. Abdel Wahid called Minawi for help, but got no response. He asked for reinforcements from Zaghawa fighters who had been given safe haven in eastern Jebel Marra, but was rebuffed. He called Minawi's chief of staff, Juma Hagar, who told him: 'Ask Minni.' Abdel Wahid's furious response was 'I am your chairman!' A rescue mission was finally mounted by the SPLA, which managed to land a plane on the flat and hard clay soils of Sindu, where Abdel Wahid had spent three days hiding in a hole in the ground, and at the end of February the SLA chairman was flown to safety.[48] Abdel Wahid recalled later,

> When the [September 2003 Abeche] ceasefire broke down, the government attacked us massively. They entered all Dar Zaghawa. They attacked me in Dreisa. I went to Wadi Saleh. The government surrounded the area. There was a seesaw battle. All my commanders knew I was the target. Dr John [Garang] called me. Roger Winter [a senior US humanitarian official] called me. They said: 'We need you in N'Djamena [for renewed ceasefire talks with the Sudan government].' The government wanted to catch me before N'Djamena.

Both Abdel Wahid and Minni Minawi made it to N'Djamena, Minawi picked up from Darfur by Winter in an American-hired charter plane. After hurriedly negotiating a 'humanitarian ceasefire' with the government on 8 April 2004 in the Chadian capital, the SLA leaders tried and failed to rebuild the unity of the movement. They agreed to return to Darfur to mend their differences. But Abdel Wahid disappeared – re-emerging weeks later with a bride – and Minawi went to Asmara. Instead of building their political cadres, the SLA's leaders became ambassadors. An 'internal–external' divide was added to the ethnic split. Abdel Wahid began to spend all his time outside Darfur, setting up an office in Nairobi and a headquarters in Asmara, and lobbying for international pressure and assistance. Fur leaders who had earlier respected him for taking on the difficult work of organizing the resistance grumbled that he had become a 'hotel guerrilla'. His failure to brief his men in the field on the political developments outside it alienated many of them.

Another split, equally important for the course of the rebellion, divided the founder members of the SLA from many older activists who had initially supported it. 'The SLA problem is a leadership problem,' Adam Ali Shogar, a Zaghawa veteran of almost twenty years' political militancy, said in 2004.[49] 'They are young and inexperienced and leave no openings for intellectuals and men of experience. They have no political system. They are not democratic. They were elected when the SLA had only a few hundred men. Now there are thousands.'

Critics began calling for a conference of commanders and intellectuals, inside Darfur, to revalidate – or renew – the leadership. In a statement made public in February 2005, a group of expatriates accused the leaders of the SLA of 'trying to deceive the world around them that their movement is united'. It said the leadership split was damaging the movement's political vision. By early 2005, hundreds of young men had deserted the movement, worried by its lack of direction, deteriorating discipline and the abusive behaviour of soldiers and commanders answerable only to themselves. They expressed doubt as to whether the SLA, as presently constituted, could reform itself. 'Be careful,' a young Zaghawa graduate warned. 'The SLA does not like criticism.'

The Justice and Equality Movement

Of the SLA fighters camped under the mango trees in Dar Masalit in March 2004, approximately a third had begun their lives under arms in the Justice and Equality Movement (JEM). Darfur's second rebel movement announced itself within weeks of the SLA, keen to step out of the shadow of the SLA and put itself on the international map. But it was weak militarily and overreached at once. Government forces surrounded its men as

they threatened the border town of Tine and, having no reinforcements to call on, they had to appeal to the SLA for rescue. Many
subsequently joined the SLA. It was a small step: the heartland
of JEM lies along the Chad border, north of Dar Masalit, and
for many in those early days geography was enough to decide
allegiance. These men were fighting for their communities more
than political ideologies.

Controlled by Islamists from the Kobe tribe, a Zaghawa sub-
group more numerous in Chad than in Darfur, JEM never packed
the military punch that the SLA initially did. But it was JEM that
struck fear into the Sudan government, even after it suffered a
series of splits that by 2007 reached into the heart of its leadership. Explaining why eight JEM delegates had been invited to
peace talks in Tanzania in 2007, compared with only three for
each SLA faction, a senior western diplomat said: 'Whenever
you meet with the intelligence people in Khartoum, it's clear
they don't give a damn about the SLA. What really worries them
is JEM.' And in JEM, specifically, its chairman, Khalil Ibrahim,
whose Kobe inner circle held the real, and some said the only,
power in JEM.

Khalil Ibrahim frightened the regime for many reasons. He
was highly educated, a superb organizer who understood the
importance of publicity and knew how to get it. As a descend-
ant of Zaghawa sultans on both sides of his family, he enjoyed
respect and support among the tribal leaders of the Darfur Native
Administration. He knew the National Islamic Front from the
inside, having supported its military coup in 1989 and having
held a number of important regional portfolios under the NIF
in Darfur, South Sudan and Blue Nile, abutting the Ethiopian
border in the east of Sudan. Most critically, he had been close to
Hassan al Turabi before Turabi's defeat by President Bashir and,
some said, he still was, although he himself vigorously denied
it. Like Turabi, Khalil wanted to rectify the faults of the Islamic
movement in Sudan; like Turabi, he believed that the power to
unseat the NIF lay with the marginalized minorities of Sudan
working together; like Turabi, it was whispered, he wanted power

for himself. The Iraqis, Khalil once said, had chosen a Kurdish president. Why then should the Sudanese not choose a Darfurian? Khartoum's fear was a two-pronged assault: JEM from Darfur and Turabi's Popular Congress Party from within.

Khalil never pretended that the neglect and marginalization of Darfur was his prime concern. His political objective, he said, was the unity of Sudan. 'The most important aim behind our movement's taking up arms is the fear of the country being torn,' he said after Khartoum granted self-determination to the South in 2005. 'We oppose the secession of any part of Sudan ... We live in the age of large blocs. We want to unite the Horn of Africa region in one state that includes Egypt, Libya, and Chad. We want a continent state [sic].'[50] If the Bashir regime remained in power, Khalil said, the South would secede from the rest of Sudan at the first opportunity. 'We will not lay down arms until after the government falls, or a fair political settlement is reached for all the peoples in Sudan's provinces.' This programme was a calculated strike at Bashir's two weakest points: the centralization of power within a Khartoum elite and his implicit surrender of South Sudan as part of the Naivasha Comprehensive Peace Agreement.

Most Sudanese Islamists believe that Khartoum was not militarily defeated in the South, but lost the battle for international public opinion. Deftly riding – and steering – the western public's revulsion at the atrocities in Darfur, JEM cadres abroad began to campaign to portray the conflict in Darfur as genocide early in 2004. A successful campaign would delegitimize the Khartoum government, foster regime change and forestall self-determination for the South. While his men struggled to hold their own in the field, Khalil set about trying to form a wider opposition front to 'finish off' the regime. 'Khalil strongly believes in a march to overthrow the regime from Darfur, Kordofan and South Sudan,' said a prominent member of Sadiq al Mahdi's Umma Party who met with him in 2003 in Germany, where Khalil announced the formation of the Union of the Marginalized Majority, the first of a succession of broader fronts that he established.[51] 'He believes the national problem has to be solved in the context of the whole of Sudan. All Darfurians feel Khalil Ibrahim is capable. He has a project, at least.'[52]

From The Black Book to guerrilla operations

The project that became JEM can be traced back to 1996, when a group of young people from Darfur and Kordofan – most of them university graduates and Islamists – met in Khartoum, and agreed that Sudan's traditional parties were part of their problems and could not provide solutions. One of the group was Abubaker Hamid Nur, an agricultural engineer with a degree in sustainable development who would become general coordinator of JEM and one of its strongest military commanders:

> From earliest youth we felt there was a problem, but we but didn't know what it was. There was too much suffering. I travelled 60 kilometres to go to primary school, in Kornoi, when I was seven; 350 kilometers to go to intermediate school in Geneina; 400 kilometers to go to secondary school, in Fasher; and 1,000 kilometres to go to university in Khartoum. It was forbidden to speak the Zaghawa language in school. In primary school, the teacher gave us a blue ticket to pass to any boy who spoke Zaghawa. At the end of the day, anyone who had had the ticket was whipped. The whole of Kutum province, with a population of more than 551,000, had one general doctor and no specialists. Women walked more than eight hours daily to get less than 60 litres of water. We were excluded from all key posts and had no way of communicating with the international community to ask for help. Why? Because a gang in Khartoum was controlling everything.[53]

Abubaker and his friends decided their first task was to educate ordinary Sudanese about the imbalances in Sudan and late in 1996 formed a twenty-five-man committee to start collecting information. The result, in May 2000, was *The Black Book*, a political and economic anatomy of Sudan that detailed the marginalization of most of Sudan's citizens. Part Two of *The Black*

Book appeared in August 2002, on the website of JEM. Making clear that JEM was fighting not only against marginalization but also had a national agenda for political change, it called for a 'comprehensive congress' to redress injustices perpetrated by 'a small group of autocratic rulers'.

Between the publication of the two volumes of *The Black Book*, Sudan's Islamist movement had been ripped asunder. The split that surfaced in 1999 had deepened into an intense power struggle whose outcome, week by week, looked uncertain. There were waves of arrests in September 2000 and February 2001, particularly in Turabi's provincial strongholds including al Fasher. Hopes for reconciliation or a resort to civilian politics were dashed, especially when Bashir won 86 per cent of the vote in the December 2000 elections, with no candidate from the Turabi bloc able to stand because of the crackdown. Meeting in Geneva on 19–20 February 2001, senior representatives of the SPLA and Turabi's Popular Congress Party signed a surprise memorandum of understanding. This pact between two parties with polar opposite ideologies led to an immediate crackdown on Turabists in Khartoum and a purge of military and security officials whose loyalty was considered suspect. The contents of the memorandum were bland: a set of common commitments to democracy and pluralism, with the major differences between the two glossed over. It did not add up to a common conspiracy to foment war in Darfur.[54]

From the outset, JEM was dogged by the suspicion that it was a stalking horse for Turabi, his stepping stone back to power in a Sudan in which the marginalized regions would finally come into their own. Its very name echoes the oldest slogans of Sudan's Muslim Brothers. The suspicion was reinforced by the fact that when the NIF split, Darfurian Islamists sided overwhelmingly with Turabi's faction. Khalil's closest colleagues insisted that he was different. At the time of the split, Khalil was abroad, studying for a master's degree in public health at Maastricht University, and was invited back to Sudan. 'Bashir and Turabi both sent people to the airport to meet him, but he went home alone,' says

Ahmad Tugod, a relative who became JEM's delegation head at the peace talks in Abuja. 'Later he met both. Bashir offered him a job as manager of Omdurman hospital. He refused. He was offered a government job. He refused. The interpretation was that he is a Turabi man. But Turabi sent him two envoys, and Khalil told them: "The Islamic movement in Sudan has collapsed."'

Khalil and his closest colleagues set about meeting with a wide range of Sudanese political activists. Among them were the civilian leaders of a nascent grouping that became the Justice Party, led by Amin Banani, a prominent Islamist from the Habbaniya of South Darfur. No agreement was reached – Banani and his group insisted that political change should come from within and by civil means only. 'Any opposition not grounded on Sudanese soil is not worth it,' said one of the party leaders.[55] A member of Khalil's office in the Netherlands, Idriss Ibrahim Azraq, travelled to SPLA headquarters in Yei and met with Garang's deputy, Salva Kiir Mayardit, but no agreement was reached. Idriss reported that the SPLA's intelligence chief, Edward Lino, was blocking his access to Garang. The SPLA's message to JEM was the same as it had been to the SLA in the Hillcrest Hotel: 'Be part of the SPLA.' This time it had a corollary: 'Bring Fur!' Khalil later met secretly with Garang in Brussels, but they disagreed on the vexatious question of religion and state.[56]

By 2002, the authors of *The Black Book* had come to the conclusion that the regime in Khartoum could not be influenced by civil politics, and an armed movement to be called the Justice and Equality Movement was in the making. The movement's spokesman would be Khalil Ibrahim, and for security reasons he would be based outside Sudan. In 2003, JEM announced itself publicly and began coordinating with the SLA. Abubaker Hamid Nur claims that JEM wanted unity with the (far larger) SLA, but the SLA refused. In October 2003, Abubaker met Minni Minawi and Abdel Wahid separately in North Darfur. Both opposed unification, saying that Darfurians would not accept Islamists again. Abubaker replied that all parties had failed, Islamists included, and JEM rejected them all. Abdel Wahid was convinced that

JEM's desire for cooperation was purely tactical. 'They are only fighting for seats [in parliament, to regain lost influence]. If they are given seats, they will not fight any longer.'[57]

A five-point manifesto made public by JEM early in 2003 was broadly similar to the SLA's but laid even greater stress on the need for national solutions, including, in later demands, a presidency that would rotate among all Sudan's main regions. The manifesto called for a unified Sudan; justice and equality in place of social injustice and political tyranny; 'radical and comprehensive constitutional reform' that would 'guarantee the regions their rights in ruling the country'; basic services for every Sudanese; and balanced economic and human development in all regions of the country. The Justice and Equality Movement rejects the idea that religion is a root cause of Sudan's problem but, unlike the SLA, does not talk about separation of state and religion. In a section of its website entitled 'Resolving the Issue of Religion and the State', it says religion has been manipulated both by the government, 'for political reasons that brought nothing good either to the people or to the state', and by the SPLA, which had 'exploited religion in order to gain western aid and support'. Islamic law should not be imposed on non-Muslims, 'and the believers of the other faiths must not oppose Muslims' attempts to apply the laws of their religion for themselves'.[58] This wording treads a fine line between constitutional secularism and enshrining Shari'a for Muslims. It is a subtle position – perhaps inconsistent, but entirely within the mainstream of northern Sudanese political thought. Sadiq al Mahdi attempts precisely the same balancing act when he insists that rights should be based on citizenship alone, not religious faith, but also argues that Muslims have the right to live in a society governed by Islamic principles.

Throwing off the past

As the rebellion progressed, and fighting in Darfur became more important than politicking in Khartoum, Khalil became increasingly outspoken in his criticism of Turabi, going as far as to tell UN investigators in 2004 that Turabi was 'the main reason for the atrocities committed in Darfur'.[59] 'Turabi will be our first enemy,' he insisted in March 2006. 'We have no contacts with Hassan Turabi.'[60] Khalil's protestations cut no ice with Khartoum, which in August 2004 convinced the Gulf state of Dubai to expel his brother, Jibreel Ibrahim, a businessman. It believed that Jibreel was in partnership with Turabi's deputy, Ali al Haj, and through him was channelling Islamist funds to JEM. These claims have persisted and neither been proven nor ever laid to rest. Unlike some Islamists, Jibreel believed Turabi still had a political future in Sudan. 'Bashir is not a very decisive man,' he said in March 2006. 'He went to see Hassan Turabi and said: "The government is in very bad shape." Turabi said: "Give Darfur what it wants. East Sudan too." If Turabi is alive he will have a future. Bashir has no popular base. Turabi does. He is very liberal.'

The relationship of Darfur to Turabi had always been complicated. For many Darfurians, support for Turabi and the NIF had had as much to do with last-chance politics as with any visceral attachment to political Islam. In democratic elections in 1986, Darfur had voted on traditional lines for the Umma Party, not for the NIF. But the Umma failed to deliver for Darfur and Sadiq was discredited by his tolerance of Libyan meddling. Turabi, however, courted all Darfurian groups, Arabs and non-Arabs, and developed a genuine constituency in the region. One of his Darfurian allies was Khalil Ibrahim, who served the NIF for the better part of a decade, holding a number of regional portfolios including health, finance and education in the North Darfur government. Khalil's supporters claim that disenchantment did not take long to set in and trace his 'conversion' to the early 1990s. 'In 1993–94, government forces lost ground in the South and Khalil, who was minister of health in North Darfur at the time, was asked to raise a battalion of Popular Defence Forces and take them to the South,' says a friend. 'He went to the South and led them. He treated Mujahidiin in Juba. It was a turning point for him. He felt that South Sudan had a cause.'

Khalil himself insists that he ploughed his own furrow for most of his time in state government, and was not a slavish follower of the NIF. In al Fasher in 1994, he says, he refused to accept the private electrical supply given to ministers and became 'the only minister living in darkness with his people'.[61] As minister for social affairs in Blue Nile in 1997, he fired northerners who had 'colonized' his department, replacing them with locals, and dismissed the director of the office for *zakat*, a cousin of President Bashir who was sending all the monies levied by the Islamic tax back to Khartoum. In Juba in 1998, he taxed Security officials who had established a monopoly on food shipped into the besieged city and were selling it at a 400 per cent profit. 'In one day,' he says, 'I raised 64 million pounds! These Security people had never been treated like this ...'

Khalil left government service in August 1998, several months before the expiry of his term as adviser to the governor of Southern Sudan in Juba, and formed an NGO called Fighting Poverty. 'We regional people, especially Darfur, have been very disappointed by the NIF,' he said,

> The AIDS of the National Islamic Front is racism. The NIF not only totally neglected our people – it punished our people. It withdrew all services, especially health and education, and by 1994 had stopped paying even a single piastre to the regions. Many schools closed, the number of children in school decreased, and there was a resurgence of illiteracy. In 1991–94, as a regional minister in al Fasher, I got an insight into the government's links to the militias. By 1991, 647 Fur villages had been burned to ashes. Our people started to blame us.

Within Khalil's inner circle, opinion about the NIF and Turabi was sharply divided, as illustrated by a coffee-table conversation in the Chadian capital N'Djamena early in 2004. Turabi had been a disaster, said one. Under him, the Islamist project in Sudan had foundered in violence and bloodshed. 'We have no reason to destroy our land and people to support Hassan al Turabi. I will not support anything that would take us back to the past.' A failure, agreed a second. Turabi had done nothing for the 'African' people of Darfur – Muslims whose devotion was second to none – even though many had supported him. 'We were marginalized in Turabi's time too. Turabi is nothing.' Turabi's Islamist promise had indeed proved to be a sham: only a handful of Darfurians were elevated to high positions in the party and the adminis-tration, local administration was still bankrupt, and above all, Khartoum had failed in its first duty of ensuring law and order. Only one person disagreed, clearly discomfited by the criticism of the architect of Sudan's Islamic revolution: 'Yes, Turabi took the wrong path,' he said. 'But you have to remember that there was a time when people would turn on the radio whenever they knew he was going to speak. Some people started talking the way he talks and smiling the way he smiles ...'

Whatever the truth about Khalil's relationship with Turabi, it is undeniable that some of Darfur's Islamists remained loyal to Turabi throughout the war, even if they took on new identi-ties in the rebel movements. One such was al Amin Mahmoud Mohamed Osman, spokesman for the Fur tribe at the 1989 peace talks. 'When the government tried to solve the problem of Darfur by force, Turabi's Popular Congress Party (PCP) stood against it, making people understand the difference between the NCP and PCP,' he said. 'This also made people forgive the PCP for its earlier mistakes. The PCP leadership at a local level began to join both movements as fighters.'[62]

Discerning the truth about JEM's inner workings is almost as difficult as seeing into the inner sanctums of the NIF. But one thing is sure: despite the strong links of JEM's leaders to the Islamist movement in Sudan, and the adherence to it of middle-ranking NIF members who still believed that Islamic values could solve many of Sudan's problems, JEM initially appealed to a not negligible number of educated Darfurians and tribal leaders who resented the marginalization of Darfur and the failure of all northern politicians, including Turabi, to do anything about it. Many who had no sympathy for the Islamist movement were attracted to JEM by the very fact that its leaders had served in government and had political skills and experience that the SLA, with few exceptions, did not have. They believed that Khalil's time in the NIF might even be a virtue: it made him privy to inside information about the government, as the subversive *Black Book* had proved, and enabled JEM to have cadres in Khartoum who might be able to attack the regime from within.[63] They saw a clear political project that was focused on the whole Sudanese nation – not just on Darfur. They liked the fact that JEM rejected the Naivasha peace deal for giving too much power to the South and not enough to the northern peripheries such as Darfur, Kordofan and the Beja Hills of eastern Sudan. Abdullahi al Tom, a Berti anthropology professor and adviser to the JEM chairman, is a former member of the Communist Party of Sudan. When the two first met in a Paris hotel, over a beer and a glass of orange juice, al Tom asked Khalil about Turabi. He was satisfied by his response. 'Everyone of our age has some sort of past. I was part of Turabi, but am not at the moment.' Al Tom joined JEM in preference to the SLA, which he felt had no coherent philosophy and an absence of institutions.[64]

Khalil brought to JEM the discipline and strategic thinking he had learned from the Islamists. He is not easily accessible, trusting his lieutenants to convey the party line and conduct the movement's run-of-the-mill, day-to-day affairs. He chooses the time and manner of his public appearances with care, meeting only the highest-level officials, and only when he has vital business to transact. At these events, Khalil projects an aura of power with an entourage of suited aides who escort him to his place and position themselves as personal bodyguards inside and outside the room. In less formal meetings, he is relaxed and approachable – and often surprisingly frank. 'Easy-going and quiet', said an SLA delegate who had dealings with him at the peace talks that opened in the Nigerian city of Abuja in August 2004. 'A good listener, objective and logical.'[65] Well into the rebellion, opinion about JEM remained divided: some believed it would never succeed in throwing off the taint of NIF Islamism; others thought that Khalil, with his energy and determination, would succeed in marking a break with the past. 'JEM has little support on the ground because of the NIF connection,' said a Darfurian prominent in the Umma Party.

> JEM is being tarred with the Turabi brush by other parties. People think the Zaghawa have great ambitions for land, money and power. But we believe that in the future JEM will progress because practically it is against the NIF. We think JEM will take the lead in Darfur. We know Khalil was an amir of the PDF, which killed many people in the South. But he was deceived by the centre. JEM are intelligent people with a good leader and clear objectives, and the Kobe know historically they cannot rule alone. But we need them to concentrate on Darfur. We don't need to focus on the whole of Sudan.[66]

'The Kobe control everything!'

Examination and criticism of JEM have always focused on Khalil's alleged links with Turabi. From the very beginning, however, JEM's tribal affiliation was at least as important as its Islamist legacy. In all key areas, JEM was dominated by Kobe – and, among the Kobe, by relatives, by blood and marriage, of Khalil himself. Unlike the Zaghawa Tuer, who provided a large recruiting ground for the SLA in Sudan, most Kobe live in Chad. Their presence in Darfur is concentrated close to the Chad border around Tine, Khalil's home town. Wadi Saira, JEM's first armed camp, is twenty-five miles south east of Tine, and it was in Tine that the formation of JEM was first announced. Many of its early recruits joined because Kobe friends and family had already done so. The movement's core was tribal at least as much as it was Islamist. But although controlled by Kobe, JEM knew it had to broaden its base if it was to be credible and accordingly attempted to reach out to other groups. One of the first to be contacted, in October 2001, was Turabi's second-in-command, Ali al Haj – not because of his links to Turabi, JEM insists, but because he was a Darfurian with a national profile. Al Haj was also the chief financial controller of the Islamist movement and had perfected, in his days in office, the art of 'retail politics' – purchasing influence through individual patronage. Although al Haj refused to join JEM, he allied himself with Khalil in the Union of the Marginalized Majority. The government's conviction that there was a direct link between Turabi and Khalil grew and was immediately reinforced by the Union's call for the formation of a broad-based interim national government, the abolition of the regime's 'oppressive' security organs and the 'release of all political detainees including Dr Hassan al-Turabi'.[67]

On paper at least, JEM did what the SLA signally failed to do: it gave itself structure and delegated authority. In January 2005, it created a twenty-one-member executive board drawn from all regions of Sudan, a fifty-one-member legislative committee, and a General Congress headed by an easterner, from Blue Nile. Members of the General Congress voted to limit the chairman's term to four years, renewable once. They also voted to change the customary Sudanese oath requiring them to obey 'conscience and religion' to 'conscience and cause'. But the issue of state and religion remained a controversial one, even within JEM. 'In public Khalil and his group say they do not want Shari'a, but in private they demand it,' said Idriss Azraq, a member of the Meidob tribe of North Darfur who led a grassroots break in 2006.[68] Non-Kobe, including several Arabs, were given a number of senior positions: Nur al Din Dafalla, a member of the Missiriya tribe, became Khalil's deputy; Khattab Ibrahim Widaa, a Ta'aisha, became deputy spokesman; Ibrahim Yahya, the Masalit former governor of West Darfur, became speaker of JEM's 'parliament'.

Real power, however, lay with Khalil and his Kobe inner circle and any attempts to challenge them were ruthlessly suppressed. In late 2003, six members of the JEM cell in the Netherlands – the first one in Europe – were seized and imprisoned in Girgira, south of Tine, as they tried to rally support for a new, non-tribal leadership.[69] They later claimed that one was hit on the head with gun butts and the others tied up with chains, that they were all beaten on their heads and body, and that two reportedly had a mixture of acid, pepper and petrol put in their mouths.

Representatives of JEM told Amnesty International the six were imprisoned because they were 'government agents', but denied knowing they had been tortured.[70]

The apparent delegation of power failed to convince even those touched by it. 'Khalil is strong and honest, but he is a tribalist,' Ibrahim Yahya said in 2006.

He is losing sympathy, especially among Masalit and Zaghawa. I told him this is not the way to victory. He didn't reply. It's a pity. The Kobe control finance, executive, everything. I am speaker of parliament and I have never received a penny! I am self-financed. The non-Kobe in JEM don't want to disrupt the peace talks. After the return from the camps we will know what to do.

Yahya did not wait that long. In mid-2007, he joined a predominantly Masalit group, the Popular Movement for Rights and Democracy, which announced its support for the Darfur Peace Agreement and signed a protocol with the Sudan government. Arabs in JEM were no happier. They had positions, but, like the Masalit, no power. They complained privately that they were not only excluded from decision-making; they were excluded from international events and therefore had no influence over Khalil's increasingly opportunistic alliance-making in the capitals of the region.

By 2008, the unresolved controversy over JEM's Islamist past and Kobe roots had split both the grassroots and the leadership of the rebel group, leaving Khalil increasingly dependent on money, guns and political backing from outside. Khalil's first government sponsor was Eritrea, but his convoluted relationship with Chadian President Idriss Deby, a fellow Zaghawa, had a strong influence on JEM's fortunes. Since taking power in 1991, Deby had stuck to a simple pact with Khartoum: each would close their common border to the other's rebels. A decade later, the grievance and vendetta among the Zaghawa he had wronged over the years meant that Deby could no longer deliver. The Kobe had been a particular problem ever since Deby double-crossed and murdered their leader Abbas Koty in 1994. At the outset, Darfur's

Zaghawa insurgencies had involved both Chadian soldiers and equipment – but not with Deby's consent. And so for the first years of the war Chadian intelligence worked hand-in-glove with its Sudanese counterparts to undermine and split the SLA and JEM. In May 2005, Khalil said that JEM had been the target of four attempts to split its ranks and weaken it – each time on the personal instructions of Deby:

> The Chadian president does not want to see us strong because we are from the same tribe. We are all from the Zaghawa tribe that is spread between Chad and Sudan ... [Deby] believes that if the Zaghawa have a chance to rule Sudan, then they will bring down his government in Chad ... Secondly, the Sudanese government is paying hundreds of millions of dollars for the Chadian government's activities ... There are disagreements but they last only for hours. They never disagree for more than seventy-two hours, only the time it takes to get the money to the Chadian side.

The first split, early in 2004, was portrayed by its leader, JEM military chief Jibreel Abdel Karim 'Tek', as a revolt against Turabi's alleged influence over the movement and Khalil's insistence on micromanaging it from Europe.[71] Jibreel, a former colonel in the Chad army, was a member of the predominantly Chadian Kapka clan to which many of JEM's fighters belonged – and he took his kinsmen with him when he formed his breakaway group, the National Movement for Reform and Development (NMRD). Colleagues said the trigger for the split was a demand by Khalil that Jibreel withdraw to Kordofan, with all his forces, in the wake of a massive government attack across North Darfur in February 2004. As Jibreel gathered his supporters, JEM attacked, killing his Kapka chief of staff, Omar Issa Rabe. Khalil blamed the split on an attempt by Chad to control JEM through the Kapka – Chad-watchers noted that the director of Deby's National Security Agency, Mahamat Ismaël Chaïbo, was Kapka – and on Khartoum's divide-and-rule. He pointed out that the assistant for African affairs in the ruling party, Hassan Burgo, was also Kapka

113

and had met Tek's supporters in Paris shortly before the NMRD's emergence. Speaking on Al Jazeera television after the split, Burgo said the NMRD represented the 'real' people of Darfur and was a death blow to JEM. In December 2004, the NMRD reached agreement with the NIF in just four days of talks in Chad.

In 2005, according to a senior JEM official, Hassan Burgo attempted to unite two JEM splinters – Tek's NMRD and the far smaller Field Revolutionary Command of Mohamed Saleh, a secular Kobe – with two start-up payments of 100 million Sudanese pounds (approximately $40,000 each at the time) paid through a trader in Tine called Shumu Hassan Saleh Burgo.[72] When Jibreel was captured in a tribal dispute soon after, it was Hassan Burgo who negotiated his release and paid his *diya*.

Along with the Kapka, the Masalit initially provided much of JEM's soldiery. But the Masalit also quickly became frustrated. As early as 2004, Idriss Azraq found deep unhappiness among the Masalit.

> They said Khalil's Kobe clan (the Angu Geyla) were controlling everything: cars, money, positions. The Masalit were so disregarded they had carts rather than cars! Khalil has no army, he only has planners; his army was mainly Kapka and Masalit. The defection of Tek and the formation of the NMRD almost finished the JEM army.

In the field, Khalil's men became notorious for attempting to buy support – sometimes with cash, sometimes just with cigarettes and Pepsis. Their efforts were not limited to Zaghawa areas: in November 2005, a UN report said JEM activists were attempting to recruit even in the Fur heartland of Jebel Marra, 'providing incentives in money, food and clothing'.[73]

By the end of 2005, Khalil had mended fences with Deby. By this time, Sudanese intelligence had decided that Deby was either unwilling or unable to rein in his fellow Zaghawa and instead decided to overthrow him by force. As Chad spiralled down into civil war, Deby began marshalling support among the Darfur rebels and quickly fastened on to Khalil as the most effective operator. The later splits in JEM all arose because of Khalil's centralized management combined with Security's offers of cash and positions. Khalil was not deterred. His ambitions reached far wider than his narrow tribal power base. Drawing on Sudanese expatriate networks and on the readiness of Idriss Deby, Isseyas Afewerki and Muammar Gaddafi to bankroll and arm Khartoum's adversaries, he was able to wield far more power than his narrow constituency would suggest was possible.

While intellectually engaging in a way that the SLA rarely achieved, JEM's main strength was always its organization and its leaders' political experience rather than its popular support. 'In 2004, we told Khalil the army had to be restructured to reflect the whole region, not just one tribe,' Azraq said. 'We were very optimistic. We called it "the second phase of the revolution". But the path of JEM paralleled the path of Turabi: in both an early emphasis on morality was replaced by corruption and hunger for power.'

Darfur's rebels, SLA and JEM, were an awkward coalition of a handful of professionals who dared to take on the burden of leadership, largely untrained Fur and Masalit villagers, Zaghawa Bedouins feuding with Arab Abbala, and a sprinkling of intellectuals, many of them disillusioned Islamists. Unlike the first generation of SPLA fighters who emerged from an army mutiny, only a minority of Darfur's guerrillas had military experience or discipline before they took up arms. The rebel groups were united by deep resentment at the marginalization of Darfur, but were not natural bedfellows and could easily be split apart. Theirs was not an insurgency born of revolutionary ideals, but rather a last-resort response to the escalating violence of the Janjawiid and its patrons in Khartoum. In the first months of 2003 these half-formed and inexperienced rebel fronts were catapulted out of obscurity to face challenges for which they were totally unprepared. They should perhaps have had more foresight. Darfur was on the brink of becoming 'southern Sudan speeded up',[74] and leading members of JEM, if not the SLA, had first-hand experience of that war.

5 | A war of total destruction, 2003–04

As rebellion welled in Darfur throughout 2002, the government's approach was half-hearted and incoherent. Some officials in Khartoum argued that the conflict was a local affair that didn't merit too much attention. But security officers saw the signs of an SPLA conspiracy to spread the civil war to all parts of the country, even while its leaders were talking peace. Hadn't the southern rebels overrun the garrison town of Torit just weeks after signing the Machakos Protocol, the key breakthrough in the peace talks, in July 2002? Hadn't they already tried – and failed – to spread their rebellion to Darfur, in 2001? And also raided and briefly occupied the eastern city of Kassala? The new insurrection was surely yet another instance of Garang's double dealing. Crush it at once, Security argued. Teach the SPLA and its foreign backers a lesson. Others saw the hand of Hassan al Turabi, an even greater menace, behind the Zaghawa militancy and the ominous Zaghawa–Fur alliance. The hardliners' problem was, the army couldn't spare the forces.

The new governor of North Darfur, General Ibrahim Suleiman, favoured a different approach: he wanted to rein in the militia and negotiate with the rebels. A former army chief of staff from the Berti tribe – a non-Arab tribe which is the largest in eastern Darfur – General Suleiman replaced Safi al Nur in April 2001. He saw immediately that the situation he had inherited was becoming 'very grave ... The violence was increasing; all the different tribes were gathering up weapons.'[1] Even more damagingly, Khartoum's failure to stop the violence was being interpreted by non-Arabs as complicity in it. 'They believed the raids against them were being agreed to by the government,' General Suleiman said. 'Otherwise, why didn't the government stop them?'

The new governor tried to stop them. He convened tribal

councils and declared 'red zones' around some of the main Arab militia camps, such as Jebel Kargo and Jebel Ju, with the aim of forcing the Arabs to evacuate them.[2] He summoned Musa Hilal, the man he considered the biggest troublemaker and a born criminal, and told him: 'If I decide to kill you, I will kill you, and nothing will happen to me.' Musa Hilal just smiled. 'I think even then Hilal knew he couldn't be touched,' the governor said.[3] When talking failed, and the militia camps proved too strong to dislodge, General Suleiman tried another approach: in August 2002, he arrested the three tribal leaders he considered the most troublesome, with twenty-one of their men, and sent them across the country to prison in Port Sudan. Musa Hilal was one of the three. General Suleiman hoped that in their absence, things would 'quiet down'. His predecessor, Safi al Nur, was critical. 'Ibrahim Suleiman was very tough with the Arabs,' he said. 'After that, the rebels went freely to Jebel Marra!'[4] Musa Hilal spent only four months in prison before he was moved to house arrest in Khartoum, reportedly after the personal intervention of Ali Osman.

General Suleiman believed the rebels' demands were negotiable. He tried to address their grievances through tribal councils and quiet contacts with the rebel leadership. The SLA were not separatists; they wanted amnesty and recognition as a political movement, a pledge to implement development projects in Darfur and autonomous powers within a federal system. But Khartoum's security chiefs wanted a show of force and could overrule the governor. Vice-president Ali Osman Taha was in a dilemma. As Khartoum's leading peacemaker, his sympathies lay with General Suleiman. But as Turabi's erstwhile right-hand man and political assassin, he was both knowledgeable and nervous about the Islamist leader's capability for bouncing back from political defeat. He smelled the hand of Turabi in the growing insurrection. Most importantly, in 2002 Ali Osman needed the support of Security chief Salah Gosh and could not challenge him over Darfur: the vice-president's priority was the North–South talks, and he could build the political capital he needed to pull off a compromise with the SPLA only if he were tough – and seen to be tough – in other parts of the country. Visiting al Fasher in November 2002, Ali Osman made clear that a military solution was possible and would be uncompromising. He warned that Darfur would be 'pulled backwards for many years' if the rebels refused to put down their arms. There would be total destruction.[5]

The fighting escalated. The rebels announced themselves publicly in February 2003. On 18 March, a fragile ceasefire negotiated by General Suleiman collapsed after Arab militia ambushed a Masalit sheikh, seventy-year-old Saleh Dakoro, on the road from Geneina to Kokota village. No one doubted that the attack was targeted: Sheikh Dakoro was a legendary horseman and the horse he was riding was known to everyone in Dar Masalit – including Military Intelligence. The old sheikh survived the attack, but was wounded and taken to hospital in Khartoum, where he died within hours of telephoning relatives to say he would be returning to Darfur 'in a few days'.[6] The word spread like wildfire: the grand old man of the Masalit, wounded by the militias in Darfur, had been murdered by the government in Khartoum! Masalit leaders issued a statement deploring his death as 'the continuation of a policy of eliminating leaders of groups and communities accused or suspected of opposing the government'.[7] They accused the government of 'exploiting international focus on the current conflict in Iraq to escalate human rights abuses in western Sudan'.

On 25 March, the rebels seized the garrison town of Tine on the Chad border and captured huge stocks of arms and equipment. Tine was the home town of Khalil Ibrahim. His organization, JEM, was viewed by the government as the military wing of Hassan Turabi's Popular Congress Party – still the major threat to the NCP in Khartoum – and the government was quick to react. On 27 March, Ibrahim Ahmed Omar, secretary general of the NCP, said, after a meeting of the party's political committee: 'We have come to the view that these events must be dealt with in a strong and decisive manner.' Ali Osman stressed 'the importance of military action to confront the repercussions' of 'armed robbery' in Darfur.[8] A major counter-offensive was inevitable. 'Khartoum will not negotiate with those who took up arms in Darfur and denied the authority of the state and the law,' President Bashir said in April, addressing an open-air rally in al Fasher. The army would be 'unleashed' to 'crush' the rebellion.

The truth of the matter, well known to Bashir, was that the armed forces had already been 'unleashed' – but to very little avail. They were making no headway against the rebels, whose hit-and-run tactics, using Toyota land cruisers to cross the semi-desert at high speed, were proving devastatingly effective. Untrained in desert warfare, the Sudanese army was losing almost every encounter, and the government was relying more and more on its air force. Badly hurt by aerial bombardment – especially in and around the Ain Siro mountains, the SLA's main base at the time – the rebels planned an attack that would change the face of the war. Unable to take the government on in the air, they decided to destroy its planes on the ground.

Early in April, government regulars and Janjawiid irregulars based in the Kutum area had attacked Ain Siro with artillery, backed by Antonov bombers and helicopter gunships operating out of the main air base in Darfur, at al Fasher. Nine rebels were killed and seventeen wounded, and the villages of Sambo and Mangori were burned. Informed that the government was planning another attack, SLA leaders held a crisis meeting in Ain Siro.[9] One of those present was twenty-three-year-old Ismail 'Abunduluk' Adam, a young man with little military experience but extraordinary personal magnetism who had joined the SLA after losing forty-six members of his family, including his father and three brothers, in the Fur–Arab war of the 1980s. The rebels soon reached a near-unanimous decision: nothing less than an attack on the al Fasher base would suffice. 'We knew the government was reorganizing,' Abunduluk said. 'We said: "We must succeed, or we will all die."' Abdalla Abakir would be the overall commander of the operation, with Abunduluk leading the unit that would attempt to destroy the planes. Juma

119

Mohamed Hagar and JEM's Abdel Karim Choley would attack the headquarters. Salah Juk, another Zaghawa commander, would go for the stores.

'The planes are ashes'

Early on the morning of 25 April, the rebels set out in thirteen vehicles – eleven belonging to the SLA and two to JEM. There were 317 men, a sizeable force, but they had only three heavy weapons – a tripod-mounted SPG-9 and two anti-aircraft guns captured in the battle of Tine. At 4 a.m., the group reached the outskirts of al Fasher where they found two government soldiers at a checkpoint taxing lorries. They took their rifles, tied them up and drove on. At the base, the troops were already out on parade. The planes – two Antonovs and five gunships – were armed and ready to fly, their engines running. Abdalla Abakir sent three cars racing between the troops and the planes. Then he fired on the first of the planes. Abunduluk remembers that

> Abdalla hit the first Antonov in the middle with an RPG. It jumped in the air and exploded. We were coming under fire, so Juma came to help. He hit the second Antonov from the front with the SPG-9. The cockpit exploded and the plane split in two. The pilots of the gunships got out and ran. Then we destroyed them too.

Shortly before 9 a.m., government soldiers waiting for air support in the Kutum area radioed: 'Where are the planes?' The response came back: 'The planes are ashes.'[10]

The rebels succeeded in capturing the storehouse, losing two men in the attack, but Juma Mohamed was wounded and his car destroyed before he could reach the headquarters. So Abunduluk took his place. He found thirteen men hiding in trees outside the headquarters and opened fire on them. Seven fell from the trees 'like birds', dead. At 9 a.m., Abunduluk drove to the clubhouse. He was thirsty and wanted a drink. Opening the door to the cold store, he discovered a man hiding inside in military trousers and a white undershirt. He recalled,

I took a Pepsi and ordered him out. I told him to sit down and open the Pepsi. I asked him where the money was. He said: 'In the bag.' I got it. I forgot the Pepsi and found some *araki* [home-brewed gin] and was ready to kill him when Abdalla [Abakir] came in. He asked the man: 'Who are you?' He replied: 'I am Ibrahim Bushra – commander of the air force, responsible for the air force in all Sudan.'

By the time the rebels controlled the base at 10 a.m., all seven planes had been destroyed, more than seventy troops, pilots and technicians were dead and Major General Ibrahim Bushra Ismail was a prisoner, together with more than thirty of his men. The rebels had captured more weapons than they could transport, including 106 mm and 120 mm mortars, four SPG-9s, eleven 120 mm anti-aircraft guns, and one 'Rubai' – a Soviet-made anti-aircraft system designed to shoot aircraft, particularly helicopters or low-flying airplanes, but devastatingly effective against trucks and light armour as well. They had gone in with thirteen cars, seen two destroyed, and come out with eighteen. Abunduluk lost four men, who were buried in the woods outside al Fasher. Thirteen others were wounded.

In more than twenty years' war in the south, the SPLA had never inflicted such a loss on the air force. The rebels were jubilant. 'The attack changed everything. We got ammunition, vehicles and weapons. Young men flocked to join us.' Indeed the attack did change everything: this was the pivotal moment that transformed Darfur's war from provincial discontent into a front-rank military danger to Khartoum. The SLA and JEM, with their lightning attacks, were running rings around the army, which had been humiliated in an unprecedented way. Khartoum insisted publicly that the trouble in Darfur was the work of 'outlaws'. But the Security cabal blamed the SPLA and Turabi, who they suspected was planning a coup, and resolved to crush the rebels who had done this – along with anyone who sympathized with them.

The government did initially continue negotiations with

the rebels, but only for as long as it took the elders of General Ismail's Missiriya tribe to mediate and obtain his release. After that, Khartoum refused to extend political recognition to the SLA and focused on mobilizing for a military solution. An operational area was declared along the Chad border and a state-wide curfew imposed. More than 150 people were arrested in a security clampdown. But the guerrillas kept the upper hand, destroying a Sudanese battalion north of Kutum in May in a battle in which they claimed they killed more than a hundred soldiers. Rapidly expanding their area of operations, SLA mobile units launched a surprise attack on Mellit, the principal town of Dar Berti north east of al Fasher. The rebels were winning almost every encounter – thirty-four out of thirty-eight in the middle months of 2003, according to UN and US data. The government feared it would lose the whole of Darfur.

The rebels were also beginning to attack civilians. One incident that especially shocked the Abbala occurred on 13 June when three young Arabs were murdered in Um Leyuna market, north west of Korma. One was a young man, Ahmed Billa, who was about to go to university; the other two a woman named Khadija Hamad and her two-year-old child, both of whom had scalding water poured over them. Worse was to follow. The very next day, in Abroha north of Kebkabiya, a holy man from the Mahamid, Faki Ismail Mumin 'Batikhtein', and his seventeen-year-old son Salih were apprehended at a well. The faki was killed, thrown head-first into the well. Salih was dismembered and the pieces were put in a leather bag tied to his camel, which returned to its home village. People saw blood running down the animal's legs as it ran through the market and tried to stop it, thinking it was injured. When they finally caught it, they discovered Salih's body parts.[11] The Arabs were outraged and demanded the return of their strongest leader, Musa Hilal.

General Suleiman was sacked as governor, Musa Hilal released from detention, and militia recruitment put into top gear. The years 2003–04 would be the bloodiest in Darfur's troubled history.

Unleashing the Janjawiid

During the height of the hostilities in Darfur in 2003–04, the government war effort had three main elements: Janjawiid, military intelligence and air force. Overall coordination was given to the minister of state for the interior, a young security officer from Kordofan named Ahmed Mohamed Haroun, who was given as much money as he needed and as much latitude with the militias as he demanded, no questions asked. In May 2007, the International Criminal Court issued an arrest warrant for Ahmed Haroun on forty-two counts of war crimes and crimes against humanity in his position as manager of the 'Darfur Security desk' and coordinator between the government's army and security services and the militias.

General Suleiman had advised against using tribal militias, convinced that a racially based mobilization would have 'terrible' repercussions on inter-tribal relations for the next several decades. His solution would have been to deploy the army: 'Send me two brigades of good soldiers,' he pleaded after the military disgrace in al Fasher. 'Just two brigades, brought up from the South, and we will end this whole thing';[12] but he also wanted to focus on Darfur's political and developmental needs: 'Hundreds of schools … Settle the nomads [and give them] water… Well-equipped, well-trained police … Health projects.'[13] But his advice was overruled. Month by month Khartoum ratcheted up its military infrastructure in Darfur – and central to its counterattack was its tried and tested militia strategy. The army played the lesser role. Bewildered by the rebels' military capacity, the army would have needed to be redeployed from the South and retrained to fight this new front with its unfamiliar style of combat. In addition, its loyalty was suspect. Large numbers of Darfurian NCOs and privates were conspicuously unwilling to put up much resistance. In the subsequent debate over whether the war in Darfur constituted genocide or not – a debate whose burden of proof, paradoxically, became a hindrance to action – one thing is certain: the people who decided to use ethnic militias as a counter-insurgency force knew exactly what it would mean. They had used similar militias since 1985 and had seen the results. Ahmed Haroun himself had been coordinator for the Popular Defence Forces in Kordofan during the vicious war against the Nuba. Now the government was organizing a replay.

When the Fur and Zaghawa first began to organize in 2001, rumours of a shadowy armed movement called 'Harakat FAZAM' – the Fur–Zaghawa–Masalit movement – circulated among Arabs in the markets of Darfur. A group of Arab traders returning from Libya was seized by Zaghawa bandits, and it was said they had been skinned alive. Then the Darfur Liberation Front announced itself with its attack on Golo, and speculation ran wild. No Arab had been consulted in the formation, or the strategy, of such a front. 'Our people asked, "Who are they going to liberate Darfur from?"' said al Sanosi Musa, a young Mahamid Arab. 'The conclusion was, they were going to liberate Darfur from the Arabs! The Arabs of Darfur are uneducated and 100 per cent brainwashed by government. People were saying in markets: "We will eliminate you!" Rumours spread like wildfire because of ignorance.'[14]

As the rebels began to build an infrastructure, Zaghawa fighters mounted a series of punishing raids on Abbala camel herds in North Darfur. 'For Abbala,' said al Sanosi, 'a camel is like a son. The Abbala hate people who attack their camels.' On the desert edge, what had been localized fights between Zaghawa and Arabs became more deadly as camel raiders began operating with vehicles mounted with heavy machine guns. In a single raid in 2002, the Ereigat Arabs reportedly lost 1,000 camels. When they tried to retrieve them, thirty-seven of their men were shot dead.[15]

In 2002–03, two powerful Mahamid clans, the Awlad Zeid and Musa Hilal's Um Jalul, lost thousands of animals. Three thousand were reportedly sold in Libyan markets, and when their Arab owners complained to the police, nothing was done.[16] Suspecting the police had been bribed by the thieves, the owners took the law into their own hands and attacked the Zaghawa merchants with knives. Six Arabs were jailed. In Darfur itself, a number of community leaders were killed. In October 2002,

Omda Mohamed al Sheikh al Hilu, his son and three others were knifed to death in the weekly market in Jebel Kaura, between Kutum and Kebkabiya.[17]

Many Arabs came to believe the 'blacks' had armed themselves only to fight the Arabs. 'The leaders said they were fighting the government, but the rank-and-file attacked Arabs,' said Salah Mohamed Abdel Rahman, better known as 'Abu Sura', a Rizegat from al Da'ien who, despite his criticism of the rebellion, nevertheless formed Darfur's first Arab rebel group, the Popular Forces Army, in 2006.[18]

As government arms flowed to Darfur's Arabs in the early months of the war, *damrat* settlements came under rebel attack. Many *damrat* by now were heavily armed, especially in the Kutum area, seen as a strategic link between Dar Zaghawa and Jebel Marra. Militiamen from the *damrat* not only patrolled roads but, beginning in February 2003, attacked and burned Fur and Tunjur villages. The attacks increased after Musa Hilal's return in June, reached a peak in August in the vicinity of Fata Borno and spread out to areas north of Kutum in September and October.[19] Safi al Nur, the former governor of North Darfur, claimed eight Abbala *damrat* were attacked between February and October 2003, beginning with the Mahariya centre at Ghreir, which had to be evacuated, and including Um Sayala, an Eteifat settlement that was becoming one of the strongest militia bases in the area and that he said was attacked on eight separate occasions.[20] The Arab rebel leader, Abu Sura, said fifteen women and children were killed in just one of the attacks on Um Sayala. He acknowledged the *damra* had become an armed camp, but said: 'There were civilians there too, yet the SLA attacked with heavy guns.'

After his release from jail, Musa Hilal made revenge against the Zaghawa his priority. He was ready to cut a deal with the Fur wing of the SLA in pursuit of that. An Arab lawyer who was one of Abdel Wahid's oldest friends led the talks with the Mahamid leader. He said,

Musa Hilal was very angry at being jailed and came every day

125

to [a secret location] in Khartoum to talk to us. Then Um Jalul camels were stolen. Two weeks later, Musa had cars and cash. He told the government he would need only three weeks to defeat the rebels. He went to al Fasher and Nyala, where he met Adam Hamid [the governor of South Darfur]. He called me from Nyala and said: 'Join us. We have money if you want it.' He had a plan to divide the Zaghawa from the Fur. He said: 'The Arab problem is with the Zaghawa.'[21]

Already fired up from the last few years' escalating tension, the Abbala tribes of North Darfur were ready to answer the government's call to arms. At first the army's Western Area Command in al Fasher distributed weapons to recruits, regardless of tribe. But thousands of Fur and Tunjur militiamen promptly defected to the rebels with their weapons. Military intelligence, staffed exclusively by officers from central Sudan, was not going to repeat this error. When 6,000 volunteers raised by tribal leaders in West Darfur arrived at army headquarters in Geneina, Arabs were armed and non-Arabs rejected. Omda Gamr Musa, a Masalit from Millebeeda south of Geneina, saw every one of the 1,000 Masalit he had assembled turned away.[22] Safi al Nur encouraged Arabs to join the militia. Separately, State Minister for Justice Ali Karti, who was a former coordinator of the PDF, reportedly flew to different parts of Darfur in an attempt to buy the support of Arab tribal leaders with fifty-kilogram sugar sacks full of cash drawn from Salah Gosh's coffers.[23]

By the end of 2003, most of the Masalit countryside was emptied and its population either driven into Chad or into overcrowded, insecure camps in government-controlled areas. The village of Mulli was one of the first targeted – two days before the al Fasher airport raid – in a pattern that would be repeated across Dar Masalit throughout the year. The attack came out of the blue on market day, when Mulli was packed with people from villages all around. Armed with RPGs and grenade launchers, and wearing the same uniforms as the regular army, Arabs stormed the mosque, on foot and on horseback, and killed ten people including the imam, Yahya Gabat. Then they attacked the market, killing another thirty people. 'The bullets were falling like rain and they were shouting: "Kill the Nuba! Kill the Nuba!"' said a twenty-eight-year-old farmer who witnessed the attack. 'They killed my seventy-five-year-old aunt because she refused to let them take her sheep and goats."[24] 'People followed them after the attack,' said another survivor. 'They went into the town, into Geneina. The wounded were taken by plane to Khartoum. Nobody complained to the government. We know these people are from the government. They say: "We *are* the government."'[25]

After Musa Hilal's return to Darfur in June, the Abbala fighters answerable to his chieftaincy began to be transformed into a full paramilitary fighting force. Their official name was the Second Border Intelligence Brigade, but their most notorious unit was a small elite force called the 'Swift and Fearsome Forces'.[26] Khidir Ali Abdel Rahman, a Fur omda from Tur in Jebel Marra, was held prisoner in Misteriha for fourteen months, from April 2004 until June 2005, and saw the barracks grow from a very basic camp to a well-equipped barracks with electricity, television, tents in place of open-sided *rakubas* for the men and guest houses for military visitors from al Fasher. Helicopters flew in two or three times a week bringing Kalashnikovs, G3 rifles, ammunition and money, which the prisoners unloaded. When the militia received their salaries, they asked Omda Khidir, an educated man, to help them read the paperwork. He saw they were being cheated. 'They were supposed to be getting 350,000 Sudanese pounds a month. But they were receiving only 200,000 pounds!'[27]

The number of government officers in Misteriha was doubled after Hilal returned to Darfur, Omda Khidir said, and two separate training camps were organized. The first came under the interior ministry and belonged to the *Ittihad al Merkazi* (Central Reserve Police), a gendarmerie originally set up for riot control. Training lasted three months. The second came under the defence ministry and training was much more rudimentary, lasting only one month. There were three types of fighter at Misteriha. The elite troops were those of the Border Intelligence Brigade, who had military identity cards and salaries. The second level was the PDF, who were given uniforms, guns, ammunition and food. They had no regular payments, but received 100,000 Sudanese pounds for every operation they participated in. Last were the *mustanfareen*, or 'reserves', young men who were recruited by force and given uniforms but not money. Those who refused to fight were imprisoned.

Darfur-wide, there were at least six militia brigades working alongside the regular armed forces – among them, the *Liwa al Nasr*, or Victory Brigade, of Abdel Rahim Ahmed Mohamed, nicknamed 'Shukurtalla', and the *Liwa al Jamous*, or Buffalo Brigade, of Hamid Dawai. Ahmed Haroun flew every few months to Darfur with boxes of cash to pay these militias.[28] Shukurtalla, an army officer from Wad Medani in central Sudan, had been sentenced to ten years' imprisonment in 2002 for abandoning the southern front. He was released after twelve months and mandated to organize militia forces in West Darfur, where he terrorized Masalit with the boast that: 'I am the Izrael [the angel of death] of the Masalit!' Dawai had also been in jail, accused of killing ten Masalit in Beida market in March 1999. The Masalit lawyer who interrogated him, Khamis Yousif Haroun, believed there was enough evidence to convict him. But the Masalit sultan was nervous about moving against such a powerful Arab, and recommended negotiations followed by compensation. Local Masalit officials received death threats, and Dawai walked free.[29] A third prominent militia leader was Ali Mohamed Ali Abdel Rahman – better known as Ali Kushayb – the second of the two men indicted by the ICC in March 2007 as commander of the militia forces of Wadi Saleh, liaison with the Sudan government, and a direct participant in murders, rapes and torture in a number of villages in Wadi Saleh in 2003–04.[30]

Under the guiding hand of Ahmed Haroun, regular and irregular forces became virtually indistinguishable. Musa Hilal reported to Khartoum, not to the army generals in al Fasher. 'You are informed that directives have been issued ... to change the demography of Darfur and empty it of African tribes,' he wrote in

August 2004 to the commander of the Western Area Command, citing orders from President Bashir himself. The means would be burning, looting and killing 'of intellectuals and youths who may join the rebels in fighting'.[31] The Western Area Command quickly became a supply line for the border intelligence, Arab PDF, militia and units brought in from other war zones, including two brigades from Blue Nile.[32] In some areas, militia were integrated into army barracks; in others, into army offensives in the field. The army supplied the paramilitaries, accompanied them as they fanned out to set up bases in outlying villages, surrounded villages as they attacked them, and participated in mopping-up operations afterwards. As arms for the expanding Janjawiid brigades rolled in, the pattern of attacks shifted – from rebel positions in the mountains and foothills to civilian targets far from the rebels. By August 2004, four months after Khartoum had signed an agreement to neutralize all militias, there were sixteen militia camps in just one of Darfur's three states.[33] Five were shared with regular troops. Three had pads for helicopters.

In January 2004, army and militia scored two successes. In separate battles they killed the Zaghawa rebel leader Abdalla Abakir and the Masalit commander Adam Bazooka. Abdel Wahid only narrowly escaped.

While Khartoum's aim was to suppress rebellion, many Arab militiamen wanted more: to take possession of Fur and Masalit lands, if not by emptying them of their inhabitants then by killing their chiefs and installing their own. Haroun encouraged them, saying in a speech to Janjawiid commanders in Mukjar, Wadi Saleh, that since 'the children of the Fur' had become rebels, 'all the Fur' had become 'booty'.[34] After years of what they perceived as discrimination by the Fur who dominated the local administration, police and market committees, many Wadi Saleh Arabs were willing recruits. 'Whether Ahmed Haroun was there or not there, it would have been the same,' remarked Safi al Nur.[35]

Starting in August 2003, according to the ICC, Security and militias worked hand-in-glove to clear a swathe of Wadi Saleh between Jebel Marra and the Chad border. A fertile area long coveted by Arabs of Chadian origin, Wadi Saleh was now crowded with tens of thousands of displaced Fur and Masalit. By the end of the year, thirty-two villages and hamlets along its tributary, Wadi Debarei, had been burned and displaced villagers had converged on the market town of Deleig. Over a period of weeks, army and Janjawiid captured and killed 172 people in the Deleig area. Some had their throats cut and their bodies thrown in the stagnant pools of a seasonal river just south of the town.[36] The burning continued. On 5 March 2004, the frightened community around Deleig woke up to find a wide area surrounded by soldiers and Janjawiid going from shelter to shelter and hut to hut, asking each man for his home village. Armed with a list of two hundred 'SLA leaders' drawn up by a local intelligence chief, Ibrahim Juma, security officers took away more than one hundred men – almost all of them displaced. In the evening, seventy-one of them were put in army trucks and taken from the police station to a wadi where they were lined up, forced to kneel and shot in the back of the head.[37] A similar massacre took place in the Mukjar area further south. This was one of the fifty crimes attributed to Ali Kushayb by the ICC, which said that 'in or around March 2004, Ali Kushayb committed, jointly with others, the murder of at least thirty-two men from the primarily Fur population of Mukjar town and surrounding areas while those men were taking no active part in hostilities, by transporting them under armed guard to their place of execution'.

The ICC indictment for Ali Kushayb presented evidence that he was responsible for virulent incitements to violence against the Masalit and Fur people. 'He had a hatred for the local non-Arab population,' said Abu al Bashar Abakir, who was Ali Kushayb's supervisor when he worked as a medical assistant in Garsila in 1993–95. 'He was a sergeant in the army until the Fur–Arab war. But he left the army and joined the Arab militias fighting the Fur after several of his relatives were killed.' Abu al Bashar said Kushayb was known in Zalingei as a member of the Borgo tribe that hailed from eastern Chad and was therefore not an Arab at all.

He was Borgo himself, with Borgo scarification, but portrayed himself as an Arab. When the NIF came to power in 1989, Ali Kushayb organized the Arabs. In the mid-1990s, before the Masalit war, he began recruiting Arabs from other areas including Beni Halba from Idd al Fursan and Ta'aisha from Rahad al Birdi. He had his own 'pharmacy' in the market of Garsila.

In all, at least 145 men were executed in Deleig and Mukjar on the night of 5–6 March 2004.[38] Another fifty-eight were killed in the Deleig area the following day. Security's counter-insurgency converged with local Arab agendas of land and chieftaincies. A week before the Deleig massacre, nine Fur omdas were arrested. All nine were shot dead in prisons in Mukjar and Garsila, near Deleig, on the same night as the mass executions in the wadis – clearing the way for Arab tribes, Salamat and Mahariya, to take possession of the area.

Bombing Darfur

The third prong of the deadly triad was the air force. As an NGO with long experience of Sudan remarked in a confidential report:

> Military aviation had made marked 'progress' in the matter of hitting its targets. Gone were the days when [Antonov] cargo planes blindly scattered barrels of explosives. The army had acquired ground-attack helicopters and tactical support aircraft whose precision was even more brutal when targeting columns of displaced persons.

In January 2004, villagers fleeing a Janjawiid attack in the Um Berro area of North Darfur intercepted, on FM, a radio conversation between an Antonov pilot and a man called Morad, a well-known military intelligence officer. 'Morad, Morad,' the pilot said. 'Burn everything! Destroy everything!'[39] The following month, Phil Cox of Native Voice Films taped the following radio conversation between an army commander and an Antonov pilot:

Commander: We've found people still in the village.

Pilot: Are they with us or against us?

Commander: They say they will work with us.

Pilot: They're liars. Don't trust them. Get rid of them.

And later,

Pilot: Now the village is empty and secure for you. Any village you pass through you must burn. That way, when the villagers come back they'll have a surprise waiting for them.

Raids like these, which needed authorization from the chief of staff's office in Khartoum, gave the lie to the government's insistence that it was not supporting Janjawiid operations at the highest level. As one of the displaced said, 'We know the Arabs. They don't have planes; they have cows! Only the government has planes!'[40] When it finally admitted to using its air force, Khartoum repeatedly failed to honour pledges to halt aerial bombardment. On the very day that Khartoum agreed to halt all offensive flights, in December 2004, several government aircraft were bombarding the Labado area east of Nyala.[41]

Although less lethal than ground forces, the Antonovs held a special terror – especially for children. 'When the Antonovs dropped bombs on us, we ran to hide under the trees,' said a young boy who survived an attack on the village of Hangala near Furawiya early in 2004. 'The bombs severed people's arms and legs ... The ones who were not killed, ran away. Three days later we came back. We used tools and cut wood from the trees and dug many graves. After we buried the dead bodies, we left.'[42]

Impunity

Regular and irregular forces operated in an ethics-free zone, as they had in earlier wars. A government official who fled to Switzerland in the early 1990s, traumatized by what he had witnessed in the Nuba Mountains, said the orders given to the government forces there had been 'to kill anything that is alive. That is to say: to kill anybody, to destroy the area, to implement a scorched earth policy ... so that nothing can exist there.'[43] In the oilfields a decade later, the orders were identical: 'If you see a village, you burn that village. If you find a civilian, you kill that civilian. If you find a cow, that cow is your cow!'[44] With the same men in power in Khartoum, the orders issued in Darfur were the same.[45] Former US Marine Brian Steidle arrived in Darfur in 2004 as a US representative for the African Union and witnessed scores of government-supported militia attacks. After one such attack, he said, the militia delivered to the AU a letter 'in which they said they'd attack this village and this village and this village and they'd burn the villages, steal whatever they wanted, and kill everybody they could. They laid it out for us. Like, "Here it is."'[46]

Impunity was an integral part of the new order. Ahmed Haroun declared his own impunity, saying in a public meeting that he had been given 'all the power and authority to kill or forgive whoever in Darfur'.[47] In North Darfur, a directive issued in February 2004 instructed all security units to 'allow the activities of the *mujahidiin* and the volunteers under the command of Sheikh Musa Hilal to proceed in the areas of [North Darfur] and to secure their vital needs'. The directive stressed the 'importance of non-interference', of not challenging Hilal's men, and instructed local authorities to 'overlook minor offences by the *mujahidiin* against civilians who are suspected members of the rebellion'.

The offences were not minor, but they were overlooked. Villagers were killed in their hundreds: shot, stabbed, butchered and burned alive. In the predominantly Kobe village of Girgira close to the Chad border, local people said that Antonovs, gunships, troops and militia from West Darfur killed 148 people in January 2004. Hobu Izhaq Azrak was raped over seven days. Her mentally retarded brother, who was seventeen years old, was shot dead as he ran away and his dead body was tied to hers. Hobu's tormentors then put grass in her hair and set fire to them both. After the massacre was over, some survivors were tied, masked and taken by helicopter to army headquarters in Geneina, where army chiefs said, 'we don't want them here' and ordered them taken elsewhere. Hobu Izhaq died of her burns in Geneina hospital in March 2004.[48] Local people told Phil Cox, who reached Girgira twelve days

133

after the attack, that 89 men, 28 women and 31 children had died in the attack, and 153 survivors perished in the ensuing chaotic escape across the desert to Chad. In Girgira, Cox found five freshly dug graves three metres long and two wide. Decomposing bodies were piled on top of each other, with loose earth tossed over them. Grain stores, the village school and mosque had all been burned. Almost every mud hut was destroyed. Cox was struck by the attackers' 'attention to detail'. 'Many hundreds of cooking bowls and utensils were littered around – they all had had a bullet put through them, rendering them useless,' he said. 'This was not just a frenzy of murder. Time had been taken to target the things that would make it difficult for the people to survive.'

In the village of Har Jang in North Darfur in April 2004, Janjawiid summarily executed a group of young men by shooting them in the back of the head. A young man who saved his life by hiding under a dead mule, the only member of his family to survive, remembered how the attackers

> took a knife and cut my mother's throat and threw her into the well. Then they took my oldest sister and began to rape her, one by one. My father was kneeling, crying and begging them for mercy. After that they killed my brother and finally my father. They threw all the bodies in the well.[49]

Sexual violence had seldom been seen in Darfur before – and never on anything approaching the scale that was now unfolding. Investigators later determined:

> The rape of individual victims was often multiple, carried out by more than one man, and accompanied by other severe forms of violence, including beating and whipping. In some cases, women were reportedly raped in public, and in some incidents, the women were further berated and called 'slaves' or 'Tora Bora'.[50]

Sexual abuse was not only rape. Early in 2003, a young Zaghawa woman called Mariam Ahmad was stopped at a roadblock and forced to watch while Janjawiid cut the penis off her three-week-old son, Ahmad. The child died soon after in her arms.[51] In Bargai, a village near Zalingei, a young mother who had just given birth to twins was killed with her legs tied to her neck, exposing her genitals. Her babies were thrown into a container of boiling water that had been brought for the birth.[52] 'You believe there's an inherent goodness in people, but you see some of these villages and it shakes that belief,' said Colonel Barry Steyn, commander of the AU's small South African contingent. 'You look at this stuff and it makes you turn white.'[53]

Minni Minawi's war

When the rebellion began, the government and the Abbala Arabs were most fearful of the Zaghawa, regardless of whether they were SLA or JEM. With links to Chad, Libya and Turabi's Popular Congress, a formidable commercial network and a reputation as fearsome desert fighters, it was the Zaghawa insurrection that most concerned Khartoum and al Fasher. And though Minni Minawi did not himself fight, it was his command of an aggressive band of Toyota-mounted warriors who were able to take the war the length and breadth of Darfur that most impressed many foreign observers, particularly the Americans.

As the rebel bands grew, some of them several hundred strong, they began looting their Arab neighbours to supply their growing forces. In 2003, a party of Zayadiya trekking with 700 camels to Libya was surrounded by the rebels. One man escaped but the other ten, along with their camels, were never seen again. What Abbala Rizeigat describe as 'the largest single incident' that targeted them was a massacre of camel-herders and traders in May 2004. A group of between sixty and seventy men were taking 700 camels to Libya when they were intercepted by Minawi's rebels and all were reportedly killed.[54] Many Arabs felt that these raids were more than just provisioning troops; they feared that the Zaghawa were aiming to drive them out of rural areas altogether. Minawi did not take his well-armed forces to Jebel Marra or Dar Masalit, where thinly defended villages were being razed by government–Janjawiid attacks, their inhabitants slaughtered and raped. His was a war of attack, not defence, and he directed his forces east to areas where, despite the war, most Arabs were living relatively peacefully with their non-Arab neighbours. One of these areas was the farmland being cultivated by Zayadiya Arabs outside Mellit, capital of Dar Berti.

In 1999, and increasingly in 2000, Zayadiya militia in the Mellit area had launched punishing attacks on non-Arab villages near Mellit, sometimes with government support and sometimes without.[55] When the rebellion came, Zayadiya farmers north and west of Mellit feared the rebels were coming to attack them – and so it proved. 'The rebel bands started small and began to grow, from twenty to fifty to a hundred to a thousand,' said Siddiq Umbadda, a development expert from the Zayadiya.[56]

From where were they going to get their supplies? They could attack a police post, or if they were lucky they could attack a lorry. But most often they would look for animals to capture and slaughter. If they went after the property of their own people they would lose support, so it is better to attack their neighbours, and it so happened that those neighbours were Arabs. The Zayadiya were attacked by rebels many times, camels and goats were taken, guns were taken, people were killed. This was repeated many times. The government played on this saying 'These people are against the Arabs, you must protect yourself.'

By early 2004, Zaghawa attacks on Zayadiya Arab farms north of Mellit had left a wide swathe of land completely deserted and thousands of families displaced, fearful of going to IDP camps, and so without humanitarian relief. Then, in March 2004, Minawi's forces attacked west of Mellit and seized a small herd of goats and a simple-minded Zayadiya shepherd. 'The people deliberated about what to do,' said Siddiq Umbadda.

One asked, 'Is this a deliberate provocation, to lead us into an ambush?' The Mahamid had learned earlier that when the Zaghawa attack and capture animals, if you go after them, you will fall into an ambush. So instead they would just go and take the same number of animals from any Zaghawa they came across. Most of the men in the meeting wanted to learn from this experience and did not want to chase after the stolen animals. But the wife of the man whose animals were taken organized a *hakkama* – a tradition whereby women sing to encourage their menfolk to be brave. She sang to insult her husband, accusing him of cowardice, commanding him to go and reclaim them by force. The husband said, 'I know I am a dead man but I will go.' So a party of more than twenty men was put together, some of them teenagers. They departed, with a little water, some guns, and one camel with ammunition. The rebels were waiting for them, with binoculars and guns ready. Early in the morning they ambushed them, and after a quick skirmish, the ammunition of the Zayadiya group was finished. One was shot. One of them told the young men, 'Run back and leave us.' Three or four made it back. Nineteen were killed and the simple-minded shepherd was still missing. But that was not the issue. Something that had never happened before then occurred. The dead men were mutilated. Their hands were broken, their mouths were slashed, their eyes were pierced, their faces branded, their mouths were filled with dung, one body was partly burned and many of the dead were shot with many bullets (mostly after they died). The next day, the Zayadiya collected their dead and brought them to Mellit where they were buried in two mass graves.

Non-Arabs also complained about the behaviour of Minawi's men. 'Minni Minawi is against Darfur,' said Mohamed Izhaq Jiddo, brother of a Tunjur omda arrested by Minawi's men and never seen again. 'With him there is no democracy, no consultation. Darfurians are not necessarily educated, but they know justice and democracy. For these things it is acceptable to take up arms. But Minni Minawi has no vision. He helped the Janjawiid by tribalizing the conflict.'

Minawi insisted that he was fighting a revolutionary war with the aim of bringing down the government, and he downplayed tribal differences within Darfur.[57] Like many self-proclaimed revolutionaries, he was as ruthless with his rivals as with his enemies. And while the government possessed an exaggerated fear of the Zaghawa rebels, the Fur if anything underestimated them. They thought they, the Fur, were the intellectuals, and the Zaghawa were simple and without ambition. This was a serious misjudgement, although one that in Minawi's case was perhaps understandable, given his credentials. Minawi was an untested youth not yet thirty years old when the rebels began organizing in 2001. He had no work experience, no military experience and among Zaghawa was of no consequence. His Ila Digen clansmen (Awlad Digayn, in Arabic) were looked down on by other Zaghawa because they were poor, had few camels and, despite the drought, kept cultivating millet. More than others, the clan had kept some pre-Islamic traditions, and were considered by many as not very good Muslims. Companions from the early days of the rebellion say other Zaghawa treated Minawi dismissively. While they had been helping Idriss Deby to instal a Zaghawa regime in Chad, he had been living in Nigeria with his uncle, a small-time business-man. But Minawi had been to secondary school and could read and write. He became known as Abakir's 'secretary'. He spoke good English as a result of his years in Nigeria and was entrusted with a Thuraya satellite phone with which to communicate with the world's media. Minawi had ambitions.

Even before Abakir's death in January 2004, Minawi had begun imposing on the movement his narrow tribalism and hatred of the Native Administration, politicians and 'intellectuals'. One of the most senior commanders then under his authority claims that the first killings preceded Abakir's death. He said: 'Abdalla was not happy. He told Minni: "We must collect all the politicians and turn a new page."' Abakir's death ended all hope of that. From being Abakir's 'secretary', Minawi promoted himself to 'secretary general', named the uneducated but ultra-loyal Juma Mohamed Hagar to be his chief of staff and stepped into Abakir's shoes, unchallenged. He promoted first Zaghawa and then members of his own Ila Digen clan to key positions in the security, police and financial offices of the SLA and to head committees.[58] The split in the movement widened, but Minawi's close aides made light of it. John Garang had used his own small clan, the Bor Dinka, to keep control of a divided SPLA, they said. Why shouldn't Minawi do the same?

'After Abdalla died, Minni was in full control,' says a senior SLA commander. 'Other tribes left him. If any strong leader emerged, Minni would get rid of him in days.' 'The Zaghawa don't want to be the leader of Darfur', says Daud Taher, himself a Zaghawa. 'Minni Minawi does, for himself. He doesn't listen to people who have experience. He pushes them away and cooperates with small boys. Many tribes hate the Zaghawa because of Minni Minawi. If all tribes hate you, who will obey you? We cannot govern Darfur by force.'[59]

Force, however, was the dominant characteristic of Minni Minawi's war, employed early in the war against one of the most senior Zaghawa chiefs of Darfur – Abdel Rahman Mohamedein, malik of Dar Tuer. Abdel Rahman's Agaba clan had wrested the chieftancy of Dar Tuer from Minawi's Ila Digen in the eighteenth century and still holds it to this day – a historic rivalry that the malik's family say has led to six members of their family being killed by his men.[60] On 27 January 2004, government troops attacked and burned Abdel Rahman's village, Um Berro. The malik set out from al Fasher to deliver food and medicines to his people, but was ambushed on the road by Minawi's men, at a village called Orshi. His family investigated what happened next, in meticulous detail, and gave the following account.[61]

Malik Abdel Rahman was taken first to Muzbat, the administrative centre of the Ila Digen, where one of Minawi's commanders, Mohamed Osman, gathered villagers under a tree and in front of them all hit Abdel Rahman with his chief's stick, a symbol of his authority, saying 'The king of Dar Tuer [whose capital is Um Berro] is like a bird in my hand!'[62] Two of the malik's relatives were raped in front of him. From Wadi Howar, where he had fled when the government began attacking, Minawi ordered the king be moved from Muzbat to Shigeig Karo, a village several hours' drive away. As the malik was escorted away from Muzbat,

139

Mohamed Osman threw sand in his face. 'This is your last day,' he said. 'If you have a last wish, tell your sister what it is!' A member of Minawi's clan, Tijani Ibrahim Mohamed, accompanied Abdel Rahman to Shigeig Karo, where the final act of the tragedy began. The malik was bound hand and foot, hanged from a tree by his hands, and beaten. After he died, he was shot three times in the head. His body was dragged around the village and left unburied.

In a rant posted on a Sudanese website, Minawi's uncle, Bahr al Arabi, denied the SLA had any hand in the malik's murder and claimed that the 'killing by government elements charged us all emotionally'. Reports of SLA involvement were 'baseless ... market rummer and iddle talk [sic] ... a campaign of calmny [sic], hate and discredit against the Ela degain [sic] first, Zaghawa second, and SLM/A third'.[63] In an interview a few days later, however, Minawi said the exact opposite. He admitted the murder. Asked how the malik died, he said: 'He was tortured and killed. But not by me. By my *shurta* [military police]!'[64] The king's family says Minawi left Darfur, for Nairobi, before Abdel Rahman was killed. But they say they hold Minawi responsible, as the commander of the SLA forces in North Darfur, for everything that happened to the malik – from his seizure to his torture and finally his death.

The war spreads south

The government offensive launched in December 2003 was designed to end the rebel challenge once and for all. It extended across three fronts in North Darfur – from Kebkabiya to Kornoi, Kulbus to Tine, and Kutum to Um Berro – and soon claimed the life of Abdalla Abakir. With their military leader dead, the rebels were thrown into disarray. At a conference held near the village of Shigeig Karo in the far north, Zaghawa commanders discussed their options. Some – including Minawi, according to one of those present – were for retreating temporarily towards Libya. Some melted into the Meidob hills after a Meidob commander, Suleiman Marajan, argued that conventional tactics could not defeat a force he estimated at 13,000 men and 450 vehicles. The only sensible course of action, Marajan said, was to lie low until the attack was over. Others fled south down the eastern side of Jebel Marra where, despite the tensions between the Fur and Zaghawa leaderships, they were taken in and hosted by the Fur. In the most significant move, one of Minawi's most powerful commanders, Jiddo Issa 'Sagor', a member of the Kaliba clan of Dar Gala, moved hundreds of SLA forces into areas of South Darfur state where Zaghawa civilians displaced by drought in North Darfur had been living peacefully since the 1980s, accommodated in the *dars* of other ethnic groups. Minawi himself moved north to the relative safety of Wadi Howar.

In the chaos of the government attack and the rebel move south, SLA forces under the command of Jiddo Issa reportedly executed scores of prisoners – both prisoners of war and civilians.[65] The same sources who first told the authors of the murder of Abdel Rahman Mohamedein said the dead included passengers from ten lorries that had been travelling to Darfur from Omdurman. They said the lorries were seized by Minawi's men on the main road between the village of Kuma and al Fasher towards the end of 2003. A Zaghawa commander in the SLA who is related to one of the lorry drivers – a civilian who has disappeared without trace – said the prisoners were held in Oriri, south of Muzbat, and killed there.[66] He said Mohamed Izhaq Jiddo's brother, sixty-five-year-old Abdalla Ali Izhaq, was among seventy-three people who were killed. 'The prisoners were held in Oriri because it was far from government-controlled areas. They were tied, shot and buried in huts.'

Mohamed Izhaq Jiddo said his brother was seized by SLA–Minawi in Kulkul market in November 2003, together with one of his sons, and accused of collecting taxes for the benefit of the government. He said the family was told the old man would be released upon payment of 3 million Sudanese pounds. The money was paid, he said, but Omda Abdalla was not released.[67] Two and a half years later, in May 2006, the family was told the two men had died in government bombing. Their own information is that they were killed by the rebels.

A second SLA commander – one of four SLA commanders who gave information about the prisoners' murder – told the authors the killings went on for almost a week:

> When the forces began to move from the north to the south of Darfur, they started to get rid of the prisoners. They didn't have the means of taking them there [to South Darfur], so they shot them. The number I know is about 80.[68] Some were killed in Oriri. But most were killed in Gorbora [a village near Muzbat] and buried in a mass grave. The man in charge of the forces was Jiddo. But everything that happened in those days happened under the orders of Minni.[69]

On 9 February, President Bashir claimed in a television address to the nation that the insurgency was 'crushed' and the army was in 'full control' of Darfur. He said 'major military operations' were over and offered amnesty to rebels who surrendered. But the war was not over; it was about to enter a new phase as SLA forces ranged ever further afield, into previously untouched eastern and southern parts of Darfur.

As the rebels began to attack police stations and other government targets in South Darfur, the government withdrew police and PDF from villages, and stepped up its mobilization of militia, wooing Arab tribes with promises of development. On 22 November 2003, the governor of South Darfur state, Major General Adam Hamid Musa, ordered the recruitment of 'three hundred Fursan for Khartoum' in the same breath as he promised to vaccinate camels and horses, and build classrooms, a health unit and twenty-four water pumps in eight villages. Three months later, in a directive issued on 3 March, the governor established an eight-man security committee composed largely of leaders of small Arab tribes of Chadian origin, which had been involved in clashes with Fur and other groups over access to land, and ordered Nyala Commissioner Saeed Adam Jaama 'to swiftly deliver provisions and ammunition to the new [militia] camps to secure the south-western part of the state'.[70]

Ten days later, the rebels struck their first major target in South

Darfur: Buram, the headquarters of the Arab Habbaniya tribe. 'They did not ask or consult with the local inhabitants,' Suleiman Jamous, the SLA's humanitarian coordinator and a friend of the nazir of the Habbaniya, acknowledged much later, after the Habbaniya destroyed a number of Zaghawa villages. 'The government was therefore able to rally the locals against the SLA. We fought again, and defeated them.'[71] In the first attack on Buram, on 13 March, the rebels were careful to attack only government targets: the Security office, police station, local administration and *zakat* (religious tax) offices, and the telecommunications centre. They announced that civilians would not be harmed.[72] In subsequent fighting, which claimed the lives of two of the nazir's brothers – deputy nazir Omar Ali al Ghali and the attorney general for South Darfur, al Ghali Ali al Ghali – the rebels entered Buram hospital, where wounded government soldiers had been taken, and killed a number of patients.[73] In a report made public on 25 January 2005, the UN International Commission of Inquiry on Darfur (ICID) quoted a government committee as reporting that thirteen civilians and some soldiers were killed in the hospital.[74] A hospital worker told Reuters that one patient died after an intravenous drip was ripped out of his arm. A second, a policeman, was shot in the head, wrapped in a gasoline-soaked blanket and set alight.[75] Until this point, many Habbaniya leaders had been critical of the government, but now they responded to Khartoum's offer of weapons for self-defence.

On 8 April, the government and movements signed a 'humanitarian' ceasefire in N'Djamena. While it was followed by expanded relief efforts, the ceasefire was soon violated by both sides. By July, much of eastern and southern Darfur was the locus of offensives and counter-offensives similar to those already visited upon West and North Darfur. In the first three days of July, soldiers and Janjawiid advancing under air cover destroyed thirty-four villages in the Birgid area, whose inhabitants also included Mima and Zaghawa. Almost five hundred civilians were reported killed.[76] In July 2004, the village of Suleia east of Nyala, on the Nyala-al Da'ein railway line, was attacked by government-supported militia who killed dozens of non-combatants, including eight schoolgirls who were chained together and burned alive in their classroom. Two months later, the government established a military base in the abandoned village.[77] More was to come: in late November, the government launched a major land and air offensive to control a number of critical road and rail supply lines. The first target was Adwa, held by the SLA. It had been attacked and looted on 18 March, with six villagers killed, according to one of the sheikhs of the area.[78] The November attack was larger, and the villagers counted 126 dead, including thirty-six children. They said the militia burned some bodies and threw others into wells to hide the evidence of the massacre. Human Rights Watch wrote, 'The offensive was extremely well planned and systematic in its approach ... The methodical way in which these strategic locations were attacked illustrates the overall coordination role of the Sudanese government; the offensive was apparently directed from Khartoum.'[79] AU officials interviewed the leader of one of the Rizeigat militias involved in the attack on Adwa, who had dawdled in the village. Mohamed Hamdan 'Hemeti', nephew of the Juma Dogolo who attacked Kidingeer village in Jebel Marra in October 2002, admitted the government–militia alliance: he said the attack had been planned for several months, and that an Antonov and two helicopter gunships were involved. After Adwa, the operation proceeded to Marla and Labado.

The 'road-clearing operation' had reduced dozens of villages to ashes by the time it climaxed in mid-December with the burning of Labado, a town packed with people who had been displaced from the surrounding areas. Survivors said some people were locked in their huts and burned to death. Others were herded into the school and killed there, as they had been in Suleia. A western military observer who flew over the area said the Janjawiid were 'fully integrated' into the army formation that advanced towards Labado.

Despite government commitments to do both throughout 2004, Janjawiid were neither disarmed nor arrested. Instead Khartoum opted for denial and, when that failed, deception.

1 Suni market in Jebel Marra, where traders and nomads came to buy grain, fruit and vegetables, 1986 (Alex de Waal)

2 Lake Gineik in North Darfur, scene of one of the first major clashes between Arabs and Zaghawa, 2004 (Julie Flint)

3 The road to
Aamo, 1985
(Alex de Waal)

4 Sheikh Hilal Mohamed Abdalla in his tent at Aamo, 1985 (Alex de Waal)

5 Musa Hilal, 2004

6 Um Jalul boys at Aamo, 1985 (Alex de Waal)

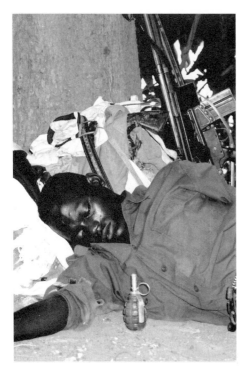

7 A Masalit rebel from the SLA in West Darfur camped in a mango grove, 2004 (Julie Flint)

8 A Masalit village in West Darfur destroyed by government-supported militia, 2004 (Julie Flint)

9 Shoba village in Jebel Marra, attacked more than a dozen times by Janjawiid, 2002

10 Abdel Wahid al Nur at his headquarters
in Suni, in Jebel Marra, 2005

11 Zaghawa fighters loyal to Minni Minawi
in Muzbat, North Darfur, 2004 (Julie Flint)

12 JEM fighters in Girgira after an attack by government forces and Janjawiid killed more than a hundred people in January 2004 (© Oliver Jobard)

13 Ismail Adam Mohamed 'Abunduluk', the SLA commander who led the unit that attacked the government airbase in al Fasher, 2007 (Julie Flint)

14 Shoba
village after
Janjawiid
attack, 2002

15 Fur rebels from Korma, gathered in Dar Zaghawa for a 'unity conference' of the SLA, 2007 (Julie Flint)

16 A food distribution in rebel-controlled Shangal Tobai, 2005 (© Jerome Tubiana)

17 The DPA signing ceremony in Abuja on 5 May 2006 (© AMIS)

18 Heavy weapons seized by the SLA from the government forces which attacked Um Sidir, in North Darfur, in an offensive designed to crush the rebels who rejected the DPA, 2007 (Julie Flint)

19 Al Salam camp for the displaced near al Fasher, 2005 (© Jerome Tubiana)

20 Bir Maza village after fighting with Janjawid and Minni Minawi's former rebels, 2007 (Julie Flint)

21 AMIS personnel with some of the AU peacekeepers killed when rebels from the SLA and JEM attacked the AMIS base at Haskanita in September 2007 (© AMIS)

22 Arab rebel leader Anwar Ahmad Khater in jail in Khartoum, 2007

Common criminals arrested before the rebellion were paraded as Janjawiid and then executed. Sham disarmament ceremonies were organized for visitors. On 27 August, the UN Special Representative witnessed 300 militiamen hand over their weapons in Geneina. They were handed back the following day.[80] The ICID reported that the government had been able to cite only one case of punishment since the rebellion began – that of a man who, apparently acting on his own initiative, had burned a single village, Halouf, killing twenty-four people.[81]

Starving Darfur

Government and Janjawiid forces destroyed everything that made life possible. Food that could be carried away was; the rest was burned. Animals that could be taken away were; the rest were killed. The simple straw buildings that served as clinics and schools were destroyed, requiring nothing more than a box of matches, and everything in them was stolen or torched. Pumps were smashed and wells polluted – often with corpses. Mosques were burned and Qurans desecrated. In 2003–04, more than sixty-two mosques were burned in West Darfur alone.[82] It was, the ICID wrote, 'a nightmare of violence and abuse' that stripped villagers of the very little they had. With few exceptions, the abuses appeared to have no military 'justification'. The UN estimated that between 700 and 2,000 villages were totally or partially destroyed.

Human catastrophe was a deliberate act. By the beginning of 2005, almost 2 million people had been driven to camps and towns inside Darfur and another 200,000 had sought refuge in Chad.[83] These destitute and displaced people were deterred from searching for wild foods or from gathering firewood by the threat of rape or death by Janjawiid. The government deployed long years of expertise in delaying and blocking relief operations with a farrago of bureaucratic entanglements. Aid workers needed visas to enter Sudan, travel permits to Darfur, daily travel permits to leave the state capitals, and fuel permits to travel around Darfur. UNICEF drugs needed to save lives were delayed for testing in

Sudanese laboratories. Vehicles were held up in Port Sudan, and on reaching Darfur were often impounded. In mid-2004, as rains threatened epidemics in the overcrowded displacement camps, rigorous registration requirements for health workers impeded the ability of relief agencies to respond to disease.[84] As so often with Sudan's wars, the death toll from hunger and disease surpassed the numbers killed by violence, and as the slaughter ebbed in the last months of 2004, the famine raged.

Starvation was not mere negligence – in some terrible instances, it was military strategy.[85] Left to their own devices, rural people in Darfur can usually find enough sustenance from wild foods to see them through months of hunger.[86] 'We don't just starve: someone must force starvation upon us,' an old woman said in 1986, explaining how her family had survived the great famine of 1984–85.[87] Death rates in Darfur tripled in that crisis and some 100,000 people perished, mostly children and old people. That was bad enough; but in 2003–04 the Janjawiid forcibly obstructed coping strategies, and people died in even larger numbers. A UN team that visited Kailak camp in South Darfur in April 2004 found a death rate forty-one times higher than the standard threshold for an 'emergency'. Among under-fives, the death rate was 147 times higher.[88] Accusing government forces of a 'strategy of systematic and deliberate starvation', they described how armed men 'guarding' the displaced had stopped food entering the camps – even the wild foods collected by the displaced themselves – and had taken it for themselves and their camels. Fortunately Kailak was soon relieved and its population moved to better-supplied camps. But had Kailak not been exposed, how many other starvation camps might have been established?

When anger over conditions in the camps became too great to continue to deny access to them, the government tried to make them disappear. In July 2004, UN Secretary General Kofi Annan visited one of Darfur's worst camps in a deserted plant nursery in al Fasher. On arrival, he found stagnant puddles and dead donkeys, but no people. No one believed the assertion that it had been cleared because it had no sanitation.[89] Annan also visited Mashtel camp outside al Fasher and found it, too, empty. Only twenty-four hours previously, aides had seen it 'brimming' with life. A government official said the displaced had been moved to the outskirts of al Fasher because Mashtel would flood when the rains came; he denied the move had been to stop Annan bearing witness. But the manner, and the timing, of the move suggested otherwise: the displaced were simply loaded into army trucks and dumped at the gates of the already overcrowded Abu Shouk camp, where some 40,000 people were living in open desert. By the end of 2004, the sheer numbers of displaced people and the growing presence of relief agencies meant that the government opted for the path of least resistance and allowed the camps to remain. Obstruction, harassment and Janjawiid attacks continued, however.

Darfur during 2004 was a firestorm of violent displacement, man-made famine and obstruction of relief. Slowly but surely, an immense relief operation cranked into gear. By early 2005, deaths from hunger and disease had dropped from the heights of the darkest days of 2004. Surveys by aid agencies show that mortality rates in the displaced camps were approaching normal levels by early 2005, and most indications showed that death rates had also dropped in the remaining villages.[90] This was a genuine but unsung success of the international response to Darfur.

Keeping the secret

Crimes against humanity like those being committed in Darfur did not bear scrutiny. From the very start of the rebellion, the government did everything in its power to black out all news from the region. The correspondent of the *Al Sahafa* newspaper in Nyala, Yousif al Bashir Musa, was arrested after publishing a report on the rebel attack on al Fasher, accused of 'spreading false information against the state', and severely beaten with sticks on his body and the sole of his only foot. Amnesty International suggested that the torture of Musa helped to intimidate other journalists. 'Red lines' issued to journalists included a prohibition against mentioning human rights abuses in Darfur.[91] Independent newspapers that pushed the bar, such as the the

Arabic-language *Al Ayam* and the English-language *Khartoum Monitor*, were suspended. Al Jazeera, the most-watched television station in the Arab world, was closed after it became the first television station in the world to report the atrocities in Darfur. Parliament was not allowed to discuss Darfur.

When the international community began to show concern over Darfur, access was simply refused. Journalists and human rights investigators were denied visas. This was nothing new: the government had never shown much inclination to let outsiders travel anywhere in Sudan. But as refugees streamed into Chad, and journalists were able to investigate there what they were unable to investigate in Darfur, measures of a different kind were needed. And so, in March 2004, army lorries rounded up Masalit tribal leaders near the border with Chad and took them to the town of Misterei, then under the control of Hamid Dawai. Dawai offered the Masalit vast sums of money to create 'security' in the Masalit area 'so no one can cross the border to Chad'. The Masalit chiefs replied: 'We don't like your security and we don't want your money.' Dawai replied: 'If you don't make this security, I will kill all your civilians.'[92] In the weeks that followed, his men burned dozens of villages around Misterei.

As it became impossible for the international community to ignore Darfur any longer, and impossible for the government to refuse all access, the pressure to keep silent grew. Sudanese human rights activists who met foreigners were arrested and held in preventative detention under emergency legislation that denied them not only access to lawyers, families and medical assistance, but also the right to be brought promptly before a judge, to challenge the legality of their detention and to be treated humanely.[93] International NGOs found themselves facing a bleak choice: to turn a blind eye to atrocities, or to speak out and risk being expelled. In May 2004, two omdas were arrested after giving the International Committee of the Red Cross information on burnt villages and mass graves.[94] Another fifty people were arrested between 26 June and 3 August 2004, most of them after speaking to foreign delegations. Police were posted outside

Nyala hospital to keep journalists away from villagers injured in Janjawiid attacks.[95] Masalit community leaders were arrested on suspicion of passing information to foreigners about attempts to force the displaced to return to their homes and, by extension, to starve in burned areas that were not receiving relief.

What was Khartoum's calculation? How could it inflict such atrocities on a civilian population, creating such a humanitarian catastrophe, and expect to escape crisis at home and censure abroad? One part of the answer is that the Darfur file was in the hands of Security, which cared not at all about internal dissent or external pressure. Indeed, many Security officers were opposed to concessions made in the North–South peace talks in Kenya and would have been quite happy to see those negotiations collapse. With Darfur screened off by the Security agencies, the rest of the government went into denial. But it is also true that the government leaders who authorized the campaigns miscalculated. They thought it would be a quick fix, like the suppression of Daud Bolad's incursion in 1991. And because Darfur has neither Christians nor oil, in any significant quantities, they thought that the western world would give them a free hand in Darfur, happy to see peace in the South at last. On both fronts, they got it badly wrong.

6 | Wars within wars, 2005–06

In January 2005, the UN International Commission of Inquiry on Darfur (ICID) declared that 'the Government of the Sudan and the Janjawiid are responsible for serious violations of international human rights and humanitarian law amounting to crimes under international law'. The ICID found that government forces and militias had 'conducted indiscriminate attacks, including killing of civilians, torture, enforced disappearances, destruction of villages, rape and other forms of sexual violence, pillaging and forced displacement, throughout Darfur'. It said 'these acts were conducted on a widespread and systematic basis, and therefore may amount to crimes against humanity'. The ICID also concluded 'the crucial element of genocidal intent appears to be missing, at least as far as the central government authorities are concerned'.[1] Two months later, the UN Security Council referred Darfur to the International Criminal Court.[2]

As the commissioners presented their report, the nature of the war was changing. The government's counter-insurgency had achieved its immediate goal of blocking the military threat posed by the rebellion, and the level of killings was reduced. Data from all sources, including the ICC, confirm this: the great majority of the killings in Darfur took place in the year leading up to April 2004, with massive spikes in July–September 2003 and the early months of 2004. Figure 6.1 on the page opposite is taken from the data presented by the ICC in its indictments.

But the government's 'success' came with bills to be paid and after twenty years of similar wars, Khartoum's generals knew exactly what to expect. The rebels had been halted, but this was certain to be only a temporary setback. The level of bloodshed and displacement meant there would be more recruits to the rebel movements and a continuing flood of weapons across Darfur's

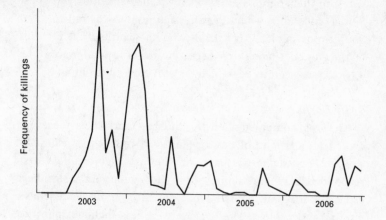

FIGURE 6.1 The correlation between time and the frequency of killings in Darfur. *Source*: International Criminal Court, 'Prosecutor's Application under Article 58(7), Annexe 3.'[3]

long, uncontrollable desert borders with Libya and Chad. At the beginning of 2005, as the ICC referral loomed, Khartoum shifted gear. It put its irregulars – now known to both Darfurians and the world as Janjawiid – in the front line.

'In the spring of 2005, there was a change of strategy,' said a senior western military official in Khartoum. Three hundred young men hand-picked from the Border Intelligence Brigade and PDF were sent to a military intelligence camp north of Omdurman for advanced infantry training by Sudanese and Russian officers.

> The training was tough and 10 per cent dropped out in the first two weeks. Those who completed the course were sent back to Darfur to work as trainers with the militias, distinguished by black berets with red leather straps. The army stayed in barracks. North Darfur was quiet. West Darfur was bands of roving men. There was only banditry.[4]

It was, perhaps, better described as a return to the politics of the frontier, in which local chiefs and military commanders assessed their options and sold their allegiance to the highest bidder, constantly defending their autonomy by defrauding and double-crossing faraway patrons who knew little of the realities on the ground. Under intense scrutiny, the army temporarily took a back seat. Security remained ever-present, controlling.

South Darfur burns

The great combined offensives that had marked 2003–04 were over. The heartland of the rebellion was reduced to ashes. As the rebels took the war east and south, the government first responded by seeking support from the big Baggara Arab tribes, especially Rizeigat, Beni Halba, Habbaniya and Fellata. These efforts mostly failed. The Baggara were less inclined than the Abbala to fight outside their own territories, especially now that relations with non-Arabs even within their own *dars* were severely strained. Their concern was to decrease, not increase, tensions. Many, especially among the Rizeigat, felt betrayed by the government. As one leader put it, 'We were always on the frontline – against the SPLA and against Daud Bolad – but we have received no reward for this. Our sons, who did the fighting, are facing discrimination and a lack of employment opportunities.'[5] As a second-best, Security turned to Arab militias from a range of small tribes across South Darfur: the Missiriya (Nitega and Jebel sections), Sa'ada, Terjem and some Mahariya groups such as the Awlad Mansour.

Almost as soon as it seized power in 1989, the NIF had begun creating chieftaincies among smaller Arab tribes in South Darfur, many of them relative newcomers from Chad. The purpose then was to create constituencies that would provide Khartoum with votes if elections ever became necessary. Now the government's needs were different and it called in its debts, demanding that the chiefs provide military backing. These militias were not all under direct government management as the Border Intelligence Guards of North Darfur had been, and Darfurians began to talk about the 'Janjawiid-ization' of tribal authority.[6] As the war spread, Khartoum bought loyalty among South Darfur's Arab tribes by promoting small or immigrant tribes that didn't have paramount chiefs, and tried to block solidarity with non-Arabs by fomenting divisions in all its usual well-honed ways.

Against this backdrop, the arrival of Minawi's aggressive Zaghawa fighters, who rode roughshod even over their own people, played into government hands by putting new strains on the already fragile co-existence of Arab and non-Arab, Chadian and Sudanese. The SLA's blocking of many of the traditional animal migration routes to the north trapped Abbala Arabs in and around Baggara areas, leading to competition for pastureland and adding Arab–Arab strains to the existing mix.

Criminality and confusion

Minawi's brief military ascendancy over a large arc of Darfur, from the far north through the east to parts of the south, confirmed the changing character of the rebellion, which in many places descended into criminality.

In April 2003 the SLA and JEM fighters who attacked al Fasher had passed through the small market town of Korma north west of al Fasher. They returned the same way. Four months later, on 16 August, militia attacked Korma, killing fifty-two people. 'They had ID cards for the Border Guards,' said one resident.[7] 'They came on horses and camels, about a thousand of them. Ten kilometres of the valley was covered by them. When they arrived they said they had been sent by the government to take all the cattle. It was because of the [rebel] attack on al Fasher.' A militia force from Jebel Si returned to the area in March 2004, systematically destroying villages, abducting civilians, including children, and taking animals. 'Eighty vehicles came,' said one eyewitness, 'they beat us, kicked us, looted everything and put it in their vehicles.'[8] Seventy-one captives were subsequently killed.

The Ereigat Arabs of Beira, north east of Korma, played no part in these attacks. Early in 2005, however, Minawi's Zaghawa forces attacked Beira and killed twenty-seven villagers. 'The Ereigat were attacked because they had not been attacked by the government,' said an Arab leader working with the rebels. 'When asked why, Minni Minawi said: "It wasn't me. It was my *shurta* [military police]."'

In areas far from their own villages, Minawi's men preyed on others in order to sustain themselves. Areas where SLA troops provided protection from the militia – at a price – were the exceptions to the rule. In most places, the rebels levied heavy 'development taxes' on trucks, market goods, livestock and even water. In SLA-controlled towns like Gereida and Joghana, the rebels also took a large share of the taxes collected by the chiefs. In some areas, the SLA forced local government officials to flee, disrupting education, health and police services.[9] In others, they attempted to impose 'revolutionary' courts in place of the traditional chiefs' courts. Arab leaders accused them of stealing cattle, killing tribal leaders and 'indiscriminately' attacking Arab villages. Nomads were especially unhappy: not only were they obliged to pay tax on their animals – in one rebel area, 500, 300 and 200 dinars per head on camels, cattle, and sheep and goats respectively – but a prohibition on horses and weapons passing though rebel-controlled areas during migration corralled their animals and encouraged the spread of disease.[10] UN officials warned that 'this heavy-handedness by the SLA could jeopardize the fragile local peace initiatives and rapprochements made by the traditional leaders from both communities to reconcile'. They urged the international community to put pressure on the SLA 'to let the animals migrate to their traditional routes to avoid a breakout of diseases that could wipe out the entire livestock of the population'. Anger against the Zaghawa rebels soon found a soft target: Zaghawa civilians who had moved south in the drought years of the 1970s and 1980s.

The locality of Shearia lies north east of Nyala. It is the *dar* of the Birgid, one of the largest non-Arab tribes of South Darfur, and is home to almost thirty Arab and non-Arab tribes including Zaghawa and Missiriya, who have been given land within the *dar*. For several decades, the Zaghawa in Shearia enjoyed relatively good relations with their hosts. But relations began to sour after the arrival in January 2004 of Zaghawa fighters from the SLA and

JEM, who by June of that year were attacking Missiriya Arabs, ignoring their long history of intermarriage with the Birgid. The nazir of the Darfur Missiriya, Tijani Abdel Gadir, complained that 'we had no conflict with other tribes until the rebels came. But the Zaghawa [in Shearia] joined the rebels and began attacking us.' Nazir Tijani claimed that 104 Missiriya were killed and ninety-two wounded in thirty-four attacks between June 2004 and May 2005.[11] As the Zaghawa became ever bolder, the Missiriya accused the Birgid of supporting the rebels.[12]

The government was quick to exploit the animosities stirred up by the rebel forces, unleashing a barrage of poisonous anti-Zaghawa propaganda. The Khartoum newspaper *Al Intibaha*, published by President Bashir's uncle, Tayib Mustafa, and famous for its venomous attacks on the opposition of all colours, featured on its front page the blueprint of a 'Greater Zaghawa State' that would allegedly encompass all of Chad, most of Libya and more than a third of Sudan, along with bites of Egypt and the Central African Republic. The paper claimed it had acquired a document that set out a Zaghawa plan to 'divide Sudan and eliminate all other tribes in Darfur'.

As tensions grew during 2004, chiefs from three native administrations in the Shearia area – including three non-Arabs: the Dajo sultan, the deputy nazir of the Birgid and the chief of the Birgid Dali – made public a letter denouncing 'continuous violations of the ceasefire' by the SLA and warning that the area was descending into chaos. The Birgid complained that the Zaghawa forces were using their villages as bases for raiding commercial lorries and Arab herders, exposing them to reprisals. The Birgid's worst fears came to pass in December 2004, when militia forces drawn from the Missiriya Nitega began to raid Birgid villages, culminating in the destruction of Khor Abeche on 17 January 2005. The African Union had been attempting to deploy troops in Khor Abeche and Nitega village ever since an incident in which the Missiriya accused Minawi fighters of stealing 150 cows and refusing to hand over the bodies of two men killed in an earlier attack. The AU and UN accused the government of 'deliberate procrastination' in authorizing the African Union Mission in Sudan (AMIS) deployment despite the fact that the Nazir Tijani 'had in their very presence repeatedly threatened the destruction of Khor Abeche'. While the government stalled, the militia struck, sending 350 men into Khor Abeche on horseback and camel, 'killing, burning and destroying everything in their paths and leaving in their wake total destruction with only the mosque and the school spared'. After the attack, the AU called for the arrest of Tijani.[13]

Generations of chiefs of Darfur's smaller tribes have retained control of their fiefdoms because of their sharp political senses. They calculate the smallest calibration of power, and adjust their positions accordingly. By this time, despite the destruction and loss of life, Nazir Musa Jaalis of the Birgid, and the other Birgid, Beigo and Berti chiefs of the area, figured that their chances were better with each other than with Minawi's men. Just four months after the Khor Abeche attack, Nazir Jaalis was ready to accept a truce with Nazir Tijani – and backing from Khartoum.[14] A meeting between Nazir Jaalis, Nazir Tijani and representatives of nineteen other tribes in the area was held at a 'Brotherhood and Peaceful Co-existence Conference' held in Shearia from 31 May to 2 June 2005, under the governor of South Darfur, al Haj Atta al Mannan. It was more defence pact than reconciliation: the Zaghawa were not invited. The aim, some said, was to build a united front against SLA–Minawi and the Zaghawa; others said, to keep the pot bubbling. Nazir Jaalis said the SLA had occupied the *hakura* of the Birgid 'by force'. He criticized the Zaghawa civilians to whom he had given refuge from drought in the 1970s and 1980s. He said they had brought 'bad new habits' of murder and armed robbery, and echoed genuine popular fears as well as government propaganda when he said they had a hidden agenda: to establish a Zaghawa kingdom that would encompass the Birgid homeland.

But the nazir went on to accuse the government too, not only for having failed to move against the rebels, but also for dismissing four hundred Birgid from the security forces and the PDF, leaving the area free for the rebels to take over. More surprising was the position taken by the Arab Nazir Tijani, who said the government had left the area vulnerable to tribal conflict by withdrawing its police and security forces. He joined his fellow chiefs in calling on the government to take responsibility for rehabilitating damaged areas, compensating victims and getting the displaced back to their homes.

Because of its strategic location linking the northern and southern fronts of the SLA's war, Minawi's forces were not going to yield Shearia without a fight. They went on the offensive. A series of rebel raids culminated in the SLA's armed takeover of Shearia on 19 September 2005, in which eighteen people were killed and a thousand camels were stolen. Two months later, government troops and a Birgid militia, created with government help to 'defend' Shearia from the SLA, counterattacked, beating and raping Zaghawa civilians, looting livestock and denying access to water points. More subtle forms of persecution by the Birgid involved refusing to purchase commodities from Zaghawa except at sub-market values. Some seven hundred Zaghawa fled to the compound of AMIS, camping outside it until a measure of order was restored and they could go home. But in January and February 2006, Minawi's forces were driven from the area and most remaining Zaghawa in Shearia either left or returned to the AMIS compound. A confidential UN report in March 2006 said,

> A deliberate strategy akin to ethnic cleansing has taken place in Shearia. Zaghawa have been forcibly evicted by acts of violence, intimidation, and economic pressure in an effort to remove any potential SLA threat to Shearia ... Despite requests and warnings regarding the imperative to distinguish between combatants and civilians in Shearia, the Sudan government and militias have failed to do so, targeting all Zaghawa in Shearia and linking them to the SLA.

In Abuja, one of Minawi's negotiating team expressed anxiety bordering on fury at the turn the rebellion had taken under

Minawi's leadership, and the damage it was inflicting on peaceful Zaghawa communities living outside their own *dar*. 'The Zaghawa are the prime losers if the rebellion fails,' he said. 'It is our land that is most affected by desertification. We are not here to transform all the victories into failures.'[15] Others were conscious of how the abuses were harming the SLA itself, by pushing Darfurians to ally with the government. Abdel Wahid claimed he had taken care to put Birgid commanders in charge of Birgid areas. 'The Zaghawa need peace,' he said. 'Darfur has become hell for them. They are seen as colonizers, not liberators.'[16]

The Baggara struggle for neutrality

Saeed Mahmoud Ibrahim Musa Madibu is South Darfur's most prestigious paramount chief. His official title is 'Nazir General', and he heads the Baggara Rizeigat, the most powerful Arab tribe in all Darfur. In his mid-seventies, possessed of a steely presence, he has inherited his ancestors' shrewd calculus of how best to guide his tribe across the shifting sands of the region's politics. He knows the history of both Abbala and Baggara Rizeigat intimately – it was, after all, his grandfather who last held paramount authority over the troublesome northern sections back in 1925. His elder brother Hassan was loyal to Khartoum all his life, and allowed thousands of Rizeigat to fight for the government against the SPLA. The Rizeigat militia was responsible for destroying a huge swathe of Bahr el Ghazal in Southern Sudan in the late 1980s. Nazir Madibu consults widely, encourages his family members to join each contending political party, and keeps his own counsel.

After succeeding Hassan as nazir in 1990, Saeed Madibu tried to steer a course between Khartoum, the SPLA and the Arab Gathering. Convinced that the war against the Dinka would be a source of unending trouble, he facilitated a local truce with the SPLA. When members of his tribe made inflammatory statements about Arab supremacy, he reprimanded them. (Like all Darfurian Arabs, Madibu has mixed ancestry and is as dark as his 'African' neighbours.) Most importantly, Nazir Madibu refused to throw his tribe into the Janjawiid war, realizing that good neighbourly relations were more important than fighting for a capricious and faraway government. Summoned to Khartoum in 2003 to meet the president and vice-president, he refused to fight, reportedly saying to Bashir, 'You are not in this chair for ever. But the Rizeigat are here for ever and revenge will continue for ever.'[17]

The old chief never faced a challenge comparable to the war in Darfur, and his nerve and authority were tested to the full as the conflict spread south and east. Government ministers tried to buy the backing of his tribe, and the governor of South Darfur tried to undermine him by recruiting sections of the Rizeigat to fight alongside the government. Foremost among these were men from the Shattiya clan of Foreign Trade Minister Abdel Hamid Musa Kasha, a rival of the Madibu family. As Minni Minawi's forces extended their operations into south-east Darfur, looting Rizeigat cattle, attacking villages and threatening to plunge the hitherto-calm Rizeigat land into bloody conflict, Madibu's Rizeigat militia fought back fiercely, and chased the SLA troops back towards their base at Muhajiriya. Seeking to avoid escalation, Nazir Madibu instructed his men to stay within the confines of their own tribal land and not to storm Muhajiriya. When the SLA persisted, and tried to encircle the Rizeigat, he sent an ultimatum: desist or we will attack. The SLA desisted.

Nazir Madibu not only refused to join the government's campaign. He also quietly mobilized the Native Administration – tribal aristocrats who are conservative but not reactionary, wedded to their own hierarchies and passionate believers in stability. The repository of family genealogies, they know that racial divides are seldom absolute and always less important than good neighbourly relations. Without the endorsement of elders of the standing of Nazir Madibu, Khartoum's Darfur war carried no legitimacy among the big Baggara tribes of South Darfur.

As North and West Darfur burned in 2003 and 2004, the Rizeigat tribal council in al Da'ien protected displaced non-Arabs who had sought refuge in their territory. Nazir Madibu negotiated an agreement with the Birgid, his neighbours to the north, to ensure that any 'misunderstandings' that might arise would not lead to bloodshed, and delegated his tribal council to establish non-aggression pacts with tribes one step further away: Daju, Beigo and Berti. He took special care to reconcile with the neighbouring Ma'aliya Arabs, a tribe which is junior to the Rizeigat in the Native Administration hierarchy. Resentful of their subordinate rank, Ma'aliya had clashed violently with the Rizeigat on occasion over the past forty years. Nazir Madibu feared, rightly, that Khartoum would mobilize the Ma'aliya against the SLA – and against him.

In September 2004 the indefatigable nazir joined a delegation of twenty-eight tribal elders to the peace talks in Abuja. He was tough with the SLA and JEM leaders – as the government, in allowing him to go, had hoped – and insisted that violence would solve nothing. But the government had not anticipated his next step. Growing in confidence, the tribal leaders flew a month later to the Libyan capital, Tripoli, to participate in a promising peace initiative in which they all agreed that the old *hakura* system of land possession should persist and that tribal authorities should be independent of government interference. But not only did the Darfurian show of independence alarm Khartoum, it worried the Libyans too, and they scuttled the process.

South Darfur is Darfur's most populous and prosperous state – the only one of Darfur's three states with an Arab majority – and the most signal achievement of Nazir Madibu and his peers was the quiet eclipse of the Arab Gathering in areas they controlled. Led from its inception in Sudan by ambitious Darfurian Arab politicians in Khartoum, intermittently funded from Libya, and opportunistically allying with Arab leaders of Chadian origin, the Arab Gathering provided ideological justification for a campaign of ethnic cleansing. During the height of the offensives in North and West Darfur in 2003–04, the rallying calls to the Arab militia were infused with racist rhetoric. But when the Arab Gathering leaders tried to rally the Baggara tribes of South Darfur, they found that their manifesto did not resonate.

When the coordination council of the Arab Gathering toured South Darfur in November 2003, it obtained verbal assurances of solidarity from the leaders of each of the five big Arab tribes (including the Fellata, the Nigerian-origin group that has become politically 'Arab') but failed to obtain the commitment of even one of these big tribes to dispatch a militia out of its home area to join the government's war – a fact glossed over in its self-laudatory report.[18] South Darfur's Arab leaders simply smothered the Arab Gathering with a strategy of polite agreement followed by indefinite postponement of action, obliging Security to mobilize smaller Arab tribes like the Terjem, Sa'ada and Awlad Mansour.[19] The Arab nazirs, meanwhile, quietly predicted that their northern cousins would regret their role in the war. As, indeed, many came to do.

Darfur's tough old chiefs made a valiant effort to fill Darfur's vacuum of government. But they were acutely aware of the limits of their power. Thirty conferences over twenty years had not solved Darfur's problems and had not removed criminals who enjoyed Khartoum's backing. The government used every stratagem to block, bribe, threaten, co-opt and discredit tribal leaders' initiatives. It stalled promising reconciliations, fearful of losing the support provided by tribal militia. It controlled access to reconciliation meetings, rescinding exit visas or blocking delegations from leaving Darfur. It spread rumours that Nazir Madibu had thrown his lot in with the rebels – pointing out that the SLA had a Rizeigat in command of its southern front and that the Nazir's younger brother, Ibrahim, was one of Abdel Wahid's senior advisers and a delegate to the Abuja peace talks.

Fearing Nazir Madibu's powers of consensus-building, the government reshuffled South Darfur's Native Administration. Taking a leaf out of the book of colonial management, Khartoum dismissed Magdum Ahmed Rijal of Nyala – the state's most senior Fur chief – and put his cousin Saleh in place, hoping for a pliant alternative. It elevated several omdas to the status of nazir, thereby reducing the magdum's power and jurisdiction. The government did not dare tamper with the status of

Nazir Madibu himself. But, in a direct challenge to his authority, and to the Rizeigat–Ma'aliya agreement he had engineered, it elevated Adam Sharif Salim, the chief of the Ma'aliya, to the rank of nazir. In November 2007, the government carved out a new local administrative unit for its allies from the Rizeigat lands in a blatant attempt to empower Nazir Madibu's rivals within the tribe. Hitherto-loyal Rizeigat in the government began to ask themselves what chaos lay in store for them if Khartoum was playing divide-and-rule with the Arab tribes. Visibly tired, Nazir Madibu faced challenges as tough as those surmounted by his great-grandfather in Darfur's bloody upheavals more than a century earlier.

The intra-rebel war

In the immediate aftermath of the offensives of 2003–04, the rebels were in disarray. Some of their leaders – notably Abdalla Abakir – were dead, others had left the field to become ambassadors for the cause in foreign capitals. Most rebel movements have a criminal fringe. In the SLA's case, criminals were rising to the top. It was not only the embattled Zaghawa migrants in South Darfur who were unhappy with the turn the SLA took under Minawi's leadership. Many SLA commanders were also – although few dared to say so to his face.

From the outset, Minawi's war had been as much against his rivals within the rebel movement as against the government and Janjawiid. Within months of Abdalla Abakir's death, Minawi launched what colleagues from the time say was his first bid to replace Abdel Wahid as chairman of the SLA. At the end of June 2004, Zaghawa forces led by one of his most trusted men, Yahya Hassan al Nil, attacked eastern Jebel Marra, reinforced by the fighters to whom Abdel Wahid's men had given safe haven when they fled the government offensive in North Darfur almost six months earlier. The plan, according to Commander Jar al Nabi Abdel Karim, was 'to kill [Abdel Gadir Abdel Rahman] Gaddura', Abdel Wahid's chief of staff, 'and declare Minni chairman'. The fighting between Zaghawa and Fur raged for several weeks before the Zaghawa were defeated and driven out. A Zaghawa commander who investigated the incident as part of an SPLA effort to mend the split in the rebel movement said Minawi's forces 'raped at least twenty-eight Fur women, looted, burned three commanders' homes, killed twenty-two civilians and three SLA'.[20]

Rivalry between Fur and Zaghawa in Darfur dates back centuries. In the middle ages, a Zaghawa empire stretched across Darfur and much of Chad. The reasons for its collapse are not recorded, but Zaghawa always resented their subordinate position in the successor states, including the Fur sultanate. Although Fur sultans married into prominent Zaghawa families and gave high positions to Zaghawa notables, the co-existence was always uneasy. The conflict between Minawi and Abdel Wahid revived animosities and split the SLA along tribal lines. It made a mockery of the movement's stated intention 'to create a united democratic Sudan on a new basis of equality' and took the pressure off the government, on the battlefield and at the Abuja peace talks. The struggle for power consumed both leaders, within Darfur and with the international community. Organizational structures were never put in place, and there was no accountability. By 2005, in the words of an Arab intellectual sympathetic to the rebellion, 'every commander [was] the president of the republic of his own area'.[21] As individual commanders took the law into their own hands, the personalities of Minawi and Abdel Wahid and their battle for leadership dictated the course, and the disintegration, of the rebellion.

Minawi also fought against JEM, which was attempting to capitalize on the bad reputation of his forces after moving south with them at the beginning of the year. Khalil Ibrahim's men had opened a 'political office' in Muhajiriya, and claimed to be attracting considerable support.[22] In May, Minawi visited Muhajiriya accompanied by Suleiman Majaran, who heard him tell JEM: 'If we get to Khartoum we will fight. Better we fight now.' Minawi reportedly told his men to close the JEM office, 'by force if necessary'. In the ensuing fighting, Minawi's uncle, Abdalla Domi, lost his life, as he attempted to lock JEM's offices, according to one account. In the following days, SLA–Minawi chased JEM's forces hundreds of miles north across Darfur, fighting them all the way. Asked why Minawi's SLA was so determined to eliminate all competition, one of the commanders who led the attack on JEM, Ramadan Jaber, a Zaghawa from Muhajiriya, responded: 'We Zaghawa are afraid. There are 177 tribes in Darfur.[23] They don't want Zaghawa. They don't like Zaghawa.'[24]

Many Zaghawa were deeply unhappy with the course the rebellion was taking, but in front of Minawi said nothing. In private, it was a different story. At the peace talks in Abuja, one of Minawi's advisers lamented the 'catastrophe' Minawi's men were visiting upon the tribe. 'The Native Administration is better than the SLA,' he said. 'The Zaghawa have a very strict moral code. Our pride and honour are damaged by these *nahab* [robbers]. There is no rule, no order. We have never experienced this kind of killing.'[25] But the abuses continued during Minawi's power grab, which climaxed in November 2005, when he was elected 'president' of the movement at a conference organized by his supporters in Haskanita, in Dar Berti, ignoring western requests that he attend a reconciliation meeting with Abdel Wahid in N'Djamena. In the ballot, Minawi received 483 of 633 votes cast. This was a surprisingly low percentage given that Abdel Wahid's faction and some of Minawi's own commanders all boycotted the conference, and that Minawi's own men threatened, beat and even imprisoned some of those who did attend, but who dared to express criticism. The conference drew up a new constitution for the movement. It granted immunity to one person: the president. 'We have completed the political unification,' said conference organizer Ibrahim Ahmad Ibrahim. 'All that remains is the military unification.'[26]

Minawi set about achieving that, once again by force, within days of the conclusion of Haskanita, sending his men to arrest three northern commanders who had attended the fifth round of the Abuja talks against his wishes. Suleiman Marajan, who had protected SLA forces during the government offensive of 2004, was captured and imprisoned in the remote northern village of

Malam al Hosh. (One of Marajan's commanders who helped him leave Darfur, Haroun Adam Haroun, was seized and tortured while Marajan was in Abuja, in the same manner as Abdel Rahman Mohamadein. His arms and legs were tied together and he was hung from a tree for three to four hours a day, three times a day.)[27] The Berti commander Saleh Adam Ishaq succeeded in repelling an attack on his village, Maw, on market day, but six people including four civilians died in the four hours it took him to fight Minawi's men off. The third commander, Jar al Nabi Abdel Karim, of mixed Zaghawa/Kaitinga parentage, talked his would-be captors down, and averted bloodshed.

The three commanders' presence alongside Abdel Wahid in Abuja should have alerted the international community to the weakening of Minawi's position. But it didn't: just as Abdel Wahid and Minawi were accepted as virtually the only spokesmen for the Fur and Zaghawa, despite the divisions within their own tribal constituencies, so the Fur and the Zaghawa were taken to speak for the SLA, leaving groups such as the Berti and the Meidob of secondary and passing interest. (The Arabs, demonized as a group, were ignored completely.) But the three commanders' rejection of Minawi's authority was the first step in the rebellion against Minawi that would drive his men out of their North Darfur heartland within a year. The three made this clear to anyone in Abuja willing to listen. 'We have decided that we will control our own areas,' Saleh Adam said.

When we return to Darfur, we will no longer accept the men of Minni in our areas. Minni gave important positions to uneducated commanders in order to control them. These uneducated commanders are treating people very badly. They get drunk, hit them, loot their belongings, take their animals, and tax them. They killed sheikhs and omdas. Civilians are complaining all the time. They tell me: 'We need peace. You SLA treat us worse than the government treated us!' They hate the SLA. All this because of Minni Minawi.

Suleiman Marajan said: 'We tried for two years to change

their behaviour. But they are illiterate and suspicious of educated people – even Zaghawa. Minni has so many problems with the Zaghawa now.' Jar al Nabi said:

> Minni Minawi divided the leaders of the movement. Some he sent abroad; some were killed, like Mustafa al Tom of Um Berro. Minni feels he's a superman, with strength through weapons. He hates educated people. He hates Abdel Wahid. When he saw how the international community greeted him at the first N'Djamena talks [in April 2004] he decided to remove him. He told a meeting near Bir Maza: 'This guy should come to the field and after he comes we will know what to do with him!'[28]

On 20 November 2005, the final round of the AU-sponsored peace talks convened in Abuja, with three rebel movements recognized for the first time: SLA–Minawi, SLA–Abdel Wahid and JEM. The African Union, United Nations and United States all believed Minawi was the strongman of Darfur. They were tragically wrong.

7 | International reaction

For a decade, Darfur's conflicts were invisible to the world, registering barely a mention even in the specialist African press.[1] The only sustained interest shown in Sudan was in the 'Christian' South. Drought and an imminent food crisis were sufficiently serious to prompt the administrator of the US Agency for International Development (USAID), Andrew Natsios, to visit Darfur in 2001;[2] but the fighting and displacement around Jebel Marra the following year went unnoticed. It was only when the war escalated in April 2003 that the first humanitarian mission was dispatched, by USAID's Office of Foreign Disaster Assistance. Over the following months, Roger Winter, the head of USAID's emergency relief bureau, visited Darfur. In Kutum, where militia rampages had destroyed a swathe of villages, he found that 'the town was already filled with IDPs [internally displaced persons] and there were Janjawiid types roaming all over. It wasn't the worst situation I have ever seen by any means but we talked to people about their experiences and heard the awful stories they had to tell.'[3] The situation was to become far, far worse in the coming months. Despite Winter's eyewitness reports, the international response remained little more than the efforts of a handful of dedicated humanitarians.

Roger Winter is a veteran Sudan activist. As head of an NGO, the US Committee for Refugees from 1981 to 2000, he championed a host of politically forsaken crises. Among these neglected causes was the SPLA, at a time when the official US position was that Garang was a proxy for communist Ethiopia. Developing a strong personal friendship with Garang over the years, Winter became an impassioned advocate for the SPLA leader's vision of a 'New Sudan' – and was duly regarded as an inveterate adversary in Khartoum. In 1987 Winter dispatched one of his staff members, Hiram Ruiz, to investigate another forgotten crisis: Chadians in Darfur. Ruiz's report was presciently entitled, 'When Refugees Won't Go Home'.[4] Focused on the CIA-led effort to defeat Gaddafi's ambitions, the US government paid little attention to the way its covert war in Chad was helping blow instability around the region, through the wanton distribution of weapons and the increasing bands of young men for whom fighting was a way of life. In 1995, Winter was the first American to fly into the SPLA-held areas of the Nuba mountains.[5] Again his early warning was not heeded: the Clinton Administration's team, focused on Southern Sudan, was very slow to take up the challenge of supporting relief operations in the mountains and it was left to Jan Pronk, then Netherlands minister of development cooperation, to lead the way in funding NGO operations there.

In early 2001, Winter surprised many of his colleagues by leaving the NGO sector to take a senior job in a Republican administration: assistant administrator of USAID, in charge of the humanitarian bureau. Winter didn't have a history with the Republicans but he was impressed by the incoming Bush administration's promised Sudan peace initiative, and took up Natsios's invitation to work together on solutions for the country which they both knew so well. In May 2003, in testimony to the US Congress Committee on International Relations, Winter warned that 'we have a new conflict zone in Darfur which is not being adequately addressed'.[6] It was only a passing remark in a lengthy presentation focused on Southern Sudan – but Winter's radar of lost causes had registered when John Garang had mentioned the SLA and encouraged him to speak to its leaders on the phone.

As the conflict escalated in 2002, the Sudan government imposed drastic restrictions on humanitarian access to Darfur[7] and the door was only levered open painfully, inch by inch. At the start of 2003, just five foreign relief agencies were conducting routine operations in the region. Winter's intervention enabled UNICEF to begin operations in North Darfur in August that year, using USAID emergency funds. Following the Abeche ceasefire agreement the next month and a visit by Natsios, the door opened another crack, and USAID committed $40 million worth of food aid in the following three months – a small figure overall, but a crucial beginning. Most donors and NGOs present in Khartoum were preparing for the reconciliation between North and South, and the launching of reconstruction projects, and displayed little interest in the western part of the country.

Winter later explained the political message he and Natsios passed to Ali Osman Taha at that time: 'We've always told the Government of Sudan, if there's a peace agreement we will normalize relations with you. Now we've said, well, if there's a peace agreement we will not normalize relations with you until the Darfur thing is addressed.'[8] At the prompting of the two men, the US embassy in Khartoum began to report 'ethnic cleansing' – a qualitative escalation of rhetoric in internal cables, but one which had only modest impact on Washington's public stand. Natsios warned that a new civil war was beginning just as the North–South negotiations were looking very promising. In December, after Khartoum had declared a state of emergency throughout Darfur and hundreds of thousands of displaced people congregated in makeshift camps, it was Natsios and Winter who took the lead in pressing Khartoum to ease restrictions on foreign aid workers and humanitarian supplies. Knowing that the relief they had committed was going to be far too little, they doubled it. But they struggled to convince the State Department to take Darfur seriously. On a visit to Darfur in January, Winter asked the pilot of their plane to fly low over some burning villages so that he and his State Department colleague, Michael Ranneberger, could see closely. 'I got it,' said Ranneberger.[9] After that, the US pushed hard for a 'humanitarian ceasefire', flying the rebel leaders to N'Djamena for the talks and sending its own emissaries, including Roger Winter, Kate Almquist, Natsios's chief policy adviser, and Mike McKinley from the State Department. Just getting to N'Djamena was a fraught affair, as Salah Gosh wanted to prevent the Americans attending the talks. Minawi agreed to fly only on the condition that two international envoys came on the same plane. Once in N'Djamena, his men only reluctantly offloaded the grenades, knives and knuckledusters they had brought with them after being warned that guns were not permitted. During the peace talks themselves, it took much American persuasion to stop the SLA delegation walking out. On the same day that the humanitarian ceasefire was supposed to take effect – 11 April[10] – a Disaster Assistance Response Team was deployed in Darfur, leading to scaled-up humanitarian operations.[11]

Natsios and Winter continued their parallel public advocacy campaign. Speaking on 3 June 2004, Natsios said, 'We estimate right now if we get relief in, we'll lose a third of a million people, and if we don't the death rates could be dramatically higher, approaching a million people.'[12] Such dramatization – even the lower figure turned out to be an over-estimate – helped focus international attention and funds on Darfur's crisis. Alongside USAID, the World Food Programme, European donors and a handful of NGOs began cranking up a response to the unforeseen emergency as soon as President Bashir announced the end of military operations in Darfur and a partial lifting of the blockade on humanitarian activity in February 2004. Six months later, 940,000 people in Darfur and 200,000 refugees in Chad were receiving food assistance in Darfur and the US government was spending $300 million on the emergency – a far more rapid response at scale than for most other humanitarian crises.[13] Setting up a large-scale relief operation in a place as remote as Darfur takes many months and by these early and unpublicized efforts humanitarian bureaucrats saved tens of thousands of lives, a claim that very few can make for Darfur.[14]

An entire cohort of humanitarian workers and activists had spent twenty years in Sudan, trying to minimize the human casualties of what appeared to be endless, intractable wars, and learning that humanitarian assistance cannot fill a political vacuum. For that reason, Natsios and Winter devoted almost as much effort to finding a durable peace for South Sudan, where two decades of war had cost a million or more lives, as they did to conventional relief work. For them, the peace talks inching forward in Naivasha held out the hope of a durable peace deal, which for years had been just a dream. And as the fighting in Darfur reached its height, the North–South peace talks arrived at a critical phase. A breakthrough occurred on 26 May 2004, when Khartoum and the SPLM signed protocols on power-sharing and the status of the 'three areas' that lay on the North–South front-line: Abyei, the Nuba Mountains and Blue Nile. That day, John Garang announced, 'We have reached the crest of the last hill in our tortuous ascent to heights of peace … There are no more hills ahead of us: I believe the remaining is flat ground.'[15] Calling it 'a paradigm shift of historic proportions', Garang indicated that he felt the formula for the 'three areas' could be a model for peace in Darfur. Khartoum agreed to accept an advance UN mission the following month. For the purposes of approving that mission, the war in South Sudan was raised at the UN Security Council – for the first time in twenty-one years of fighting. Darfur reached the Security Council within a year of rebellion breaking out, on the coat-tails of peace in South Sudan.

The man who took the job of heading the UN Mission in Sudan on 18 June was Jan Pronk, a hard-nosed and plain-speaking Dutchman, veteran of his country's politics and the Horn of Africa. He was well aware of how successive Khartoum governments had obstructed and manipulated humanitarian relief over more than twenty years, winning almost every round against divided and ineffectual UN agencies and their western backers. Pronk was steeped in politics, ready to tackle the highest level of leaders but also to go right down to the grassroots. During his tenure in Khartoum, he visited Darfur several times a month on average, meeting with villagers and displaced people. Never one to keep his opinions private, he wrote a weblog.[16]

The UN mandate – and Pronk's – covered the whole of Sudan, and involved supervising the entire six-year 'interim period' determined in the Naivasha protocols and finalized in the January 2005 Comprehensive Peace Agreement (CPA). The intention was that, during this period, Sudan would be fundamentally reshaped, with democratic elections, power-sharing between the former enemies, an equitable sharing of the national wealth (especially oil revenue), demarcation of the internal North–South border, the transformation of the SPLA into a political party, the creation of an autonomous Government of Southern Sudan and finally, in 2011, a referendum on self-determination in the South. To Pronk's annoyance, the mandate did not cover the negotiations between Khartoum and the Darfur rebels. Knowing that an unresolved crisis in Darfur would fatally undermine the CPA and aware that the world expected a visible UN presence in Darfur, Pronk devoted much of his immense energy to Darfur.[17]

One lesson that Pronk had learned from his long experience in dealing with Khartoum was that leverage and pressure achieve little unless they are applied in a coordinated, consistent and strategic manner. Ten years earlier, fearing that uncoordinated efforts would cancel each other out, he had created the 'Friends of IGAD'[18] to coordinate Western support to the Inter-Governmental Authority on Development, the sponsor of the North–South peace process. It was a far-sighted initiative, and coordinated international action in support of the IGAD peace initiative was critical to its success. There was nothing comparable in Darfur. The Americans, who had taken the lead on the humanitarian response and saw themselves as the main stewards of the North–South agreement, tended to take initiatives without consulting others; the European Union jealously guarded a special role awarded to it as deputy head of Darfur's Ceasefire Commission. A confused tangle of responsibilities became another enduring theme, with the UN often becoming competitor rather than coordinator. Pronk was not innocent of this himself. In August 2004, convinced the Janjawiid could not be disarmed in thirty days, as the Security Council had demanded, he announced a plan to create 'secure areas' around displaced camps – but without consulting the rebels or clearing the plan with humanitarian agencies, many of which were sharply critical, arguing that it would facilitate the government's forced relocation programme. Like many such initiatives and deadlines, there was no follow-up, and the idea faded.

Despite all the obstacles thrown in its path, the humanitarian operation began operating at full throttle in the middle of 2004, shortly after Khartoum had completed its destruction campaign in North and West Darfur. The site of the world's worst humanitarian crisis became the locus of the world's largest relief effort, with world attention only briefly distracted by the Indian Ocean tsunami. The worst predictions for a million dead, or even half of that number, did not materialize. Best estimates for the numbers who died of hunger and disease during the years 2003–05 are in the region of 150,000.[19] The evidence also shows that during 2005, mortality rates in Darfur came down to levels comparable to those before the war – levels 'normal' for a desperately poor and under-serviced region.[20] Each military operation and tribal clash since then has brought in its wake a localized crisis of nutrition, but no humanitarian disaster on the scale of 2003–04. Under extraordinarily difficult constraints, the humanitarian operation in Darfur achieved remarkable successes.

'Africa responded with its heart, not its head'

The African Union became peacekeeper and peacemaker in Darfur by default, because no other organization would take on the challenge. President Idriss Deby of Chad was acutely aware that a crisis in Darfur could herald his own demise, and began mediating between the government and rebels in September 2003, achieving a forty-five-day ceasefire that neither side respected. Something much more robust was needed when, under pressure from the US and the Europeans, the talks reconvened in N'Djamena six months later. The AU was drawn in first as witness, then as co-mediator, and then tasked with sending ceasefire monitors and troops to protect them. The AU responded in the bright morning of what South African President Thabo Mbeki called the 'African Renaissance'. Established in Durban, South Africa, in July 2002, taking over from the nearly moribund OAU, the AU's constitution has bold liberal aspirations, including the duty of intervention in the affairs of a sovereign country in the event of grave human rights abuses or humanitarian disaster.[21] A year later, Alpha Konaré was elected as the AU's first fully constituted chairperson. Konaré had been the democratically elected president of Mali, and, unlike so many of his peers, had stood down when his term was up. He had also presided over a peace agreement with Tuarag rebels. Energetic and domineering, Konaré took Africa's top job amid high hopes.

A few weeks after the N'Djamena talks, Darfur was raised at the AU's Peace and Security Council at AU headquarters in Addis Ababa. Konaré played tough, insisting that the Sudanese ambassador leave the chamber after making his presentation. 'Africa must not only act in Darfur,' he said, 'Africa must be seen to act.' The council mandated the African Union Mission in Sudan (AMIS) to dispatch 120 military observers to monitor the ceasefire and 350 troops to protect them. Although an armed humanitarian intervention was possible under the AU Constitutive Act, the Council didn't consider any options beyond those stipulated in the N'Djamena Agreement – traditional ceasefire monitoring – and the troops were not mandated to protect civilians. The AU advance party of sixty monitors arrived on the ground just six weeks after the ceasefire – a rapid start for any organization, let alone a novice in peacekeeping. Konaré flew to Darfur shortly afterwards. On arriving in al Fasher, dressed in his accustomed Muslim robes like a Darfurian tribal chief, Africa's top civil servant did not behave as a well-pressed bureaucrat, cocooned in an air-conditioned land cruiser. Instead, he gave his entourage the slip and, accompanied by just one security officer, spent the night in a displaced camp, to see for himself how Darfurians were living.

All the problems that bedevilled the AU's peacemaking and peacekeeping mission, which ultimately earned the scorn both of Darfurians and foreign activists, were foreshadowed in those early months. The N'Djamena Humanitarian Ceasefire Agreement signed on 8 April was a fatally flawed document. For one thing, it had no maps. Professional military officers on both sides warned that a ceasefire agreement without maps was unworkable. How could the ceasefire be monitored if the belligerents' locations weren't known to the peacekeepers? But the crisis in Darfur was threatening to unravel the progress made in the North–South talks, a vast humanitarian crisis was looming, and the US and

UN wanted Khartoum, Chad and the AU to organize a quick fix. Khartoum had sent General Ismat al Zain, head of the Western Regional Command, to N'Djamena for the talks and he called his superiors to ask for more time to push for mapping. The reply came back, 'We need a signed agreement tomorrow.'[22] The professional soldier dutifully concurred, and later bit his lip and refrained from saying 'I told you so' when SLA and JEM forces opened new fronts in the east and south of Darfur. Ismat himself systematically resupplied his forces in violation of the UN's arms embargo. Neither the army nor the Janjawiid respected the ceasefire. The AU monitors, the weakest of all the parties on the ground by far, could only watch and complain.

The most serious problem with the N'Djamena agreement was that it existed in two versions. A typewritten text was signed by the delegates of the SLA and the Sudan government on 8 April. But later that same day, the government delegation approached the Chadians and insisted that an extra sentence be added to paragraph 6. Following the typewritten sentence, 'The Sudanese government shall commit itself to neutralize the armed militia,' the AU representative, Sam Ibok, wrote in, on the instructions of the Chadian foreign minister, 'The forces of the armed opposition should be assembled in clearly identified sites.' Ibok says he expected the text to be passed back to the movements for their agreement, but it wasn't. They would never have agreed to rounding up their fighters and putting them in camps where they would have been static targets for the air force and army. Instead, a Chadian government stamp was affixed to it, and to this day Khartoum insists that the agreement includes a clause linking its obligation to 'neutralize' the Janjawiid to the encampment of the SLA and JEM.

The AU was rashly optimistic – the UN would never have sent in peacekeepers without a far stronger ceasefire agreement. With no maps, one AMIS officer said, it was 'mission impossible' from the outset. 'Africa responded to Darfur with its heart, not with its head,' said Abdul Mohammed, an adviser to the AU. Initially, most Darfurians were enthusiastic and welcomed the African troops. At the minimum they represented a gesture of solidarity and a sign that Africa cared, and in many cases their presence translated into practical improvements in security. 'We saw some good African Union commanders [who] really made a difference locally – when they organized patrols to go with the women to collect firewood; when they would try to defuse conflicts between some rebel groups and some Arab militias; to organize a migration, for instance, of cattle along certain roads,' said Fabrice Weissman, head of mission for Médecins Sans Frontières in 2005–06.[23] Displaced people around Nyala reported that AMIS patrolling in the first months of the mission reduced attacks on their camps.[24] In Fata Borno, displaced people tethered their animals overnight close to the AMIS base, where the floodlights and sentries kept them from being stolen. In Tawila, a frontline of the war, thousands of displaced villagers sought safety in a camp they built themselves right on the edge of the AMIS compound. 'If these soldiers leave,' said one, 'we will be slaughtered.'[25]

Many of AMIS's early successes came down to dynamic leadership more concerned with results than rules. General Festus Okwonko of Nigeria, its first force commander, breached protocol and pushed the limits of his mandate, opening new sectors wherever he thought there was likely to be trouble. Brian Steidle, an American former marine who served as a ceasefire monitor, described Okwonko as 'phenomenal ... We would escort humanitarian convoys and do a lot of extra work we weren't supposed to be doing. We actually had been told not to do it but he allowed us to do it.'[26] In November 2004, Okwonko went as far as to warn that the government was *planning* an offensive. Challenged by Khartoum over this breach of protocol, Konaré backed up the Nigerian general, who had just been given a marginally stronger mandate: he could now protect civilians under threat, but only if he came across them in the course of his routine operations. At this point there were just 135 military observers and 310 AMIS troops in Darfur.

But AMIS could not sustain its early successes. Neither its leadership nor its capacities matched up to the expectations that its soldiers would not only monitor, but protect civilians at risk. The political head of the mission in Khartoum, Baba Gana Kingibe, often seemed more concerned with his business interests and political ambitions at home in Nigeria, where he was seriously considering a bid for the presidency, than with the challenge of running the AU's flagship mission. Kingibe had sharp political sense, but he rarely delegated and never drew up a strategic plan. His micromanagement paralyzed everyone: every phone call to a senior official or movement leader had to be approved by him. In the field, his men needed better communications equipment, more armour and bases designed for defence in case they came under attack.

'AMIS was weak and appallingly resourced. It neither had the capacity to ask for what it needed nor the ability to manage what it had,' said a western officer who liaised with AMIS for a number of years.

> There was also too much African pride and 'big man' command and control. No man was or is big enough for this. As a few, non-African countries paid for absolutely everything – from helicopters to food to knives and forks to sandbags, to vehicles, to wages, to beds – the AU preferred to blame these countries rather than take responsibility. Why did it never manage to formulate a simple requirement for telephones? How can you have operations rooms and logistics management with no telephones? Why were there no sandbags? Probably because, like us, it was more important to be there and be seen to be there than actually to do something. And money was involved. Lots of it. The majority of the mission was and is made of determined, dedicated and capable people. But people who are unpaid, unfed, under-armed, unvisited (apart from the al Fasher abyss), with a meaningless mandate, being shot at, with no idea what is going on, are unlikely to make a difference in Darfur, where it is hard enough anyway.

While most international attention was focused on AMIS's limited numbers, armour and mandate, leadership and morale were more important in the field. Okwonko had shown what a tiny force could do. His successors showed that a larger force could be less capable. Steidle described the next force commander:

> He was horrific. He had a totally different perspective. We got cut off from the humanitarian convoys. He wouldn't allow us to meet with humanitarian organizations. What we'd do is find out where everyone was and notify them for security reasons. We'd say they were headed to attack for a village, so don't go there or pull your people out. Under this new commander, we weren't permitted to share this information. But we did it anyway. He cut that off. He'd say no humanitarian people in the compound. Through pressure from all the monitors and from international pressure and a lot of pressure from the US embassy, we got him out of there in three months. He got booted from his command.

The credibility of AMIS died a death of a thousand cuts, in matters big and small. In every community across Darfur, there was a complaint. Near Kutum in North Darfur, an AMIS patrol came across a robber in the act of stealing a donkey. The soldiers didn't intervene or pursue the thief but merely assured the owner that they would file a report. In Gereida in South Darfur, AMIS was tasked with creating a demilitarized zone after the SLA took over, but was incapable of doing it. The Joint Commission (the political oversight body for the Ceasefire Commission) met rarely and had no mechanisms for following up its decisions. As insecurity grew around IDP camps – both as a result of Janjawiid activity and rebel threats after the Darfur Peace Agreement was signed – AMIS officers in many locations began to rely on the government representatives in their observer bases in the countryside for intelligence and even force protection. In March 2006, Sudan air force officers painted their aircraft in AMIS colours and used them for a number of military activities – resupplying garrisons and bombing, which was proscribed by the ceasefire. AU troops took photographs of the repainting – an act of perfidy prohibited by the Geneva Conventions – but their political masters stayed silent. They didn't even file reports on the incident.[27]

Between May and August 2006, the Darfur Peace Agreement, and the subsequent decision to expel from the Ceasefire Commission the rebels who hadn't signed the accord, destroyed what remained of the AU's impartiality and with it the troops' security and ease of movement. Attacks against AMIS escalated, leaving more than forty peacekeepers dead by the time their mandate ended on 31 December 2007. A mission that began with the hope that Africans would solve Africa's problems ended with its troops sitting ducks, unable to protect even themselves. Many Darfurians felt pity, asking, 'What soldiers cannot even defend themselves?'

Opening the eyes of the world

Until March 2004, Darfur's crisis unfolded in the typical manner of African civil wars, unremarked in the world's media, with horrific human suffering, barely mitigated by low-key diplomacy and uphill efforts to get a modest relief programme in gear. Almost overnight that changed. The UN's humanitarian coordinator in Sudan, Mukesh Kapila, called Darfur 'genocide' and said, 'the only difference between Rwanda and Darfur now is the numbers involved'.[28] He wanted international troops and an international tribunal. Kapila wasn't the first or the most senior UN official to speak out on Darfur – Jan Egeland, the under-secretary-general for humanitarian affairs, had visited Darfur in early December and said that the humanitarian situation 'has quickly become one of the worst in the world'.[29] But Kapila was blunter and his timing was critical – on the eve of the commemoration of the tenth anniversary of the Rwanda genocide, just as the UN Secretary-General Kofi Annan and other world leaders were preparing their 'never again' speeches. The day before the 7 April anniversary, the *New York Times* published an opinion column by Samantha Power entitled 'Remember Rwanda, but Take Action in Sudan',[30] which drove the point home, and – as Power intended – impelled Bush to refer to Darfur.

Kapila's UN colleagues had not been impressed by his professional performance – he had offended many staff members and donors – and his contract had been terminated, contributing to both his anger and outspokenness. Not did they support his provocative comments. Taye Zerihoun, head of the Africa section at the UN's department of political affairs, remarked, 'some at the UN felt Kapila was irresponsible in characterizing what was happening in Darfur at the time as genocide without consulting the leadership at HQs'.[31] Zerihoun and other staff at UN headquarters in New York were afraid that Kapila's use of the word 'genocide' would push the UN into calling for armed intervention and capsize the Comprehensive Peace Agreement. The US State Department had the same concerns. Its senior officials had abandoned the regime-change policy of the second Clinton Administration three years earlier, making progress towards ending the much longer and bloodier North–South war as a result, but still feared that Congressional lobbies hostile to Khartoum had the power to revive an agenda of aggressive intervention. Nor was this lost on Ali Osman: he ordered his delegates to the ceasefire talks in N'Djamena to sign an agreement the very next day. A ceasefire was sorely needed, but the document hastily agreed in the Chadian capital created as many problems as it solved.

Even as the massacres ebbed, a mass campaign was in train which would lead to a million Americans sending postcards to President Bush clamouring for intervention to end 'the first genocide of the twenty-first century'.[32] Darfur was being mentioned in the same breath as the Holocaust. The US Holocaust Museum and American Jewish World Service created the Save Darfur Coalition, which soon became the hub of a vast network of American groups involved in Darfur: the Genocide Intervention Network and Students Taking Action Now! – Darfur (STAND), college students, Jewish community groups and churches.

The activists pressed their case throughout the summer of 2004, beginning with a bipartisan effort by members of Congress to call the events in Darfur 'genocide', in the hope that – in contrast to the US's shocking silence and inaction over Rwanda – calling the crisis by its 'correct name' would force an international intervention. On 24 June, Congressman Donald Payne, a

Democrat and a leader of the Congressional Black Caucus, and Senator Sam Brownback, a conservative Republican, introduced concurrent resolutions in the House of Representatives and the Senate declaring that genocide was occurring in Darfur. Four weeks later, the resolutions passed unanimously. The activists were frank in explaining why they were focusing on the 'G-word' – they believed that once the Administration declared 'genocide' it would be legally committed to military intervention. The underlying theme was that the world was witnessing the latest instance in a criminal sequence that ran from the Nazi Holocaust, through Cambodia and Rwanda to Darfur, and because American power *could* stop it, America *must* intervene and do so.[33]

Two days after the Congressional resolutions were introduced, the State Department began preparing to send a team to investigate the atrocities in Darfur.[34] Coordinated by the Coalition for International Justice, the investigators were prevented from going to Sudan but interviewed Darfurian refugees in Chad in July and August. They were shocked by what they found, and their legal experts advised that the scale and nature of the atrocities, and the evidence for racially and ethnically based motives among the perpetrators, obliged them to conclude that it was indeed genocide. The conclusions were duly passed to the State Department.

Confident that abiding American interest in Sudan was focused on the South, and enjoying a close working relationship with the CIA on counter-terrorism, President Bashir shrugged off the rising concern over Darfur. He spurned a compromise proposal Konaré put to him for an African inquiry into Darfur similar to the international panel the OAU had set up after the Rwandan genocide. The Rwanda panel wrote a fine report with human rights at its heart and recommendations framed by the politics of peace and stability[35] and Konaré's envoy hinted to Sudanese Foreign Minister Mustafa Osman Ismail that a similar African panel might forestall a UN inquiry. The African Commission on Human and People's Rights was already concluding a fact-finding mission, whose report spoke of 'war crimes and crimes against humanity' overwhelmingly committed by the Sudan government, but stopped short of using the word 'genocide'.[36] But Bashir rebuffed the AU[37] and set up his own commission. Its report, released in January 2005, was so unbalanced that even some of its own commissioners were furious. It concluded that crimes had been committed by all sides, and more effort was needed to call the perpetrators to account. Equivalence was presumed where none existed. No one was named, no government culpability admitted and not one perpetrator was apprehended.

Bashir misjudged the level of international outrage, especially in America. He saw that the US had not been prepared to do much to help AMIS beyond releasing a pair of planes to transport AU troops for a day or two. He knew that the administration did not want to change its Sudan policy, given its determination to complete the Naivasha talks, its cooperation with Khartoum on counter-terrorism, and its lack of stomach for any military entanglement in the shadow of Iraq. But Washington was generous with words, and more than ready to condemn human rights violations in very strong terms. It was also election season, and Democrat contender John Kerry was taking advice from some of Clinton's former advisers on Sudan – at least one of whom was active in the Save Darfur Coalition – and saw political advantage in denouncing Bush for failing to stop 'genocide' in Darfur. Having taken his own legal advice – which was that the Genocide Convention does not specify a duty to intervene – Secretary of State Colin Powell decided it was safe to take the moral high ground and pre-empted Kerry. In written evidence to the Senate Foreign Relations Committee on 9 September, he catalogued the horrors of Darfur and noted that 'despite having been put on notice multiple times, Khartoum has failed to stop the violence'.[38] He concluded that 'genocide has been committed in Darfur and that the government of Sudan and the Jingaweit bear responsibility – and genocide may still be occurring'.

The following week, at American behest, the UN Security Council established the International Commission of Inquiry on Darfur (ICID). The ICID worked fast and finished its report in little more than three months. Published on 25 January 2005, it confirmed, in detail, the pattern of abuses described by the State Department and the African Commission. It found no evidence of genocidal intent 'as far as the central government authorities are concerned'. Attacking, killing and forcibly displacing civilians did not 'generally' indicate intent to annihilate that group. In Darfur, the report said, 'it would seem that those who planned and organized attacks on villages pursued the intent to drive the victims from their homes, primarily for the purposes of counter-insurgency warfare'.[39] This echoed the belief of many NGOs including MSF, one of the earliest to respond to the crisis, that the war in Darfur was in fact 'more akin to "pacification campaigns" carried out by European armies during periods of colonial conquests than to the methodical destruction of part of its citizens' as in Rwanda.[40] The UN report said that individuals – including government officials – may have possessed genocidal intent, but this was 'a determination that only a competent court can make on a case by case basis'. It proposed prosecution in an international court and submitted a sealed list of fifty-one individuals for criminal investigation. Ten were high-ranking members of the central government; seventeen were local government officials; fourteen Janjawiid; and three officers of foreign armies; seven were rebels.

Three days before its official release, the ICID report was passed to Khartoum, which leaked the 'no genocide' finding, ignoring the corollary that 'the crimes against humanity and war crimes that have been committed in Darfur may be no less serious and heinous than genocide'. Some activists accused the UN of lacking backbone, although what the UN did next showed more verve than the US's empty determination of genocide. The UN Security Council referred Darfur to the International Criminal Court – the first ever such referral, and the one international action to date that has truly worried President Bashir and the Security cabal.

'The biggest activist movement since anti-apartheid'

Powell was mistaken if he thought that using the 'G-word' without altering policy would satisfy campaigners and draw the sting of Darfur as a partisan issue in US politics. Media attention to

Darfur grew, increasingly critical of US policy, and the genocide-intervention narrative persisted. English-language media attention to Darfur increased from fewer than fifty newspaper articles in March 2004 to almost 1,300 in August.[41] A survey of opinion and editorial columns in major American newspapers found that Darfur was compared to Rwanda three times as often as to South Sudan, and that the tenor of almost all articles was the need for military intervention.[42] The biggest boost to American popular interest was an event wholly unrelated to Darfur: the 11 September 2004 release of the feature film *Hotel Rwanda*. The engagement of Don Cheadle, who played the lead role in *Hotel Rwanda*, and other actors including Mia Farrow and George Clooney, ensured that press coverage stayed at the astonishing level of about 500 articles per month throughout 2005 and beyond. The celebrities' message was that genocide was continuing and only coercive action – if not military intervention, then sanctions – could end the catastrophe.

By 2005, Darfur had become the focus of what one veteran campaigner and policymaker called 'the largest American civic activist movement on Africa since the anti-Apartheid campaign'.[43] Few could have predicted that a previously unknown Muslim region, lacking historic ties to the US and without natural resources such as oil in significant quantities, would become the recipient of so much activist and celebrity attention. That attention had an immediate impact: Khartoum could not persist in its refusal of humanitarian operations; and aid organizations in Darfur have not had to scramble for funds. But it also had a downside. The level of interest increased Khartoum's suspicion of American motives, catapulted often incompetent rebel leaders out of obscurity and on to a world stage awash in dollars, and created a simplistic moral fable that portrayed the crisis as a battle between good and evil. In the words of an experienced UN political adviser on Sudan, 'getting a sensible view heard is like shouting out in the middle of a crowd'. The advocacy officer of a major international relief agency acknowledged that the campaigners, and their demand for foreign troops for civilian protection, 'have kept Darfur on the agenda when many just wanted it to disappear', but lamented that they were 'easily influenced by certain elements of the rebel movements' and 'generally unaccountable – especially to the very people in Darfur that they purport to speak on behalf of'.[44] She wrote:

> Many activists were hugely detrimental in terms of looking for solutions. They created mass hysteria which limited the ability of decision-makers to pursue legitimate options. They have no concept of the fact that Sudan is a country and Darfur is just one part of it. These groups sucked up the space available for seeking solutions to the immediate needs of the people on the ground in Darfur because they focused all the attention of decision-makers on the far-fetched, long-term and debatable notion of a 'military solution' to the conflict, and of a UN-led intervention being the panacea to all Darfur's problems. For many humanitarians on the ground, the takeover was a far-off objective that we all knew would probably not work even if it did occur because no matter what people believe, you can't bring peace and safety for civilians to a place as big and complicated as Darfur by the barrel of a gun – even if it is 20,000 guns.

The most extreme activists went as far as to denigrate those who were risking their lives every day to get aid into Darfur and to get cool explanations of the crisis out. The same relief worker said:

> We were not only fighting the Sudan government. We were also fighting our own allies. I've been called some really bad names – a genocidal supporter and friend of Bashir for suggesting that what is happening in Darfur is not genocide; crimes against humanity maybe, but not an attempt to exterminate a race or ethnic group – and so have many of my colleagues. Not only were we followed and monitored on a daily basis in the country; we were vilified when we went out as well.[45]

Years of apolitical relief work in South Sudan had been widely criticized for failing to grapple with the causes of hunger and displacement.[46] The response to Darfur swung to the opposite extreme. What some aid staff in the field called 'genocide hysteria' had a negative impact on humanitarian work as some agency headquarters focused on advocacy at the expense of assistance. 'The relentless media campaign understandably led many to focus on genocide or ethnic cleansing as being *the* "protection issue", and overshadowed other concerns,' said Fabrice Weissman. 'If Darfur was the scene of a holocaust, if displaced camps were extermination camps, the priority was not to increase relief assistance but to wage a war against the Sudanese regime and its allied militias.'[47] By the time the activist campaign gathered momentum in 2005 and 2006, violence was no longer the biggest killer in Darfur: that was diarrhoeal diseases and malaria. But some aid agencies were not interested in building latrines. Weissman again: 'A lot of NGOs were more concerned with documenting atrocities and proving that genocide was going on. For them, feeding the displaced was like giving sandwiches to the survivors of Auschwitz. Anything less than military intervention was not acceptable.'[48]

In 2006, Save Darfur sponsored a vast advertising effort driving home the message that genocide was being committed, 400,000 had been slaughtered and even more would die without immediate military intervention or pressure such as sanctions and divestment. This message was not welcomed by the mainstream relief agencies in Darfur. 'It took us a year and a lot of our resources to stop Save Darfur [demanding unilateral intervention],' said the humanitarian official quoted above. 'They finally said they would only talk about it as a last resort.'

Another criticism of much activism – and nearly all reporting – was that the description of the crisis as a genocidal onslaught by 'Arabs' against 'Africans' led to the demonization of all Arabs, and a denial of assistance to Arabs fleeing from violence against them. This led to deaths among Darfur's Arabs. There was a near-total failure of communication between international agencies and peacekeepers and the Arabs, whose forces controlled many of the roads along which the agencies needed to move. The first coverage of the Arab victims of the war by a major newspaper was in 2006, fully three years after the war began. One reader responding to the article e-mailed the author photographs of an Arab who had suffered full-body burns after being set alight in his home by Zaghawa rebels two years earlier. The photos had been sent to human rights groups, he said, but had not been picked up or investigated. One of the groups contacted by him said it had been 'too busy' documenting government abuses. An Arab intellectual in Khartoum who had tried to encourage Arabs in Darfur to give their side of the story – 'factually, not dismissive and denying' – quoted some as saying that 'they told many Western media, but that information was never published'.[49]

'Things are getting worse'

Alongside 'genocide' and calls for intervention, the refrain throughout 2005, 2006 and 2007 was the blanket assertion that 'things are getting worse'. A tabulation of statements from some of the most prominent activists and advocacy groups between April 2005 and August 2007 found that variants of this refrain – assertions or predictions of deterioration – accounted for all but seven of 134 statements.[50] Yet these warnings do not correspond with increased civilian deaths from violence, hunger or disease. Graphs of deaths from violence show huge peaks in August–September 2003 (in North Darfur) and January–March 2004 (in West Darfur), with a third, smaller peak (mostly in South Darfur) later in 2004.[51] From February 2005, known violent deaths ran at approximately a hundred a month, increasing to between two and three hundred in 2006 and 2007.[52] Whereas the great majority of violent deaths in 2003–04 were due to attacks on civilians by the army and Janjawiid, from 2005 onwards most were caused by fighting among rebel groups and competition for pasture land among Arab militias – both of whom often fought with weapons supplied by the government, whose attacks continued. Banditry was also a problem. A Reuters tally of casualty figures contained in a December 2007 UN human rights report indicated that at least three hundred people were killed in some twenty land and air attacks documented by the UN in the six preceding months – an average of fifty a month.[53]

On the basis of purely demographic and epidemiological indicators, death rates were reverting to normal. By 2007 mortality rates and malnutrition had come down to 'well below emergency thresholds and in many IDP camps well below pre-war levels'.[54] In the field of relief, 'things are getting worse' applied, most disturbingly, to attacks on humanitarian workers. These climbed dramatically, with a 150 per cent surge in incidents against humanitarian staff in three months in 2007,[55] for example, and seven deaths in the single month of October 2007. While most incidents were criminal – land cruiser hijackings to resell in Chad or convert into battle wagons – aid agencies were also the targets of political violence. In late 2006, the Kutum office of the International Committee of the Red Cross was overrun by gunmen who got on the roof of the building and fired at the staff through the windows, aiming in the direction of ringing telephones and shooting to kill. In Gereida, staff members of Oxfam and Action Contre la Faim were assaulted. International agencies saw their work demonized in the Sudanese media and portrayed as part of a conspiracy against Sudan. Public rhetoric by western leaders and advocates confounded the problem, said one aid worker. 'What appeared to be strong and important statements in the US or UK had a negative impact in Sudan, where they fed into a very public paranoia that the West was only interested in Darfur to justify taking Sudan's oil and stealing Muslim territory as they claimed had occurred in Iraq.'[56] As a result, relief agencies shrank the spaces in which they operated, and fewer people received assistance. In the middle of 2007 the indicators of malnutrition began to tick upwards again. Nevertheless, 'things are getting worse' did not apply, objectively, to health, nutrition or mortality during 2005 and 2006.

The numbers of displaced people climbed sharply during 2003 and 2004, and continued a steady rise thereafter – as much because of rampant insecurity as because of war. Conditions of life across much of Darfur were unconscionable, and criminal impunity still ruled. But the unanimity with which commentators diagnosed deterioration, without the slightest nuance despite the immensity of Darfur and the multiplicity of its conflicts, ignored and distorted a much more complicated reality.

Activists and senior UN officials – most obviously, Emergency Relief Coordinator Jan Egeland – sounded dire warnings about 'those beyond the reach of aid', to the point of claiming that 'we are at the point where even hope may escape us'.[57] But in many 'no-go' areas for international agencies, such as Ain Siro in North Darfur, local people 'beyond the reach of aid' were not suffering famine or sustained assault. Rather they were mending their societies, making local reconciliation agreements with their Arab neighbours and patiently rebuilding their lives with the little that was left to them. In the Ain Siro mountains, a woman who had walked across militia-controlled areas to exchange life with aid in an IDP camp for life without it in the 'no-go' mountains said 'life is good here', despite continuing fear of militia attacks.[58] Clinics abandoned by foreign relief workers continued to function, kept scrupulously clean and under tight lock and key when not in use. The main school in Ain Siro village not only kept going without inputs from UNICEF, but organized an end-of-term 'graduation' ceremony in which hundreds of children received certificates and a shake of the hand, and noisily appreciated a school play in which a young woman in love overcame her parents' objections to win the man of her heart. Rebel commanders who attended the ceremony said what they needed most was not relief, but peace.

Once the twin narrative themes of genocide and 'things are getting worse' were established, they could not be shifted. In May 2006, a *Washington Post* editorial was headlined: 'Still a Genocide: There Should be No Ambiguity About Darfur'.[59] More than a year later, Andrew Natsios tried to make the point to US senators that the situation was complex, killing was reduced, and the 'genocide' label was not a good or even a helpful fit. Senator Robert Menendez was not interested in Natsios's niceties. He just wanted an answer to the question, 'Do you consider the ongoing situation in Darfur a genocide, yes or no?' Six times he repeated the question, brushing aside Natsios's attempts not to pander to such gross oversimplification.[60] 'What do you not understand?' Menendez hectored. But it was he who did not understand – or did not care to.

August and September 2006 saw a veritable avalanche of predictions of imminent disaster, linked to Khartoum's obstruction of UN troops and the expiry of AMIS's mandate on 30 September. On 5 September, the activist Eric Reeves told a reporter that the government was working to drain Darfur of foreign witnesses as it prepared for a final battle, 'a genocidal black box'.[61] Reeves said: 'There are very likely more than 10,000 conflict-related deaths per month.'[62] UN officials on the ground, in Darfur, estimated the correct figure at closer to two hundred deaths a month from violence, while mortality from hunger and disease remained comparable to pre-war levels and well below emergency thresholds. Nine days later, George Clooney addressed the UN Security Council at the invitation of the US government:[63]

> Now, my job is to come here today and beg you, on behalf of the millions of people who will die – and make no mistake they will die – for you to take the real and effective measures to put an end to this. Of course it's complex, but when you see entire villages raped and killed, wells poisoned and then filled with the bodies of its villagers, then all complexities disappear and it comes down to simply right and wrong ...
>
> So after September 30th, you won't need the UN. You will simply need men with shovels and bleached white linen and head stones. In many ways it's unfair, but it is nevertheless true, that this genocide will be on your watch. How you deal with it will be your legacy – your Rwanda, your Cambodia, your Auschwitz.

In September, the 'ongoing genocide' was composed, in the main, of the deaths of approximately one hundred Sudanese army soldiers, most of them raw conscripts who thought they were going to oversee a peace agreement, who were killed when their position at Um Sidir in North Darfur was overrun by SLA forces. The next month it was a similar story in Kariari, on the other side of Darfur, only with higher army fatalities. Over the following year, the best available information suggests that the death toll from violence continued to average around two hundred a month: a total of about 2,500 individuals killed in violence, half of them government soldiers and Arab militiamen. Mortality rates from hunger and disease did not rise. But no one in the activist community corrected earlier predictions; never was there a more clear-cut case of truth being the first casualty of war – as Hiram Johnson had warned the US Senate almost ninety years earlier – and Clooney's apocalyptic rhetoric resonated. On 16 September, demonstrators at simultaneous rallies across the world donned blue berets to demand that UN troops be sent at once to 'save Darfur'. A 2007 survey of global public opinion found that 83 per cent of Americans thought that the UN had a right or responsibility to intervene in Darfur.[64] This sustained Darfur as an issue in domestic US politics. As the early campaigning for the 2008 presidential election moved into gear, all candidates were required to take a muscular stand on Darfur. The activists demanded no compromises with evil. The Sudan government has no friends in US politics so there was little pushback from an ever-escalating round of demands for more and tougher action against Khartoum, regardless of whether it would relieve – or exacerbate – the suffering in Darfur.

The responsibility to protect

For Khartoum, the prize of peace was not tranquillity and development in rural Sudan, but normalized relations with Europe and, especially, the United States. During the North–South peace talks it had been a simple and attractive American position – peace followed by normalization – that enabled Ali Osman and his supporters to convince sceptical colleagues that they should persist. Ali Osman's rivals, especially security chief Nafie Ali Nafie, argued that the Americans would always want more, no matter what was agreed, and that international involvement was a slippery slope that would end with enforced regime change. Nafie was quite explicit about his belief that the US government, increasingly in tandem with the British and (after the election of Nicolas Sarkozy) the French, had a clear objective of removing the Bashir regime from power.[65] He considered the variations in policies between the CIA, which was cooperating with Khartoum on counter-terrorism, and the White House and Congress as 'a division of labour' rather than a difference of opinion. 'Either we will win or they will win,' Nafie said, 'why should we dismantle ourselves on their behalf?'[66]

Ali Osman's arguments persuaded fewer of his colleagues as the Naivasha talks dragged on and the role of the international community grew ever larger – until the UN special representative enjoyed powers over a multinational peacekeeping force, and an internationally chaired Assessment and Evaluation Commission presided over such matters as internal troop deployments and the national budget. By the time of the peace-signing ceremony in Kenya in January 2005, the attitude of most senior members of the government was, 'This is Ali Osman's gamble, and we will wait and see if it works.'

President Bush's special envoy for Sudan, Senator Jack Danforth, reassured Khartoum. Danforth's dislike of self-determination for the South was no secret, and he had made clear that he did not advocate regime change. But Powell's genocide determination shook Khartoum's confidence. Sudan's leaders feared that President Bush was serious when he spoke of 'bringing justice' to the Janjawiid,[67] and of living up to the note 'not on my watch' he is reported to have scribbled in the margin of a report on his predecessor's abandonment of Rwanda.[68]

The height of hostilities in Darfur in September 2003–April 2004 coincided with Washington's push for completion of the Naivasha peace agreement. This, along with counter-terrorist cooperation, was the US government's priority at the time. There was a momentary waver when there was discussion of prioritizing Darfur over the North–South talks, but the rebels' lack of preparedness and the prospects of a long drawn-out peace process persuaded diplomats – eager for a rare piece of good news from the Arab world in the midst of the Iraq débâcle – to consummate

Naivasha first. The case was clinched by Garang's promise that he would make Darfur his first priority as soon as he joined a Government of National Unity.

There was, however, no single point of authority in the last months of the first Bush Administration. Only when Deputy Secretary of State Robert Zoellick took charge in early 2005 did a political strategy begin to crystallize. Having previously been US trade representative, Zoellick had planned to make relations with China the centrepiece of his tenure as deputy secretary, but quickly found he was spending his time on Darfur. One senior American diplomat said of Darfur, 'These are the issues of our children's generation. Look at all these college kids and the issues they care about. That is what is driving this. It's the new reality of foreign relations.' He went on, 'The president spends more time on Sudan than on China. Our task is to allow him to get his priorities straight.'[69] To his credit, Zoellick engaged with Sudan more than any other American politician of cabinet rank had done. A meticulous strategist and studious reader, he visited the country four times in the course of 2005. But it is hard to escape the conclusion that he too saw Darfur as a distraction from the bigger issues like China – something that should be fixed with a short, sharp injection of attention and pressure. The US government simply didn't commit the level of personnel or resources needed to get to grips with a complicated war. The embassy in Khartoum was always short-staffed and there were never sufficient military advisers in the field or at the peace talks. Zoellick's stint at the State Department lasted barely eighteen months, too short for the kind of sustained engagement required to end a war. He resigned in August 2006, leaving a vacuum at the top of Washington DC's policymaking that Assistant Secretary Jendayi Frazer was not able to fill. One American adviser in Sudan complained, 'There has been a lack of US engagement. When Bosnia happened, we sent two heavy hitters: Dick Holbrooke and Wes Clark. Bashir is wary of the US. Minni [Minawi] got Bush, Bashir not only got a woman, he got a black woman [Frazer].'

Zoellick thought Darfur needed peace *and* protection. He

believed that Ali Osman and John Garang could reach a North–South agreement that would serve as a foundation for peace in Darfur, even though this process excluded Darfurians and limited Darfur's options for power-sharing. After Garang's death, he banked on Ali Osman, developing a personal rapport that was, for the embattled vice-president, a double-edged sword. For Ali Osman, Washington's very public confidence in him carried high risks. He was increasingly isolated from his colleagues in government and became a target of their intrigues.

For Zoellick, protection of Darfurian civilians was a job for international troops. He had been greeted by AU troops on his first visit to al Fasher in April 2005, and dispatched members of his staff to Darfur to support and evaluate their capabilities. He immediately saw that AMIS was out of its depth. The fundamental problem was neither numbers nor mandate, but organization – lack of it. Corruption began at the top, and Darfurians began to call the mission, contemptuously, ABIS: African Business in Sudan. The initial deployment had gone smoothly, in large part due to the dedication of a tiny staff of planners in Addis Ababa. But the key post in the AU Commission – head of peacekeeping operations – remained vacant while governments intrigued as to who should fill it. The AU was so weak in capacity that it did not have the ability even to recruit essential staff. It ran its Darfur operation with fewer personnel than the Sudan desk of a small NGO – and frequently diverted them to other tasks. When the bi-annual summit was imminent, AMIS field commanders who phoned Addis Ababa often found no one around to take their calls.

The European Union had a fund to support African peacekeeping operations, but it was designed only for small and rapid deployments, not for missions on the scale of Darfur. The UN has a system of mandatory payments for peacekeeping operations which means that it can deploy first and fund itself later. The AU, without wealthy states to finance it, was reliant on running cap in hand to foreign donors every few months. The original budget of the monitoring mission was just $26 million, which was raised to $221 million six months later and $465 million a year after that. Soldier-for-soldier, AMIS was much cheaper to run than any envisaged UN force – by comparison, the UN–African Union Mission in Darfur is budgeted at over $2 billion for its first year, when its troops' strength will be well below the projected 26,000 men, and little different from AMIS's peak strength. However, donors had to plunder other budgets to finance AMIS; they didn't find all the money, and much of what they did provide got stuck in AU headquarters in Addis Ababa. By early 2006, peacekeepers' salaries were paid weeks, then months, in arrears, and in some cases Sudan government officials and security officers stepped into the breach, offering sweet deals to fill the gaps. In one base, local officials even provided the food for AMIS soldiers who were left without rations.

Contemplating the débâcle that was fast becoming AMIS, senior officials at the UN Department of Peacekeeping Operations had two reactions. One was, 'We could do better. Having run peacekeeping missions for fifty years, we have mechanisms to make sure troops are paid on time and properly equipped.' The other: 'We wouldn't have gone in to Darfur without a proper peace agreement and we don't want to go in now because we will fail too.' The political leaders of America and Europe wanted only to hear the first.

In Burundi, the AU had initially sent in peacekeepers who were later transferred to a UN operation, switching their green helmets for blue UN ones: 'rehatting'. In theory, AU capacity could have been built up while it ran the Darfur operation, or innovative solutions could have been found. Some AU staff advocated putting the Rwandans in charge of the force headquarters. But in the event, the AU was simply not capable of building its own institution and running AMIS at the same time. Handing over to the UN seemed a sensible proposal. There was, however, one important difference between Burundi and Sudan. In Burundi, the AU, the UN, the government and the warring factions all wanted UN troops. In Darfur, the AU was reluctant to let go, the UN didn't want to take the job on, and the Sudan government

195

soon learned that obstructing the transition from AU to UN would tie down the energy of the international community. Jan Pronk saw this coming and warned against it. But in America, the clamour for a military intervention was such that any other option was not politically acceptable.

The proposal to 'transition' AMIS to the UN meant radically different things to different people. For the troop-contributing countries – principally Nigeria, Senegal, South Africa and Rwanda – it meant rehatting their existing contingents, being assured of salaries, and having stronger administrative and logistical support. It was agreed from the outset among the AU, UN, Khartoum and major donors that a UN force would have a 'predominantly African character'. This would not be the NATO force activists had demanded and the displaced in Darfur had come to believe was possible. For the US government, it was a convenient way of shifting the burden and covering its back. If the UN succeeded, the US could claim credit; if it failed, the UN could be blamed. The stratagem, in playing to the gallery, cynically ignored the UN's poor record in coercive peacekeeping and civilian protection.

For the Darfur activists in America, the UN was heralded as a form of military intervention, implementation of the principle of the 'responsibility to protect'. Vast amounts of energy were devoted to pushing for UN troops. The International Crisis Group published a report entitled 'To Save Darfur' that devoted about seven times as much space to peacekeeping (almost all to the plan for UN troops) as to peace. It later published another entitled 'Getting the UN into Darfur'. The high expectations for what UN peacekeepers would do was frankly astonishing to those in the UN's Department of Peacekeeping Operations and others who had witnessed UN peacekeeping operations from Sierra Leone to Congo. Many believed the deployment was doomed to be, in the words of a UN official in Khartoum, 'an announced disaster'. A mandate under Chapter VII of the UN Charter that allowed the troops to use force would mean little unless there was a plan for how that force could be used successfully, and there was not. With few exceptions, humanitarians did not want tens of thousands more armed men and, if they had to have them, wanted to know exactly how they intended to 'protect'. A confidential NGO report of April 2006 included the following:

> A kind of propaganda is going on, with Egeland stating the UN agencies are 'paralysed' in Darfur due to insecurity and that there is therefore a need for a strong UN force to be deployed. For sure parts of Darfur are inaccessible for the time being, but it is quite an overstatement to declare that UN agencies are paralysed and I don't see how the deployment of UN troops could improve access ...

MSF warned,

> An international intervention in Darfur presents tougher problems than Kosovo, East Timor and Sierra Leone. Those were small areas, held by well-identified armed groups, and the overwhelming majority of people living there agreed to foreign intervention. An invasion of western Sudan could end in a blood-bath that would include civilians, like Operation Restore Hope in Somalia (1992) and Operation Iraqi Freedom. In addition, a non-consensual intervention would *inevitably* [italics in original] result in the collapse of ongoing aid programmes ... one of the most effective aid operations of the last twenty years.[70]

Some believed the mere threat of UN intervention had increased the dangers facing humanitarians. Khartoum, said MSF's Fabrice Weissman, had responded with 'xenophobic propaganda, likening all foreigners to "new crusaders" motivated by hatred of Arabs and Islam – therefore encouraging armed elements operating on the roads and generally drawn from nomadic clans to target relief workers'. 'In all likelihood,' he continued, 'the increased violence against humanitarian personnel results from a deliberate strategy by the government aimed at confining aid organizations to garrison towns [and] also at resisting the threat of international intervention by holding humanitarian workers hostage.'[71] Some in MSF believed that their operation in Darfur had been a first casualty of this backlash against the UN. On

197

11 September 2006, four MSF staff – three Sudanese and one expatriate – were beaten and threatened with death by masked, armed men who told them: 'We don't want any foreigners here'. The attack took place on a road controlled by a government-supported militia exactly eleven days after the Security Council passed the resolution creating the UN–African Union Mission in Darfur (UNAMID). The message many relief workers took from the attack was this: 'If you want to send in troops, OK, but it will be at the cost of humanitarian workers.' 'We are caught in the middle of a struggle between the international community and Khartoun,' said Weissman. 'I don't see how international troops can secure relief without becoming party to the conflict. Peace can only come as a product of the global stabilization of Darfur.'

There was no need to look further afield than Sudan itself for evidence of the shortcomings of UN peacekeeping. In neighbouring Kordofan, the twenty unarmed monitors of the Joint Military Commission (JMC), set up to monitor the 2002 Nuba Mountains ceasefire, not only kept the peace for three years, but also helped calm potential flashpoints for intercommunal violence, disarm combatants, support the provision of humanitarian aid, and facilitate conflict resolution and the free movement of civilians and goods. After the CPA was signed, the JMC was replaced by a full-strength battalion of UN Mission in Sudan (UNMIS) peacekeepers which presided over a sharp deterioration in security. A report by Britain's Overseas Development Institute in December 2006 said local people attributed the growing insecurity to 'the inability of UNMIS to monitor the situation on the ground with equal effectiveness'. It said one of the most recurrent issues was 'the lack of disarmament of militia, particularly of former PDF fighters ... Another persistent complaint was the lack of patrolling by UNMIS, both on foot and by helicopter ... The area in which communities feel the handover from the JMC to UNMIS has left the greatest vacuum is local level reconciliation work.'[72]

What should have been the simplest part of the plan for bringing UN peacekeepers to Darfur – getting AU and Sudanese approval – turned out to be costly and complicated. As Pronk predicted, it consumed most of the time and effort of most senior policymakers in Washington and allowed AMIS, neglected, to grow steadily weaker until troop strength at the time of the take-over was down to fewer than 6,000 men. Khartoum suspected an American plot behind the plan for UN troops. At the end of 2005, Bush was asking his advisers whether the US military could shoot down Sudanese military aircraft or 'send in helicopter gunships to attack the militias' if they attacked IDP camps. A senior official familiar with the episode said, 'He wanted militant action, and people had to restrain him ... He wanted to go in and kill the Janjaweed.'[73] The 'restraint' option was to accelerate the policy of UN peacekeepers.

Bringing in the UN meant ending AMIS. Many in the AU felt the ground for the transition was prepared at the expense of their men in Darfur. With some activist voices once again drowning out balanced debate, there was brutal, blanket criticism of the AU's shortcomings. 'I don't know of one incident where the African Union has protected a village or a woman,' one well-known activist was reported as saying.[74] While this may have helped convince western leaders that the UN was far superior to the AU – and more than indispensable, the *solution* – it was counterproductive in Africa: African pride was at stake, and the AU dug in its heels. It took much arm-twisting by the Americans for the AU Peace and Security Council to consider handing over AMIS to the UN. The UN wasn't keen either. Kofi Annan had been head of peacekeeping before becoming UN Secretary-General and, his spine stiffened by the bloody chaos of Iraq, wasn't going to be bullied into accepting an impossible mission. Annan insisted that the UN couldn't send in blue helmets without a peace agreement first. So Khartoum's consent and a peace deal were needed. To deliver on both, the Americans relied on Ali Osman – but on UN troops, they were to discover that President Bashir had the last word, and for a peace deal, the man in charge was Majzoub al Khalifa.

8 | The Abuja peace talks[1]

Dr Majzoub al Khalifa Ahmed was a master of Khartoum intrigue. Physically, he was an imposing figure, sweeping into the negotiating chamber like a king crocodile with his minions swarming around him. His gimlet eyes darted around the room, missing nothing. A dermatologist by training, Majzoub had, in his medical days, represented the doctors' union in pay negotiations with the ministry of health, gaining a reputation for wearing his employers down with his persistence, inflexibility and grasp of detail. Always meticulously prepared, Majzoub pounced on his adversaries' every incoherence and inconsistency. As governor of Khartoum in the 1990s, he insisted that women sit in the rear of public buses and enter separately from men, and devoted inordinate attention to ensuring that the minutiae of decrees like this were scrupulously enforced. Majzoub was as vexatious to his allies as he was fearsome to his adversaries, at one point driving Turabi to exclaim, in reference to his dermatology, 'Even his speciality is superficial!' Turabi might equally well have asked how Majzoub acquired a hide so thick that he was able to maintain his humourless smile no matter what barbs were fired his way. To some he resembled a small-town merchant, one of the northern *jellaba* who traded soap, sugar, razors and every other imported consumable and knew every price down to the last cent. It was for him that the term 'retail politics' was coined by Congress Party members, as awed by his encyclopaedic grasp of the mechanisms of patronage as by his obliviousness to the demands of broader strategy.

In 2004, Majzoub took Darfur's political file, and held it in the face of repeated challenges from his rivals in Khartoum until his death in a car accident in July 2007. When he returned to the Abuja negotiations after a break in January 2006, he insisted that the president give *him*, and not his arch-rival Vice-president Ali Osman, full responsibility for negotiating the final deal. Bashir did not want a repeat of Ali Osman's secret dealings with John Garang in Naivasha and granted the authority he demanded. When the Abuja peace process ended in failure in May 2006, the greatest share of the responsibility for that failure fell on Khartoum's chief negotiator. The negotiations had many flaws, but at the end of the day it was Majzoub's stubborn arrogance that kept a fair peace out of reach. 'With Majzoub in charge, we will never have an agreement,' remarked a senior security officer from Khartoum, who added that the obstruction was too powerful to be removed. A more strategically minded politician could have accepted enough of the rebels' demands – or even their need for symbolic victories – to have made an agreement possible. But relishing point-scoring, and the prospect of delivering the cheapest possible deal to Bashir, he spurned the grand compromise.

Majzoub's approach to negotiation was to compile a file on every single individual in the opposing camp and try to buy them off one by one, with money or positions – or both. As the talks moved through successive rounds, Majzoub won more and more clients in rebel ranks, including some of the negotiators and advisers. He outlined a political accord with Abdel Wahid al Nur in February 2006, and for a moment it looked as though he would follow it up with a formal protocol that would pave the way for a peace deal and an electoral pact with the Fur tribe, one of the NCP's main aims in Abuja. The AU had placed the principals in adjacent rooms on the top floor of Abuja's Chida Hotel, partly because each was entitled to what were rather grandly called 'VIP suites', but also because one important duty of a mediator is to provide a location where the leaders of the contending parties can meet privately. This they did, and in the first week of February, there was anticipation that a deal was being struck between Majzoub and Abdel Wahid. Majzoub's main contacts included Hafiz Yousif, Abdel Wahid's boyhood friend, and Abdel Rahman Musa, his delegation leader. A professor of ancient languages at a French university, Abdel Rahman had established a link with Khartoum over the preceding months and was distrusted by most SLA commanders. In Darfur, government trucks began rolling, taking food to Abdel Wahid's forces in Jebel Marra. But at the last moment, Abdel Wahid backed away. According to Abdel Wahid, 'Majzoub's interest was competing with Ali Osman. He was not interested in Darfur. He wanted to tell Bashir: "Ali Osman cost you a lot in Naivasha. I am bringing you a very cheap deal."'[2]

As chairman of the Sudan Liberation Movement (SLM), Abdel Wahid was his own worst enemy. He failed to set up structures or delegate authority. Many of those who worked closely with him complained that his most important meetings were held one-on-one and he never made a note of what had been discussed or decided. The next day, he often did the opposite of what he had promised.[3] Most frustrating to his colleagues was his chronic indecisiveness, fatally combined with an insistence that he alone make any important decisions. Abdel Wahid paid lip service to the need to expand and formalize the structures of the SLM, but never did anything about it, seeing in every new proposal a challenge to his own position and authority. In March 2006, his insistence on going it alone was one of the factors that led a group of nineteen prominent commanders, mainly Zaghawa but also Masalit and Meidob, to 'freeze his powers'. The trigger for the split was Abdel Wahid's decision to pull out of the single negotiating team with SLA–Minawi and JEM, deepening suspicions that he was secretly negotiating a separate deal with Khartoum. In a statement issued on 6 March, the group of nineteen, or G19, deplored their chairman's determination 'to go it alone to consolidate his dictatorship and marginalize all the institutions of the Movements'. They accused him of having a 'narrow-minded personal agenda, surrendering himself to the desires of his entourage, incapable of performing the functions of leadership, while arrogating to himself standards of perfection, because to him, the determinant of leadership is how much one is admired by the others'. The G19 said Abdel Wahid had become 'a quagmire of inflexibility, rigidity, grudge [and] division'. They called for a Transitional Revolutionary Council led by Khamis Abakir 'to collectively administer the affairs of the Movement until such time as a congress can be held' and not later than June that year. They demanded 'full coordination between the Movements' negotiating delegations in Abuja' and pledged to 'commit ourselves, as a matter of strategy, to full transfer of power to the people of Darfur after the Darfur–Darfur dialogue'.

What the G19 statement did not mention was a growing conviction among many of its signatories that Abdel Wahid – in his 'Minniphobia', as his colleague Ahmed Abdel Shafi put it – was thinking of forming common cause with the government against the Zaghawa. 'From the beginning of this round [of talks] Abdel Wahid has been saying: "We will go to Khartoum without JEM and Minni Minawi,"' said Jar al Nabi Abdel Karim, one of the prime movers of the G19. 'He is against the Zaghawa as a tribe.' Another signatory of the G19 statement, Meidob commander Suleiman Marajan, said two of Abdel Wahid's confidants had told him: 'We are taking steps with the government, especially Mohamed Yousif [a Fur minister from Jebel Marra and delegate on the government's Abuja delegation] to protect our people from the Zaghawa.' When Marajan asked how, they reportedly told him: 'We will take weapons from the government and then use them against the Zaghawa.'[4]

Abdel Wahid forcefully denied these allegations, stressing that he opened Jebel Marra to the Zaghawa in 2001 in the face of opposition from many Fur. But one of his oldest friends, and a founding member of the SLA, said he was stressing to Abdel Wahid the need for an alliance with the Arabs of Darfur – at the expense of Zaghawa. He said,

All Arabs are with Abdel Wahid, but they are given no status. We need a political plan for social unity under the SLM. It would be led by Fur and southern Rizeigat. All tribes will join except the Zaghawa. They will join a political party. To get the Arabs to join you must give them an enemy. That enemy will be number one, the Zaghawa, and number two, the government of Sudan. We need to put the Zaghawa as the enemy. Fur and Arabs are 75 per cent of the population and political force in Darfur. Arabs will not join unless they have an enemy.

Abdel Wahid, he said, was 'very interested'. Suspecting a new alliance was in the making – especially in the wake of the Birgid–Missiriya pact in Shearia – Minawi's hostility to Abdel Wahid deepened.

Majzoub's negotiations with Minawi had a very different approach, based on offering him money and positions. Khartoum's negotiator was much less interested in an electoral pact with the Zaghawa and also assessed that for Minawi – as indeed for Majzoub himself – the main function of the peace talks was not to explore the areas of political compromise, but to assess relative strengths, calculate the price of a deal and then take the decisions that would guarantee survival. Minawi was a latecomer to Abuja, and until the final stages of the talks was the least ready to compromise. The day after he signed the Darfur Peace Agreement (DPA) he explained, 'I calculated the balance of power and I realized I had to sign.'[5] In his rise to power, Minawi had relied on the patronage of Libya and Chad, and he feared that they would turn on him. In the final months of the talks, Minawi's forces in the field were crumbling. But the Americans refused to see his decline. Like most of those involved, they backed him as Darfur's strongman, believing he could deliver an agreement and giving him an importance far beyond that which his political and popular base warranted.

For Majzoub, at that time, a peace deal was a ticket to personal prestige and international legitimacy for the government. The details of how it would work on the ground were unimportant. He read the AU and internationals well and knew that they too wanted a quick political fix. Some American diplomats privately recognized the problems of short-circuiting the long and tortuous process of negotiation, but hoped that a deal in Abuja would bring the rebels into the Government of National Unity and a UN mission to Darfur, at which time the real issues of security and conflict resolution could be properly addressed. The main critics of this sequence were the AU's security advisers – several of whom insisted that a flawed deal would make things much worse. On the back of an American meeting with the two SLA factions in Nairobi in November 2005, African security experts, among them Jeremy Brickhill, a former guerrilla fighter from Zimbabwe, and Mulugeta Gebrehiwot, a former Ethiopian guerrilla commander who became commissioner for demobilization, drew up a plan for negotiating a ceasefire. Far more than just stopping shooting, a ceasefire involves restrictions on movement, mechanisms for organizing the supply and rotation of troops, communications systems, and modalities for reporting and investigating reported violations. Hard enough where there are regular armies in the field, it is even more complicated when there are multiple irregular forces, especially highly mobile ones like the Darfur rebels. Brickhill and Gebrehiwot estimated that it would take six months to complete assessment, training and confidence-building measures, and a further three months to negotiate a ceasefire that would hold. They pointed out that the most important commanders were not in Abuja and that without their involvement, any agreement would be worthless. However, Gebrehiwot said later, 'We were rebuffed by our chairman [the AU's General Chris Garuba] and by the AU mediation team saying, "Why complicate things?"'[6] Brickhill argued that it was not only unwise but dangerous to short-cut these steps, but with the deadline for completing the whole process just seven weeks away, the AU dismissed the proposal as too 'leisurely'.[7]

Fighting and talking

The war never stopped while the Abuja talks were on. After a lull during most of 2005, fighting intensified during the final round of the talks – from November 2005 to May 2006. For Minawi, JEM and the government, the main event was the battlefield; the negotiations were a sideshow.

Minawi's immediate objective was not to defeat the government but to eliminate his rivals and emerge as the undisputed, internationally recognized leader of the SLA. The Abuja talks resumed on the heels of his Haskanita convention, with Minawi claiming leadership of the SLA as a result of his 'election' in Haskanita but in reality increasingly weak on the ground – opposed even by some Zaghawa who thought the Fur tribe should retain its historic leadership role in Darfur. In February 2006, fearing a deal in Abuja between Abdel Wahid and Khartoum, and seeking to bolster his ebbing strength in North Darfur, Minawi went on the attack. Driven out of the Haskanita area in March by a militia attack, his forces retreated towards Korma, north east of Jebel Marra, and asked Abdel Wahid's commander there for care for the wounded. The commander, Mohamed Abdel Salam 'Terrada', accepted Minawi's men, against the advice of most of his colleagues in the field and in Abuja, and they entered Korma. Once in, however, they demanded that Abdel Wahid's men leave. In the fighting that ensued, they captured one of Abdel Wahid's commanders, Mohamed Issa, and killed him.[8] Abdel Wahid's regard for the AU plummeted when it said nothing about the most serious ceasefire violation for months. The US, busy encouraging Minawi to participate constructively at Abuja, also stayed silent. 'Instead of expanding in the government area, Minni is expanding in our area!' exclaimed Abdel Wahid.

As the negotiators returned to Abuja, Khartoum attempted to strengthen its hand by engineering the overthrow of the regime in N'Djamena as the most efficient way of destroying the rebels' supply lines and rear bases. Conflict in Chad had been simmering for some time and Sudanese Security was not slow to seize on the chances that arose either to overthrow President Idriss Deby or, at the least, to force him into cooperating with them. Darfur's war had begun with Chadians in 1987 and as soon as full-scale hostilities erupted in 2003, Chadians predicted that it would end in their country too. For that reason, Deby was quick to try to mediate between Khartoum and the rebels, and Chad sat as formal co-chair of the Abuja talks alongside the

AU. After Chad's involvement in the war became too obvious to conceal, in March 2006, the AU pressured the Chadians to step down, which they did. But no western government was ready to push the kinds of political reforms that would prevent civil war in Chad unless France took the lead – and France supported Deby, who allowed French military bases on Chadian soil. By the middle of 2005, the presence of Chadian opposition forces in Darfur, armed and supplied by the Sudan government, was attracting international attention. Early in December, Deby made public a dossier which, he said, proved Khartoum's complicity with those who sought regime change in Chad. The ten-page dossier contained a photograph captioned 'Chadian rebel training camp' and showing President Bashir with Chadian rebel leader Mahamat Nour and his men in an unidentified place of semi-desert.[9] On 18 December Nour's forces attacked the border town of Adré, but were beaten off by Chadian army units with French support. Deby declared that Chad was in a state of war with Sudan and increased his support for Darfur's rebels. The next month, Deby brought Khalil, Minawi and Khamis Abakir, the SLA vice-chairman whose Masalit forces were mostly based in Chad, to N'Djamena to coordinate the counter-offensive.

On 13 April 2006, a Chadian rebel column – armed, supplied and organized by Sudanese security officers in Darfur – attacked N'Djamena and was repulsed only after French military planes based at Abeche intervened. A rebel commander captured in Chad told AU investigators 'the Sudanese intelligence people were our contacts ... We were given transport, communications. We were well equipped.' The commander, Colonel Adoum Maratis, said the security officers also helped recruit rebels, including children as young as twelve, from displaced camps in Darfur.[10] For Deby it was a fight to the death and he used all his resources – including oil revenues seized in contravention of an agreement with the World Bank – to buy arms and allies. He cut a deal with Khalil Ibrahim and among the forces defending the Chadian capital were JEM troops, some of whom briefly occupied the Sudan embassy. Khartoum supported this blatant attempt at regime change in Chad just as the Abuja talks were entering their endgame. Victory would have hugely strengthened Ali Osman's hand; failure meant that a deal with JEM in Abuja would be impossible for the time being. But not all the Zaghawa were lost to the peace process: the Americans had succeeded in splitting Minawi off from JEM and Deby, who considered him an unreliable ally, and now concentrated their energies on bringing him into a deal in Abuja – even by threatening him with sanctions at the UN if he failed to cooperate.[11]

Confusion in Abuja

The Darfur peace process came hard on the heels of the Naivasha North–South peace process but unfolded in a completely different political context.[12] When Senator John Danforth visited Sudan in 2001, as President Bush's special envoy, few thought the chances of peace were better than one in ten. Not wanting to be associated with a failure, the US preferred a low-profile approach fronted by others. Only when peace was near did the Americans start claiming credit for it. The chief mediator, a former Kenyan army chief of staff, General Lazarus Sumbeiywo, appreciated the assistance of the troika of 'friends' of the process – the US, Britain and Norway – but zealously protected his independence from what he regarded as their tendency to meddle too much. Sumbeiywo believed that a Sudanese war required a Sudanese solution.

Salim Ahmed Salim's appointment as chief mediator for the Darfur conflict in early 2005 seemed an inspired choice. African and Muslim, he was one of the continent's most accomplished diplomats and had served sixteen years as secretary-general of the OAU. He is unassuming and a good listener. He delegates and consults, and is not afraid of excellence among his colleagues. But he was not Sumbeiywo. The Kenyan general was a proactive mediator, canvassing the views of ordinary Sudanese and flying off at the drop of a hat to pre-empt crises. Salim made just one visit to Darfur and avoided the vortex of Khartoum politics. For him, the task of a mediator was to facilitate the parties coming together, not to pursue them and corral them into agreement. He took the post of chief mediator believing that the hard work in Sudan had already been done by others. At no time did he consider reshaping the peace process, as some recommended, by widening it outside the rigid formality of the negotiating chamber to involve other sectors of Darfurian society.

A longtime champion of African liberation movements, Salim began with genuine sympathy for the rebel cause and saw at once the acute imbalance in capability between government and rebels. He spent many hours with the SLM leaders trying to coach them in the craft of liberation through negotiation. Yet he was conservative in what he expected a government to concede. The AU is an association of states, and states deplore anarchy. While recognizing that Khartoum was the source of most of Darfur's problems, Salim also believed that any solution had to come through Khartoum – the government could not simply hand Darfur over to the rebels in the same way as the northern government had withdrawn from the South in the wake of the Comprehensive Peace Agreement. When the movements demanded the removal of all military aircraft from Darfur in March 2006, for example, Salim's instinct was to see this as a defence minister would. What sovereign government would ever make such a concession? he asked, especially when facing a military threat from a hostile neighbour like Chad?

Salim has a keen eye for political dynamics and as he came to grips with his task he became gloomy about what was possible in Abuja, even though he had seen many liberation movements at first hand and was not surprised at the divisions that plagued the SLA and JEM. He was insistent that the AU would recognize no additional rebel movements – this would be tantamount to encouraging splinter factions, he said. What made Salim despair was the rebels' readiness to bask in the international spotlight, seemingly in no hurry to leave Abuja (and their generous per diems), while ordinary Darfurians suffered in miserable camps and unserviced villages. He saw no figure of Garang's stature, ready to move beyond the politics of anger towards articulating a real political programme. He knew from his own frustrating encounters that the government was intransigent. He also knew that the AU had few cards to play, especially after Africa rejected Bashir's bid to be president of the AU in January 2006, and that only the Americans could provide the leverage needed. Above all, he was acutely aware of his own marching orders: the Comprehensive Peace Agreement was inviolable.

The first five rounds of the peace talks were consumed by government ceasefire violations, recrimination and procedural issues. It was only at the final round of talks held in the Chida International Hotel on the outskirts of Abuja that the substance of a peace deal began to be discussed. And even during this final round, held without a break over six months, very little real dialogue took place. The atmosphere in the hotel was stifling. At once grandiose and jerrybuilt, the Chida managed to look pretentious and cheap at the same time. Every room was taken by the Sudanese delegations, mediators, support and office staff, foreign diplomats and observers. The government and rebel delegates bumped into one another all the time, in the corridors and at breakfast, yet the delegation leaders hardly ever met to negotiate. The talks resembled proximity talks in which the mediators shuttled between the sides with proposals, seeking to fashion consensus on key points. Even the last, hyper-charged hours on 4–5 May were a series of parallel negotiating sessions, with rebels and government sitting down in the same room only when the time came to sign the agreement they had reached apart.

The AU, UN and internationals, especially the US, were impatient for a deal. They repeatedly set deadlines and sent senior figures to Abuja to demand that the process be expedited. Each new deadline gave only a few weeks' grace, making it impossible for the mediators to craft a strategy. Each high-level visitor was a distraction for the already overstretched mediation staff, who had no option but to respond to the commands from above. When the North–South talks faltered, Sumbeiywo had banned visits from outside and at times even prevented observers from accessing the parties; when they threatened to collapse, he took the process to a distant location (Nanyuki) to keep outsiders out. But Salim lacked both the will and the clout to keep the internationals at arm's length. He allowed the deadlines to become the strategy, giving up on a negotiated agreement and relying on international pressures to force one.[13]

Deadlines came and went, with each failure bringing only new demands for speed. Finally, the American determination to bring the UN to Darfur created a real deadline. At a meeting in Paris on 8 March, Ali Osman told Zoellick that once there was a peace agreement, he would personally propose a UN peacekeeping mission to Bashir. Two days later, in a marathon session of the Peace and Security Council, the AU agreed to hand AMIS over to the UN in September 2006. Returning from Paris, where he also met with Zoellick, Salim instructed his mediation team to draw up a comprehensive text that covered all the areas of power-sharing, wealth-sharing and security arrangements. Under pressure and running out of patience, Salim resolved that if the parties could not draw up a blueprint for peace, then the mediation would. As soon as the UN Security Council had been briefed, Salim set a deadline for the parties to reach an agreement. That deadline was 30 April.

Drafting the Darfur Peace Agreement

The three mediation commissions took very different approaches to drafting their proposals. Wealth-sharing made good progress. The government's negotiator Dr Lual Deng, a member of the SPLM's negotiating team in Naivasha recently appointed as minister of state for finance and economic planning, went to great lengths to explain to the movements the provisions of the CPA – what worked and what didn't, what could be remedied and what couldn't. His patience and expertise brought agreement on most contentious items. But Lual put his foot down on compensation for individuals who had suffered losses during the war. Southerners had neither asked for nor been offered individual compensation, and their war had been much longer and bloodier than Darfur's. Lual argued that the funds for reconstruction and rehabilitation were sufficient to cover the needs of the dispossessed; Abdel Wahid had already publicly promised that he would deliver compensation to every war-affected family, and wouldn't yield. It was not just that he considered compensation a basic right; his own ability to deliver, as leader, was at stake. In the end, Lual sought compromise by conceding the idea of a compensation commission that would examine individual cases and a short-term compensation fund that could make quick payments to the neediest. As the negotiations approached their conclusion, the main issue still outstanding was how much compensation money would be immediately available.

But the power-sharing track was stuck. Until March, progress was glacial, and then it froze entirely. Both sides had hardline positions and neither would budge an inch. The rebels presented their opening demands: a single Darfur region (reversing the administrative reform of 1994 that created three states), the post of a vice-president, return to the region's borders at independence,[14] and a sharing of posts in the executive, legislature and civil service commensurate with Darfur's population. Majzoub rejected them all: 'Not possible, at all, at all!' Even the smallest concession, he insisted, would cross Khartoum's red line. The movements' delegates responded with equal intransigence – at one point the SLM–Minawi negotiator responded to a proposal on the borders that met the rebels' main demand by saying 'Not accepted!' and walking out of the hall. A retired Ethiopian ambassador, Berhanu Dinka, presided over the meetings, growing more and more exasperated with the lack of any negotiation. His patience snapped just once when he shouted at the unyielding rebel negotiators, 'Do politics! You are here to do politics!' When Salim asked him to begin preparing a final text, Ambassador Dinka held no further plenary sessions, stopped meeting the rebels and devoted his attention to compiling mediation proposals. He took this task seriously and carefully explored Majzoub's 'red lines'. He insisted, for example, that the mediators could not accede to the rebel demand for a single region for Darfur, because, he claimed, this would violate the logic of the CPA and encourage similar demands in other marginalized areas. Challenged by other members of the AU team, Dinka stood his ground and agreed only to the compromise of a *transitional* regional authority for Darfur, pending a referendum on Darfur's status. The rebel delegates were bewildered and enraged by the inactivity in the power-sharing commission over the last six weeks of the process, not least because a number of important items, including control of local government, had not once been raised for discussion.

The all-important security arrangements track was chaotic. Chris Garuba, the retired Nigerian general who headed the commission, tried to run the talks as a part-time affair while attending to his business empire and became frustrated when he couldn't. US security advisers ducked in and out, staying for short periods only. Garuba sidelined Norwegian Brigadier Jan-Erik Wilhelmson, who had run the small but exemplary ceasefire monitoring mission in Kordofan. Wilhelmson and the other security specialists assigned to the commission were deeply sceptical that an approach based on merely negotiating a text could work. Jeremy Brickhill and Mulugeta Gebrehiwot repeated their view that any agreement should be taken to the field commanders before a comprehensive peace plan was drawn up and proposed a timetable of an additional two or three months. When this advice was spurned again, the two did not return to Abuja.

Under these inauspicious conditions, a ceasefire text was hammered out. Proposals for an 'enhanced humanitarian ceasefire' were presented on 12 March – and immediately rejected by all parties. The government delegation led by General Ismat al Zain was the most dismayed. Generals and military intelligence officers sat in a row as the main points were outlined to them. Ramrod upright at first, they were slumped in various postures of dismay and disbelief after an hour, like a line of fortifications under fire, as they read the proposals and heard how they would be required to withdraw their troops, restrict their aircraft and sit in a strong Ceasefire Commission on equal terms with the rebels. General Ismat rejected the document in its entirety and threatened to walk out if it were not rewritten from scratch. 'Are you saying take it or leave it?' he demanded. Sam Ibok, in the chair, faced him down, betting that Ismat had been ordered by his political masters to stay. 'We will go through the document, paragraph by paragraph,' said Ibok. Ismat compiled a long list of objections, but remained.

Stymied, the mediators adopted the approach of parallel discussions, shuttling backwards and forwards with every new amendment to the text. They asked the government and each rebel group to map their military positions in order to compile a confidential 'master map' which would allow AU security advisers and AMIS officers to begin planning how to enforce a ceasefire and protect IDP camps and humanitarian supply routes. The planned ceasefire itself was a three-stage process: disengagement, redeployment of armed groups and limited disarmament. This was further complicated by the presence of irregulars not represented in Abuja, including Chadian rebels, and the highly mobile nature of the rebels. The complexities grew as the talks progressed, resulting in a document that was hard to understand and would have been extremely difficult to implement. The strongest element of the ceasefire, which was accepted by all sides, was a series of staged, reciprocal actions: the rebels would only redeploy and begin to disarm when the government had completed the redeployment of its army and militia units. Disarming the Janjawiid posed a major problem. Not only was there was no agreed definition of 'Janjawiid', but coercive disarmament was never a practical possibility. Disarming a militia by force entails fighting it, and this approach had left hundreds dead and the objective not accomplished on the only occasion it was attempted in Sudan.[15] The only viable process in such a huge theatre is voluntary disarmament, but the Darfur Arabs were not invited to Abuja to negotiate how this might be done. A third challenge was planning the policing of IDP camps. The UN was not willing to take on powers of arrest and detention, the rebels had no policing capabilities, and Sudanese police could not operate inside the camps because they were not trusted by the displaced. The only solution was a 'community police force' drawn from the IDPs themselves and trained by international civilian police.

General Ismat was a professional military officer to the core. If confronted, he fought back; if asked to find a solution to a problem, he looked for it. Ismat was a decent and practical man and, like most regular officers, he disliked the Janjawiid. He knew the havoc that Khartoum's military strategy had unleashed and wanted practical measures to control the militia and police the camps. But his political masters did not. On more than one occasion after he backtracked, he later said he had been misunderstood. The mediators smiled and accepted, realizing that his superiors had overruled him. But they also knew that Ismat's instructions were to stay at the talks come what may, and that his aim was to produce a working agreement. So the security team pressed on, exploring territory far behind Majzoub's red lines and bringing into their blueprint – most infuriatingly, for Khartoum – the reform of paramilitaries, including Musa Hilal's Border Intelligence Brigade, and the involvement of an international security advisory team to oversee the security arrangements.

On the instructions of the US delegation, which was handling the proposal of transitioning AMIS to the UN, the ceasefire text referred to 'AMIS' throughout. There was no mention of the UN. The AU's lawyers explained that when the UN Security Council authorized a handover to the UN, any references to AMIS would automatically be transferred to refer to the new UN force. However, as the draft text increased the administrative, logistical and reporting burdens on the peacekeepers, doubts grew among the mediators about whether the security plan was feasible for any force. The AMIS force commander, General Collins Ihikere, spent a month in Abuja with two staff officers transferring the maps to his laptop and making estimates for the force size needed. But the AU's security advisers worried that it could all go terribly wrong unless the security text was tested against the realities of the field. General Ismat also demanded that the AU send a mission to verify the locations of the different forces on the ground before an agreement was finalized – he didn't want to repeat the error of the N'Djamena ceasefire. The Americans promised a mission to do the mapping immediately after a deal was signed.

Despite the signs that Ali Osman's position was weakening with respect to his rivals, including Majzoub, the AU and the US put great store in the ability of the vice-president to snatch a deal. It had been Ali Osman's face-to-face talks with Garang in late 2003 that had provided the breakthrough in the Naivasha talks, and the mediators hoped he would do the same for Darfur. Along with a high-powered delegation that included the security chief Salah Gosh, Ali Osman arrived in Abuja on 7 April. There was a keen sense of anticipation. Surely there would be a breakthrough. But where, and how?

Ali Osman met privately with the two SLM leaders. After his first meeting with Abdel Wahid, in which the two discussed ideals of democracy and pluralism, Ali Osman asked, 'Why are we fighting this man?' They agreed on most points. Ali Osman's side insists that they eventually made a deal, but didn't announce it because they wanted to bring the others on board first. Abdel Wahid insists not.

> I was very optimistic at first, but I got an impression Ali Osman was not powerful. He offered me the job Minni [now] has. But he offered nothing on the Janjawiid. Security is everything. Then we can come to power-sharing and wealth-sharing. Everything collapsed because they wouldn't give us a very clear plan with a timeframe. They think security is how many armed men are to be integrated [into the government's forces]. For me that is not the issue. It is the last issue.[16]

The Americans were present for all but one of Ali Osman's meetings with Minawi and quickly realized that Minawi was most concerned with his own gains in any deal. He wanted the rank of general for himself and Juma Hagar – a demand on which the Sudanese army command choked. Ali Osman did not meet Khalil – his forces were busy defending N'Djamena for Deby.

Ali Osman stayed in Abuja for three fruitless weeks. Although he extended his stay twice, he was unable to get an agreement. As

Abdel Wahid had realized, less unfocused than he often appeared to be, the vice-president's position was not secure enough for him to stay on to explore bold compromises that might have led to a breakthrough. Ali Osman's last morning in Abuja on 1 May was downbeat and confused. Members of his delegation argued over breakfast as to whether it was worth staying. Salah Gosh and the head of the SPLM delegation, Yasir Arman, were among those who advocated making one final effort focused on Minawi. Others were sceptical, saying that Minawi was neither strong nor strategic enough to cut a deal. Abdel Wahid's signature was taken for granted. The Sudanese said he had assured Ali Osman and President Obasanjo that he would sign. The top job was earmarked for him. What more could he want, they said?

Forcing the peace

With neither Majzoub nor Ali Osman managing to cut a deal, Salim moved to the 'Plan B' he had been preparing since early March: to put on the table a set of proposals covering all contentious issues as a basis for further negotiation. The eighty-seven-page document was presented to the delegations in English on 25 April and a plenary was called immediately, before the Arabic text was ready. It caused uproar in the armed movements, whose delegates accused Ambassador Dinka of backtracking without warning. Some of Abdel Wahid's aides, including his power-sharing negotiator Ibrahim Madibu, a model of reason and restraint, were visibly furious. The discussions they had had before February had led them to believe that power in Darfur would be shared evenly between the government and the movements. What they had here was 50 per cent for the NCP and 50 per cent shared among all others, including independents – in effect, a guarantee of working majorities for the NCP. On top of this, the Transitional Darfur Regional Authority wasn't as strong as they had hoped it would be. All the posts below state level, including the powerful commissioners who ran local government, remained as they were – on Majzoub's self-serving assertion that they were civil servants, not party members. The appointment of tribal chiefs was passed over, leaving them hostage to a government which continued to have the power to hire and fire.

On the evening of 25 April, Majzoub played a blinder. He was filmed by Sudanese TV in the plenary session holding the document in front of his chest and saying 'We have the Darfur Peace Agreement'. He told Salim that he intended to initial the text that evening, despite the fact that in two key places – the number of rebel fighters to be integrated into the army, and the government downpayment into the compensation fund – the document merely had 'X'.

Salim was dismayed. This wasn't the plan at all. He managed to forestall Majzoub and avoided receiving him in the mediation office to initial the document. But it was clear that the strategy for closing the deal was going seriously awry. Salim had hoped for a final round of bargaining in which the movements might yield some ground on those proposals most favourable to them in return for the government making concessions elsewhere. Majzoub had killed that. And by signing up to some provisions in the security arrangements that he had rejected earlier, including the downsizing of all paramilitaries in Darfur under the supervision of an official appointed by the rebels, he had shown that his talk of red lines was bluff.

No one had expected all the parties to agree at the same time. Ten months earlier, the Declaration of Principles had been signed first by JEM, which had then pressed the SLA into a last-minute agreement.[17] The mediators wanted to get the agreement of Abdel Wahid, whom they considered the most unpredictable, first. They thought the US would then be able to pressure Minawi, and finally the government, into signing. But Majzoub had turned the tables. On previous occasions he had taken a week to respond to any mediation paper. By agreeing to sign on this occasion within a few hours of seeing the proposals, he raised suspicions that he had known them in advance and considered them good for the government.

With the deadline just five days away, the crisis was acute. When Salim announced a new deadline of 30 April, in line with the recommendation of the UN Security Council, few took it seriously. Several of the mediation team even took breaks in April, confident that negotiations would continue into late May or June as thorough discussion of the issues required. But this deadline was serious – and completely unworkable. For months the talks had resembled a wagon with a wobbly wheel, lurching from one rut to the next. Now, suddenly, they were about to become jet-propelled. In March, the rebels had taken a week to study and respond to the ceasefire text once it was available in Arabic. How could they read, discuss and come to a position on a document that was five times as long in just five days, with only two days to study an Arabic translation that was littered with errors, each of which needed an explanation? They couldn't. They suspected a trap, and they said no. Salim proposed to 'stop the clock' while Deputy Secretary Zoellick and a high-level American team flew in from Washington DC and President Obasanjo freed up his schedule. This was 'Plan C', a salvage operation. 'My boss is not excited about this trip,' wrote one of Zoellick's aides as they packed their bags to leave.

Zoellick arrived on 2 May, followed soon after by Britain's secretary of state for international development Hilary Benn, Canada's UN ambassador John Rock and the European Union envoy for Sudan Pekka Haavisto. Between them they composed a quartet of high-level negotiators intent on 'enhancing' the draft AU text in such a way that Abdel Wahid and Minawi would sign and the government would stay on board. They consulted JEM, but doubted there would be agreement from Khalil Ibrahim given his Chadian involvement.

In three days of intensive shuttling between the parties with revisions to the text, Zoellick focused on security arrangements, particularly the numbers of rebel fighters to be integrated into the army. He replaced the AU's 'X' with a number – 8,000 – and strengthened the details for controlling and disarming the Janjawiid, imposing a deadline of five months for the militias to be confined to specified areas and disarmed. Majzoub and General Ismat al Zain argued each point. They insisted that 5,000 was the maximum number of SLA troops they could absorb in the army and Popular Defence Forces, saying that the total rebel forces in the field numbered scarcely more than this.[18] As the US and Sudan government teams argued late into the night of 2 May, Sudanese generals paced up and down outside the Chida Hotel, accosting mediators to ask, 'What are the Americans really after?' Why, they wondered, did the Americans want so many of Minawi's people in the Sudanese army? And in such senior positions, right up to general and brigadier! They pushed back hard, with success: the figure was reduced to 5,000 to be integrated into the army, with 3,000 given unspecified non-military training.

Hilary Benn's small British team set to work enhancing the power-sharing provisions to make them more acceptable to the movements. Theirs was an even tougher task. The rebels' objections were much more far-reaching, and the government's position was that it had already accepted an agreement – the draft Majzoub had flaunted on television. Might he reject an 'enhanced' agreement altogether? In reality, Majzoub's strategy was bluff – his political future depended on returning to Khartoum with a deal – but he managed to convince the AU and the internationals that he had the option of saying no. The British added in a quota of local commissioners and their deputies to be given to the movements,[19] increased the powers of the senior assistant to the president, the most senior position awarded to the Darfurian movements, and tried to shift the allocation of state-level posts back towards parity. Majzoub objected to each concession – and even attempted to sneak an extra NCP nominee into each state assembly.

On wealth-sharing, Majzoub offered a downpayment of $30 million into the compensation fund. None of the international team imagined that this would become the problem that it eventually did. It was a first contribution, not a ceiling. But, based on expansive statements by Abdel Wahid, displaced families were hoping for amounts up to $1,000 each.[20] To deliver, Abdel Wahid needed at least $100 million.

Presented with the revised text on 3 May, the movements'

leaders seemed satisfied with the security arrangements, but still objected to the power-sharing proposals. More revisions were made and on 4 May, when Minawi told Zoellick he was satisfied, the Americans were ready to proceed. Obasanjo reported that he had Abdel Wahid's promise of a signature on a 'fair' agreement, and Salim and others considered this a fifty-fifty chance. Attention turned to procedure: if the parties still would not sit down together, how was the deal to be concluded? It was decided to hold a session in the presidential villa as the midnight deadline approached that night, asking the rebels first whether they agreed and then bringing in the government.[21]

President Obasanjo chaired the meeting and orchestrated the questioning of the three rebel leaders. For six hours, starting at 11.15 p.m., the same question was posed to Minawi, Abdel Wahid and Khalil: 'Will you sign the Darfur Peace Agreement?' Since Minawi's agreement was assumed, he was summoned first. But while he accepted the revised security arrangements – as did Abdel Wahid, while even Khalil told the mediators that night that he found them 'mostly acceptable'[22] – Minawi surprised the mediators by rejecting the document because of its power-sharing provisions. He wanted parity of representation at the level of the Darfur states. Zoellick was unsympathetic. 'I cannot believe that you are dropping peace for a few more seats.' Abdel Wahid had the same demands, plus increased compensation, and the response was the same. 'Don't overlook what you have gained. Do not drop peace for these minor issues.' Khalil was defiantly rejectionist, saying, 'I cannot sign. The document needs radical modifications.' Obasanjo shouted at him, 'You are utterly irresponsible. What the hell are you saying?' And then, 'JEM, you can go!'

Obasanjo and Zoellick cajoled, threatened and promised. The Nigerian president threatened that Darfur would be forgotten. America's deputy secretary of state told Abdel Wahid, 'If you pass up this historic opportunity, to whom do you intend to turn? If you pass this up you will remain victims for ever.' He warned that there would be 'accountability for actions' before the UN Security Council. Zoellick read out letters from President Bush promising to 'strongly support' implementing the accord and to 'insist on holding accountable all those who are not supporting the implementation'. Similar letters were written for Khalil and President Bashir. Khalil's was never handed over. Minawi wavered, but still did not agree; he seemed to accept the argument of Zoellick and Benn that representation at the state level was a 'detail', but demanded more time to get his commanders' consent. Having been let down once already during the night, Zoellick insisted on a positive outcome, to which Minawi said, 'Inshallah there is no deception we shall come at the time agreed upon with all blessing.' Obasanjo hesitated, then commented that the answer was 'partly political and partly divine, half carnal and half spiritual. Minni, we take that.' He granted Minawi an extension until 9 a.m. and summoned Abdel Wahid back.

Abdel Wahid returned to the hall at 4.25 a.m., his position unchanged. He said his commanders and IDP camp representatives were insisting 'we must include our negotiating platform, our just negotiating platform'. A majority of his delegates in Abuja were in favour of signing. Several of them told mediators that Abdel Wahid had decided to sign, pending only a phone call from his 'chief adviser', Ahmed Mohamadein Abdalla, who was in Canada at the time. They quoted Mohamadein as saying: 'Hold on, there will be developments in our favour.' Abdel Wahid strenuously denies this. What is not in question is that, on returning to the negotiating session, Abdel Wahid demanded 'an American and British guarantee for implementation like in Bosnia'. Zoellick was infuriated. 'I don't know what more you want than a statement by the president of the United States that I will strongly support the implementation of the peace accord' – a promise that must have rung very hollow to the SLA chairman after the non-implementation of all previous agreements. Zoellick offered support for making the SLM into a political party and concluded, 'What more can I give?' What Abdel Wahid wanted, and Zoellick couldn't give, was NATO troops. The *Washington Post* had recently reported that the Bush administration had 'settled on the idea of sending up to several hundred NATO advisers to help bolster AMIS'.[23] Abdel Wahid wasn't going to accept any second-best security guarantees. Obasanjo concluded the session with Abdel Wahid by saying, 'You are throwing away your chance for compensation, for power-sharing ... If you win the elections you will be in charge. You want to throw that overboard. That I cannot regard as responsibility. The story can be told one day and you cannot hide it ... We shall be here at nine. If you want to see us, we will see you. Otherwise au revoir.' It was a few minutes before 5 a.m.

Minawi returned to the negotiating hall at nine o'clock as requested, looking exhausted and expressionless. He told Obasanjo, 'We have accepted the document with important reservations concerning power.' There was a pause as Obasanjo and others realized that 'objections' had become 'reservations', and Minawi would sign. Minawi couldn't bring himself to speak the name of Abdel Wahid, but did say that no agreement would work without the other movements, and asked for more time to 'persuade our brothers to sign'. He was not granted it.

Majzoub and his delegation had spent the whole night waiting. for their turn. Their minds had long ago been made up: they would accept, but cite major reservations. Majzoub spelled out his reservations – all of them in security arrangements, which he considered detrimental to the government – and then said he would sign. 'If you feel that the amended document should remain as it is, there is no reason for us to object. We shall accept and cooperate in the implementation.' There were two signatories, and a deal of sorts. Obasanjo set the signing ceremony for 1 p.m., an hour and a half away, waving aside Majzoub's request for a delay so that Bashir himself could fly in for the consummation of the peace.

Those seeking certainty will not find it in Sudanese politics – or Nigerian communications. Abdul Mohammed, one of the mediation advisers, had remarked, 'If you want to see what corruption does to a country, come to Nigeria.' And indeed, many times over the course of the previous months, inefficiency stemming from corruption had created logistical and communication problems that disrupted the negotiations. In the few final days, even the simplest communications kept breaking down as telephone calls – sometimes just to locate a negotiator, or fix an appointment – became problematic: most of the scratch cards for mobile phones came with most of their air time used up, stolen before sale. At this crucial juncture, too, the Chida International proved unable to print even five copies of the DPA. A fuse blew and no electrician was on hand to make repairs. So the signing ceremony was put on hold.

As 1 p.m. approached, Majzoub and his delegates took their seats in the hall. Minawi was meeting his commanders in a side room. Abdel Wahid strode down the driveway towards the waiting press corps. Intercepted a few yards short, he was confronted by Obasanjo, who sprang into the posture of a boxer. 'You let me down!' he said, his fist in Abdel Wahid's face. 'You are our baba [father],' said Abdel Wahid, rocking back on his heels, 'not just the baba of Nigeria but the baba of Darfur, of all of Africa. But I am demanding the rights for our people ...' Obasanjo seized him by the collar and pulled him into a side room. 'I need to talk to you, boy!' For more than two hours, Obasanjo, Zoellick and Benn pressed Abdel Wahid to sign. Without stronger guarantees, he refused – and left. His chief negotiator, Abdel Rahman Musa, assembled thirteen delegates who were determined to find a way of signing the agreement. Minawi also vanished for an hour after receiving the news that his brother had been killed in fighting that morning, and the American delegation was near to panic as they tried to locate him. When they found him, they insisted that he stay in the villa and not return to the hotel to meet his commanders who, they feared, would hold him hostage. Majzoub and his delegation sat unmoving in the hall as if to say, 'We are here, but where are the rebels?'

Minawi reappeared at 5.30 p.m. He looked haggard and apprehensive. Juma Mohamed Hagar was next to him, glowering in his fatigues. Obasanjo spoke: 'Will you attach your signature?' He paused. 'Unless the right spirit is there this document is not worth the paper it is written on ... This is a defining moment in the history of Darfur.' He called on Majzoub and Minawi to come forward. The copies of the DPA were ready for signature and most dignitaries were present. Jan Pronk had arrived late in the morning; Alpha Konaré had already left to catch his plane. The two men came forward to sign. It was a joyless climax. Majzoub waited for Minawi to sign before he bent down to do the same. A moment of drama was injected into the proceedings only when Abdel Rahman Musa and his group burst into the hall and demanded the chance to sign too, causing Majzoub, at last, to smile.

Obituary on Abuja

Majzoub lost his smile. The next day, for the first and only time during the Abuja talks, he looked uncertain of himself. He had cornered himself into signing a deal with the rebel leader whom Khartoum least desired to have on its side. What Khartoum wanted was an alliance with Abdel Wahid to forge a winning electoral base for itself in 2009. But despite the split in Abdel Wahid's group, most Fur were united in opposition to the DPA. Worst of all, the agreement was bringing about the Darfur Arabs' greatest fear: a Zaghawa with power over Darfur. General Abdalla Safi al Nur expressed the Arabs' public line on that day: 'Minni fought us 100 per cent. Now he must make peace with us 100 per cent.' But even as a dozen Darfurian Arab chiefs waved their sticks in celebration at the signing, some were muttering 'betrayal'.

The tragedy of the Abuja talks was that Abdel Wahid wanted to end the war and get people back to their homes, not least for his prestige and authority as the now-disputed SLA chairman. Khartoum wanted a peace deal with Abdel Wahid for its international legitimacy and electoral success in 2009. But the AU failed to broker the marriage. The Americans especially came to put their store on Minawi, describing him in public as the most powerful rebel leader and in private as businesslike and straightforward – everything Abdel Wahid wasn't, they said. Seeing the preference for his arch-rival, Abdel Wahid – already a difficult man – became frustrated and petulant, and less and less able to give clear and convincing expression to his genuine concerns. The DPA was broken-limbed from the moment that Abdel Wahid refused to sign.

The DPA was an agreement built on sand. As the Abuja talks ended, the warring parties did not trust each other enough even to sit at the same table and talk to each other. A fundamental misunderstanding was never addressed: what was the DPA *for*? The international community saw it primarily as a buttress to the main event – the Comprehensive Peace Agreement – and a way of bringing Darfur into the process of national democratic transformation. This was why the internationals considered the power-sharing provisions less important; these were seen as a *transitional* arrangement until elections, for a maximum of three years. The rebel leaders saw a peace agreement as a means of addressing the root causes of the war by resolving the *permanent* status of Darfur. They wanted something that gave Darfur many of the same rights and guarantees as the South, including its own government and its own army for the interim. The government wanted a deal to end its international ostracism, confident that it could discard later the parts it most disliked. As Majzoub put it on 5 May, 'Discrepancies will be remedied.'

Without trust, guarantees became the key. Abdel Wahid looked for political guarantees for the devolution of political power and resources in Darfur, and didn't find what he wanted in the DPA. The text's rollback from parity of representation was too much to swallow, and he wasn't satisfied with the carrot of elections that might never take place, fearing that even if they did, they would not be free and fair without strong, sustained international pressure. The rebels' strongest card in the DPA, on paper, was control over the reform of all Darfur's paramilitaries, but Abdel Wahid feared that the security arrangements would be controlled by Minawi and the government, neither of whom he trusted. Without his central demand – an autonomous Darfur region with veto powers in Khartoum – Abdel Wahid looked for strong international guarantees. With NATO's armies already spread thin, in Afghanistan and the Balkans, and the US isolated internationally by its war in Iraq, it was a futile quest.

Returning to the Chida Hotel late on 5 May, Sam Ibok admitted that more could have been done to get Abdel Wahid on board. 'We could have given him the region,' he said. Salim was exasperated with Abdel Wahid and urged all the international diplomats in Abuja to shun him. But at Ibok's insistence he kept the door open for Abdel Wahid, announcing that the DPA would remain open for signature until the AU Peace and Security Council convened on 16 May. The vast majority of rebel delegates left Abuja. But Abdel Wahid and his team remained behind, believing the DPA could be made acceptable with relatively minor modifications, and for the next few days Abdel Wahid focused on getting a 'supplementary agreement' which would address his remaining issues. Salim was insistent that the most that could be offered was AU assistance in the implementation of the deal. The Americans feared that even minor tampering with the text would unravel the whole agreement and lose Minawi. Majzoub had regained his composure and demanded that Abdel Wahid sign first and renegotiate later.

At this critical juncture, the political terrain shifted. The DPA had been sprung on Darfurians without consultation. No one had attempted to explain the agreement to them, and none of them had read it. All they knew was that their leader had refused to sign and the AU was asking them to forfeit their political demands: a single autonomous region for Darfur and the vice-presidency in Khartoum. Abdel Wahid became a hero, his defiance celebrated in demonstrations in IDP camps across Darfur even while he continued to seek a solution out of the limelight, for once. One of the IDPs' main complaints was the reported absence of individual compensation – even though this was conceded, in detail, in fourteen paragraphs, one of which provided for 'interim awards of monetary compensation without proceeding to a full hearing of the claim ...' A barrage of activist criticism of the DPA followed. 'We're asked by the Abuja agreement to forget how many of these militia murderers have already been incorporated into the various military and security services in Darfur,' thundered the activist Eric Reeves, apparently unaware that the DPA not only reduced government forces but also government paramilitaries, under the control of a rebel commander and an international team of security advisers. The agreement, Reeves said, was 'disgraceful'. It put 'hundreds of thousands of lives at risk'.

Unceremoniously ejected from the Chida Hotel when the AU stopped paying their bills, Abdel Wahid and his team had moved into a small, shabby, cockroach-infested hotel, and it was in these miserable surroundings that the final drama of Abuja was played out. Abdel Wahid veered between exuberance, when he heard that the deadline for signing the DPA had been extended, and amused defiance when he listened to radio reports of demonstrations in which displaced people shouted 'Abdel Wahid, *shab wahid*' – Abdel Wahid, one people! As the demonstrations spread from camp to camp, the founder of the SLM sensed both a powerful surge of popular sentiment and a new political opportunity for himself. His position hardened when his attempts to salvage the agreement were rebuffed. The leader became a follower. 'I can sign,' he said, 'but I can't take my people. I have no magic wand.' Abdel Wahid had spent six long months in Abuja without a break – longer than any other delegate – and had vowed to leave only when he had a peace agreement in his hands. On 17 May, as he packed his bags to leave the city empty-handed, he reflected,

> If they give me twenty-four hours or twenty-four days or twenty-four years I will not sign ... If the whole world has come – and this is exactly what happened – and tells me to sign, I will not sign. In this document there is no guarantee that the people will return to their original homes, village by village, valley by valley. They want our people to remain in poverty, to remain open to attack again when the international troops leave. This is no solution. This agreement gives them nothing, they are like slaves. Before we started this revolution the people were living in their villages ... at the minimum I must be able to take them back to their villages, before we even begin to go ahead.

The last hopes of an agreement that might possibly be made

to work – if the North–South agreement held and international attention remained focused on Darfur – were fading in the gloom of the tawdry rooms of a downmarket Nigerian hotel. Some in Abdel Wahid's team were close to tears. Without Abdel Wahid, and without a Darfur Peace Agreement, the prospects for peace and democracy in Sudan as a whole had dimmed. The next few years would be, as tribal leaders visiting Abuja in the final stages of the talks had warned they would be, 'a war of all against all'.

As Abdel Wahid departed from Abuja, the AU extended for a second time, to 31 May, the deadline for him to sign the DPA. Just days before the deadline expired, SPLM leader Salva Kiir invited Abdel Wahid to South Sudan to discuss a pact that could lead to him joining the peace. At first he agreed. But senior SPLM figures regarded the Darfurians as wayward sons who could be brought into line simply by knocking their heads together, and their behaviour now reflected this: without telling or consulting Abdel Wahid, they also invited some of his most bitter critics in the movement. He was furious, and performed an about-turn. 'I am the chairman of the SLA and I am the person who will decide who is there or not. These people are creating fractions.'[24] On 29 May, feeling disregarded by the Americans and disrespected by the SPLA, Abdel Wahid gave a vote of no-confidence in the peace brokers – the representatives of the AU, EU and Norway who were trying to facilitate his travel to South Sudan. He received them in his flat in the middle-class suburb of Lavington. 'Remember these words,' he said. 'All of you, the international community, will create big chaos in Darfur, endless fighting, endless suffering, endless chaos.' When next he was seen, it was in Asmara, in the company of Khalil Ibrahim.

9 | Endless chaos

On the evening of 5 May 2006, Minni Minawi looked isolated and apprehensive – as if he had just signed his own death warrant rather than an acclaimed peace treaty. Eighty days later, he shook the hand of President Bush in the Oval Office, smiling for the cameras. Two weeks after that, he was appointed Senior Assistant to the President, on paper the fourth most powerful man in Sudan, and took possession of an office in the Republican Palace just across the lawn from Omar al Bashir's. His immediate neighbour was Nafie Ali Nafie, Assistant to the President, in theory his junior but in practice a man with infinitely more power than he had. There was no fanfare. Minawi's elevation to the five-man presidency[1] was little more than decoration; his windowless office, in the months that followed, little better than a holding cell.

By the time he arrived in Khartoum to claim his prize, the DPA's sole rebel signatory had lost his North Darfur tribal heartland and power base. The slow but steady erosion of support that had been afflicting him had accelerated with the Haskanita conference of November 2005, and after he signed the DPA the few remaining areas he controlled in North Darfur fell like dominos, notwithstanding government support. On 12 July, in the first serious international criticism of him, the UN's humanitarian chief, Jan Egeland, said 'indiscriminate killings, mass rape, beatings, looting and the burning of villages' by his faction had displaced 8,000 civilians in ten days. But Minawi's aggressiveness failed to stop his rout. Muzbat, the administrative centre of his own Ila Digen clan, fell on 14 July. As Minawi prepared to fly to the US on 20 July, he lost Oriri, despite the gift of government weapons and trainers flown in to instruct his men in their use.[2] On 6 August, the day he arrived in Khartoum, he lost another toehold: Sayyah. His men were forced back upon their South Darfur strongholds,

Muhajiriya and Gereida, where they were soon being accused of abuses including rape, torture and summary executions.[3]

Thirteen months earlier, John Garang had entered Khartoum as a hero. The largest crowds ever seen in the capital turned out to roar their approval of a man who had fought four successive governments over more than twenty years. Onlookers climbed the floodlight towers of the stadium to catch a glimpse of the guerrilla-turned-statesman, whose vision of a 'New Sudan' had kept alive the dreams of millions all over the country. Minawi had been scheduled to arrive in Khartoum on 5 August, but postponed his journey as Bashir hesitated to issue the decree formalizing his appointment as Senior Assistant. The DPA allowed the movements to put forward three names for consideration, and a Zaghawa it considered little more than a hoodlum was the government's least-favoured option. But Minawi and his men insisted that he be the only candidate, and Bashir reluctantly concurred. By this time the peace accord was looking more like an alliance of military opportunity, and part of the deal was expelling the groups that had refused to sign from the AU-chaired Ceasefire Commission and Joint Commission, the bodies that handled all the key security issues.

Thousands of policemen and soldiers, backed by rooftop snipers, were stationed along the avenue from Khartoum airport to the Republican Palace in the expectation that Minawi's arrival would generate public protest, as had attempts to take the DPA to Darfur's displaced camps. But in the event, the mood of the day was indifference. On 5 August, only a few hundred people, mostly schoolchildren and students, gathered in Khartoum's Green Square to greet Minawi. When he finally appeared twenty-four hours later, the government organized no welcome and the few who turned out on the airport road were there to protest against him. Minawi arrived in Khartoum a much-diminished figure.[4]

'We can kill anyone who is against this agreement'

Nothing in Minawi's past suggested that he would one day, still in his mid-thirties, become the highest-ranked Darfurian in Sudan since the Khalifa Abdullahi at the close of the nineteenth century. Not only was he, in the words of his peers, 'semi-uneducated', but 'the only time he ever worked', according to Sherif Harir, was three months spent teaching in the primary school of the little village of Boba, near Furawiya, before he left Darfur for Nigeria. Many times during the Darfur war, observers predicted that Minawi would not survive. He surely had too many enemies and too bad a human rights record to be acceptable either to Darfurians or to the international community. But he was given prominence by the ineptitude of Abdel Wahid and his failure to consolidate the SLM as a political organization, and by the hard logic of peace talks: those who have fought most brutally are often cut the sweetest deals. And Minawi was no fool when it came to matters of survival: he invested considerable time and energy in charming key US diplomats, who were flattered by his enquiries after their health and their families, found him a 'fast learner' and argued his corner in State Department discussions on how to tackle Darfur.

On becoming the sole rebel signatory of the DPA, despised in Khartoum and rejected in Darfur, Minawi embraced the Americans, travelling with American minders and consulting them daily. His weakness and abuses became too flagrant for even his admirers to ignore, but the US was committed to the DPA, which President Bush had demanded and endorsed, and which Zoellick had signed as a witness and guarantor. As a legal document, the DPA was held in higher regard in the State Department than in Khartoum – not least because it remained the basis on which the UN could send troops to Darfur. America was stuck with Minawi, and his apologists hid behind the fig leaf of 'there are no angels', even as they acknowledged that 'he has no support. If we don't support him, he's dead.'[5]

Minawi quickly reverted to type. On past record, President Bashir's first instinct would have been to seize the moment militarily and unleash the army, but his troops weren't ready and the international spotlight was on him, so he held back. As the US put the AU under pressure to challenge the non-signatories, with Zoellick asserting publicly that 'the AU would confront with force any party that tries to weaken or foil the agreement',[6] Khartoum helped Minawi try to impose the DPA in the only way he knew – by force.

Determined to make the agreement work, the AU foolishly became a partner in this project. The DPA had been written in anticipation that all the rebel movements would join, and included provisions for the AU to provide technical assistance, supplies and logistics to the rebels once they had signed. In the event, AMIS's fidelity to this particular element of the agreement, while disregarding others, put it on one side of a continuing war. By August, the AU had become 'the enemy' of the non-signatories, its men and its vehicles as much a target as the government's, for several months.[7]

The AU began its cooperation with Minawi by flying his chief of staff and close relative, Arko Suleiman Dhahia Domay, to the village of Bir Maza, in the heart of the territory controlled by the rebel commanders who had rejected the DPA, known as the 'non-signatories'. Here, on 20 May, Arko Suleiman waved his pistol in the air and told a crowd of hundreds summoned from villages all around: 'We can kill anyone who is against this agreement!'[8] One of those who was against it, wanting better compensation and stronger security guarantees for the displaced, was Suleiman Jamous, a long-time critic of Minawi's abuses who had first opposed the Haskanita conference and then attempted to challenge Minawi in the vote for 'chairman'. Arko Suleiman promptly arrested him. When a delegation of seventeen villagers visited Minawi's camp to enquire about Jamous, they too were arrested. Arko Suleiman told them, 'I can shoot Jamous and sodomize any of you.' The group was then made to hand over knives and *hijabs* (protective talismans that usually contain Quranic verses). They were stripped naked, bound and beaten for five hours. Three were paraded, still naked, around Bir Maza in a pick-up truck.[9] Photographs taken after their release showed rope marks and cigarette burns.

Minawi's violence spread. In the Korma area, a predominantly Fur and Tunjur area whose control had been contested ever since

Zaghawa fighters seized it in March 2006, Minawi's forces killed seventy-two people in the first week of July in a five-day orgy of burning, raping and looting. Villagers were told they were being punished for opposing the DPA. A survivor in the village of Deker, where at least fifty-eight non-combatants died, reported seeing men in police and army uniform alongside Minawi's fighters.[10] Amnesty International said the ferocity of the killing and looting had led local people to call Minawi's men 'Janjawiid 2'.[11] The AU-chaired Ceasefire Commission did not meet to hear any complaints. It was deadlocked, with Khartoum and Minawi insisting that its task was only to implement the DPA's security arrangements, no longer to represent all the parties and investigate and adjudicate reports of ceasefire violations. On 20 July, AU officials met Jar al Nabi Abdel Karim, the military spokesman of G19, in Amarai, and threatened the non-signatories with sanctions. The rift was sealed. 'AU planes supported Minni in Bir Maza and Kulkul, taking his wounded away,' Jar al Nabi said later. 'AU cars took petrol to Minni. They helicoptered his men to Oriri with weapons in big boxes. I told them, "there can be no cooperation with the AU because the AU is fighting us. The AU has become our enemy."'[12]

Despite being ready to accept 'declarations of commitment' to the DPA by splinter groups from SLA–Abdel Wahid and JEM, the AU refused to recognize that the SLA non-signatories who had ousted Minawi had what he lacked – popular support, including from the Native Administration chiefs whom Minawi had bullied, imprisoned and even killed. One of the first things G19 leaders did on driving Minawi's forces out of North Darfur was to mend relations with the Native Administration, consulting with chiefs on the way forward and asking them to reopen the traditional courts Minawi had replaced with 'revolutionary' courts, even for cases involving civilians.

'The SLA is good now,' Omda Hamid Manna, kidnapped and tortured by Minawi's men in 2003 and held to ransom for 25 million Sudanese pounds, said in March 2006. 'Minni denied us our rights. His men took our animals and collected our money. They took food aid from civilians. No one protested. If you protested, you were killed or beaten. Today the SLA respects our rights. There is a very big difference with the days of Minni.'[13] Other chiefs echoed these sentiments. Minawi's SLA 'treated civilians very badly', said Omda Yousif Dili of Bir Maza, who worked with G19 leaders to protect the families of Minawi's commanders after they fled fom Bir Maza in July 2006, leaving their wives and children behind. 'They took money and animals at the wells, money from shops in the market and two to three sheep a month [from herders]. They took oil, sugar and beans from the WFP store. Every commander ate a sheep a day. After signing the peace, they took sixty young men from this area at gunpoint for training in Atroun,' on the Libyan border.[14]

Abuses such as these led to a wave of popular reaction against Minawi and speeded the expulsion of his forces from most of North Darfur. When the security mediators drew up their maps in Abuja, Minawi had marked virtually everywhere north of Kutum as being under his control, refusing to acknowledge that anyone else had any power outside Anka, Jar al Nabi's home village. Three months later, commanders moving in the orbit of G19 controlled it all. 'It was easy because we have a mission, a political vision against injustice and marginalization,' said Meidob commander Suleiman Marajan. 'Minni Minawi has no mission. I have good relations with my people. Even if I have only ten soldiers I can last long in Darfur because I have my people. But Minni Minawi is not going anywhere. Without the sea, the fish will die.'[15] Part of the non-signatories' mission was building local peace. 'Peace with Arabs is not only possible. It is a must,' said Abunduluk, the young man who helped destroy the government's planes in al Fasher in 2003. 'Darfur is for Darfurians. Not all the Arabs are bad. No tribe can destroy a tribe.'[16]

Minawi's unpopularity in Darfur was soon reflected in government-controlled areas that had no previous experience of rebel authority. 'Minawi's troops are coming to IDP camps in al Fasher threatening civilians and looting their property,' a human rights activist warned in August, a few days before Minawi ended his first visit to the state capital and travelled to Khartoum. 'Many IDPs are leaving such camps to other areas where there are no Minawi men. They went into a school in Zamzam camp and beat a female teacher. No one controls them. They are becoming bandits in the town. In al Fasher itself, they are drunk and drugged and living in the prostitutes' area, unfortunately driving AMIS cars ...'[17] Much the same was true in Khartoum over the following months. The SLA office in the Muhandiseen district of Omdurman became an area to avoid due to frequent disturbances and on 26 March 2007, ten policemen and three SLA members were killed in a shootout there. Drivers along the Nile Avenue, where everyday civilian traffic passes in front of the palace gates, were frequently terrified by Minawi's gun-toting escort of desert warfare-style technicals.

'What peace are you talking about?'

By the time the DPA was signed, about one-third of Darfur's population was displaced, living in camps or towns. The initial trauma of murderous attacks had given way to a life of unending internal exile in wretched slums. When an AU team visited the camps in 2007, it heard messages of anger and hopelessness. 'We were never anything but poor, but at least [in our villages] we had dignity. Here we have no dignity, we are not living like human beings.'[18] Rations from the World Food Programme sustained life in the camps, where people resorted to the kinds of menial livelihoods that their parents would have despised and pursued only in the most desperate famine years – working for a pittance as day labourers on building sites or as domestic maids. Camps provided little protection from violence. Inside the camps there were inter-tribal fights, gang wars and rape, and on the perimeters, or when people ventured into the rural areas, a constant threat of attack by militiamen and bandits.

Challenging the old rural order, a new hierarchy of camp leaders sprang up, whose old-fashioned title 'sheikh' belied the fact that their power base was different and new. Usually, the camp sheikhs were those who had established the first shelters and organized the first relief distributions. Most of the old rural aristocracy had fled to the towns, where they or their close families owned houses, often forfeiting the trust of their destitute and displaced tribespeople. One group of camp leaders, who requested anonymity, said, 'We have lost confidence in the Native Administration. Ninety per cent of them are NCP, 90 per cent didn't come to the camps with us – or when they come, they just come to give us government propaganda.'[19] Stripped of the autonomy they so valued, desperately impoverished, and living with constant insecurity, the camp residents sought a new brand of leaders able to articulate their sense of anger and powerlessness. Like the Native Administration leaders they belittled, the new leaders utilized their control over resources to win support, often becoming substantial merchants and power brokers themselves. As the larger camps like Kalma grew into mini-cities, where government officials and policemen feared to tread, the displaced populations emerged as powerful political forces.

The leaders of Darfur's displaced have no troops, but they do command the attention of the media and visiting politicians. Camp leaders across the region use mobile phones and *Thurayas* to hold regular telephone conferences, to exchange news and decide their strategies. Hundreds of foreign dignitaries and journalists have visited the most accessible camps near Darfur's main cities, and the camp representatives have become well practised at receiving them and conveying their message within the few minutes that special envoys grant them. Despite the ease of access to the camps, it was only a year after the signing of the DPA that the AU itself organized its first extensive consultations with IDPs, as part of the 'preparatory consultations' for the Darfur–Darfur Dialogue and Consultation, a process of involving Darfurian communities in peacemaking. The AU team was politely received, notwithstanding the camps' sometimes violent rejection of the DPA. These were not meetings in which the visitors tapped their feet in impatience, whispering to aides that it was time to move on. Rather, the IDPs chose their own representatives and spoke in their own time. The AU's Darfur dialogue leaders listened to complaint after complaint about AMIS without becoming angry

or defensive, with none of the unnatural haste that had character-
ized the closing stages of the Abuja talks. Abdul Mohammed, who
led the consultations, reported after three days in Zalingei:

> People focus on nostalgia and the life they have left behind
> alongside the imperative of returning and reclaiming their land.
> They feel they have nothing to lose and therefore are developing
> a sense of fearlessness. They have rejected much (not all) of the
> old leadership. They are angry at the GoS [Government of Sudan]
> and the AU. A new consciousness is being formed ... One aspect
> of this new consciousness is Fur nationalism. I was struck by the
> fact that many young people insisted on not speaking Arabic and
> used only the Fur language and English.[20]

In rural Darfur, people spoke of *harb* (war) or *mashakil* ('the
troubles'). In the camps, they talked of '*ibada*' (genocide).[21] In
common with exiles the world over, prolonged displacement
crystallized both an idealized past life and a set of rock-hard
political demands. The demand for return was not a return to the
status quo ante, despite a language of nostalgia and an appeal to
tradition. It was a vision of a militant new Darfur in which the
older generation of Native Administration had passed the baton
of leadership to a new and younger class of men and women.
The camp leaders had little enthusiasm for compromise, be it
the horse-trading of a peace deal or the rough and tumble of
electoral politics. With remarkable unanimity, they demanded
the protection of international troops, an organized return home
and a new political world in which their preferred leaders would
wield power both in a single Darfur region and in Khartoum.
And their leader of leaders was Abdel Wahid al Nur, in whom
they declared complete faith. The same group of camp leaders
quoted above said, 'All of us back Abdel Wahid. He can give us
any guarantee and we will accept it. If he says, "My guarantee
is this empty can of Pepsi," we will accept. On the guarantee of
Abdel Wahid and the international community, we can go [home]
even without compensation.'

The camp leaders trusted the AU almost as little as they trusted the government, and their contempt for AMIS was undisguised. 'At the beginning, cooperation with AMIS was good,' explained one camp leader. But after May 2006, relations took a disastrous turn.

> One day they conducted a big meeting in the AU compound, with sixty-four camp sheikhs. The subject was the DPA. They distributed some books and reviews about the DPA and peace. I was given the chance to speak, so I thanked them for coming and asked them, 'What peace are we talking about? Is this the peace that has been signed or the peace that is coming? We don't see any peace now.' The AU person said, 'This is a big question, let us leave it for the future.' I insisted that they should answer the question. But they closed the meeting and postponed it for another day. The next day I was arrested by Security, so I began to suspect that they had told Security what we had said.

In most of the camps, people protested against the DPA even before Abdel Wahid finally left Abuja. Unprepared for this, AMIS had no police units with experience of crowd control. The clumsy AU response – which led to one fatality that first week – made things worse.

> After the arrival of Minni in Khartoum, we protested in all the camps, and the police came with forty vehicles from three different forces to confront us. AMIS protected us from police harassment. But after that they withdrew. Then the government forces came and shot a seventeen-year-old boy, and arrested six people and injured two – one shot in the foot and one beaten with an electric cattle prod. The body of that boy lay where he had been shot. I called AMIS to come but they refused. It stayed there until I took the body at 5 p.m. to bury it. The next day AMIS came and went to see the grave and took photos. That was all.[22]

The AU came under suspicion of giving intelligence to the government. 'I discovered that AU reports are sent to the government of Sudan and we are arrested,' said one camp leader. 'Now if I see AMIS troops in the street I do not even look at them.'

'Whatever we say, the Sudan government will know,' said another. 'We stopped cooperating.'

As AMIS prepared to hand over to UNAMID, many of Darfur's camps were outside government control. Neither police nor army could enter Kalma, just outside Nyala, and large parts of other big camps were no-go areas for government officials and soldiers. On the perimeters, militiamen harassed the camp residents when they ventured out to visit the towns or to search for firewood, creating a climate of fear. Inside, armed men associated with one or other of the rebel factions, or with the camp sheikhs, or with mafia-style rackets, put down roots and imposed their will.

At independence in 1956, Khartoum was a town of 250,000 people and only 8.6 per cent of Sudan's population lived in urban areas. Fifty years later, more than 40 per cent of the country was urbanized – a figure that excluded the displaced and illegal squatters. Khartoum's registered population had grown to 4.5 million and – if IDPs and squatters were added – well over 7 million in a national population of 40 million.[23] This was the result of extreme inequality in social and economic opportunities – the bias detailed in *The Black Book* – combined with decades of conflict in the peripheries. The great unanticipated and unwanted consequence of the Sudan government's civil wars was that millions of people from uprooted communities had found their way first to provincial towns, and ultimately to the metropolis. Even with peace, few were likely to return to their homes. The economic opportunities of booming Khartoum were just too great when compared to the hardships of neglected rural areas ravaged by conflict. The mushrooming urban population posed political and security challenges for the ruling authorities – their town was becoming an unwieldy mega-city demographically dominated by 'black' southerners and westerners. At the height of its ideological fervour in the early 1990s, the government demolished squatter settlements around Khartoum and relocated their inhabitants to 'peace cities' where they would pose less of a security threat to the metropolis.[24] Subsequently it reverted to manipulating tribally based leaders to try to control the sprawling settlements.[25]

Darfur reflected Sudan's urbanization in forced and accelerated microcosm.[26] Before the war, 18 per cent of the region's
population was urbanized. By the end of 2005, if IDPs in large
towns were included, the figure had more than doubled to 42
per cent.[27] With every passing month, IDP numbers increased.
By 2007, with an urban population of 1.2 million plus 300,000
people in IDP camps, Nyala had become the third largest city in
Sudan and home to more than one in five Darfurians.

In the last months of 2007, security officials canvassed the
breakup of Darfur's IDP camps and the forced dispersal of their
inhabitants. These vast concentrations of angry and politicized
people were a frightening proposition. Better, they argued, to
have smaller camps where a more compliant leadership could
be imposed. But, as with similar threats to the southern displaced over the years, the effort was thwarted by the sheer scale
of the task. Darfur wasn't Khartoum, where governments could
be toppled by urban protest. Local officials resorted instead to
a divide-and-rule approach. Their plan: a typical combination
of threat and bribery, including purchasing the loyalty of camp
leaders – many of whom were becoming small-town politicians
and businessmen with interests in real estate and trade, and a
stability of a sort. A generation of Darfurians was growing up
without farms, trees and the rhythms of rural life – and also
without having to walk for hours to find water.

For some North American activists, however, the only way of
analysing Darfur was through the lens of 'genocide'. One proclaimed that Darfur's displaced camps were set to become the
new frontline 'in Khartoum's genocidal counter-insurgency war'.[28]
He compared the camps to 'concentration camps'. In September
2007, Luis Moreno-Ocampo, the prosecutor of the International
Criminal Court, echoed this rhetoric, saying that Ahmed Haroun
now 'controlled' the camps and had turned them into concentration camps. Three months later, Moreno-Ocampo told the UN
Security Council that Khartoum's campaign against civilians suspected of supporting the rebellion was now in its 'second stage'.
The first stage, he said, was the 'criminal plan coordinated by

Ahmed Haroun' in which 'millions of people were forced out of their villages and into camps'. This took place in 2003–04 and the ICC had indicted Haroun for his role. Now, '[w]e are witnessing a calculated, organized campaign by Sudanese officials to attack individuals and further destroy the social fabric of entire communities. All information points not to chaotic and isolated acts but to a pattern of attacks.'[29] While acknowledging continuing government repression of some relief agencies, especially in the heat of the controversy over UNAMID, not everyone working in the camps agreed with Moreno-Ocampo. 'People are always trying to look for a scheme behind these events,' said a relief worker based in Nyala. 'Bad things happen, but it is probably nearer to a random approach than anything structured.' The prosecutor spoke of the 'slow destruction of entire communities ... in full sight of the international community'. The basis for this claim appeared to be that Haroun had been appointed as minister of state for humanitarian affairs. It failed to acknowledge – perhaps even to understand – that the conflict, and the government's strategies, had changed significantly since the Wadi Saleh massacres of 2003–04 which formed the basis of the case against Haroun. Terrible things had happened, with long-lasting destructive consequences, but not all of them were the criminal fruit of the government's war.

Life in the camps was dire and security was bad – especially at the perimeters – but the parallel stretched the meaning of 'concentration camp' well beyond breaking point and could be considered an insult to the survivors and victims of Nazi concentration camps. The Ministry of Humanitarian Affairs has only modest control over the camps. Khartoum undoubtedly fostered violence towards camp residents, but this fell far short of a policy of genocide. It was far more concerned with two much graver threats: the continuing military capability of the rebels and, even more so, the turncoat Arab militias.

'God willing, on our way to Khartoum'

A month after the exodus from Abuja, a group of ambitious Darfurian opposition leaders – several of them veterans of decades of struggle – met in the Eritrean capital Asmara and drew up the 'founding statement' of a new 'National Redemption Front' (NRF), the *Jabhat al Khalas*, to fight the DPA. Alongside the signatures of Khalil Ibrahim, Ahmad Diraige and Sharif Harir (the latter two the Sudan Federal Democratic Alliance) and the SLM's early vice-chairman, Khamis Abakir, a space was left above the typewritten name of Abdel Wahid al Nur. The Fur leader flew to Asmara, but then declined to join the Front, believing it was designed primarily to relaunch JEM, 'with different initials', and distrusting the Eritreans' motives in sponsoring it. His opinion was that 'they want oil and money, that's all. They have no concern for Darfur.'[30] The NRF announced a structure – a leadership council with a rotating presidency and a general secretariat responsible for daily executive affairs – but like JEM's it boiled down to one man: Khalil Ibrahim. The only meaningful military organization in the NRF was Khalil's. His standing army was small but, as an Eritrean official pointed out, it could 'grow at any time' thanks to his anonymous but munificent donors.[31] And the main motive of JEM's chairman was to harness Eritrean support to build a broader platform for his dream of taking the war across Darfur's borders as a first step to taking over Khartoum. In March 2006, Khalil had met Ali Osman in Libya and claimed the vice-president had agreed to JEM's demand that Darfur be reconstituted as a single region and given a vice-presidency in the central government. If either of these promises were broken, Khalil said, 'war will continue and we will take the whole cake'.[32] The NRF was his grab for the whole cake.

On 3 July, JEM attacked into Kordofan, hitting the town of Hamrat al Sheikh, the capital of the nomadic Arabs of the Kababish tribe. Although claimed in the name of the NRF, the attack combined the forces of JEM and elements from two loosely affiliated SLA splinters – G19 and SLA–Unity – led by Suleiman Marajan. But the operation was essentially JEM's: Khalil's men had three vehicles to every one for the SLA, and the overall commander was JEM's general coordinator, Abubaker Hamid Nur. Attacking in some fifty vehicles, light trucks and land cruisers mounted with machine guns, the rebels destroyed the national security office, police station, the emergency section of the local hospital and a telephone relay station. They stole cars and looted market stalls and private homes. The governor of North Kordofan, Faisal Hassan Ibrahim, said twelve people were killed – eight policemen, two security officers and two women.[33] One of the women was Mariam Khamis Jamous, the sister of SLA humanitarian coordinator Suleiman Jamous and one of many Zaghawa married to Kababish. Jamous telephoned the nazir of the Kababish, al Tom Hassan al Tom, to apologize for the attack. 'The rebels were in a hurry to say: "We are still here and alive as an opposition,"' Jamous said. 'I told them it was a mistake. Our agenda is in Darfur. We should not lose the sympathy of the world by spilling instability to other parts of the country.'[34]

Jamous underestimated Khalil's ambitions, which had hardened after Abuja. 'JEM now wants regime change,' said a senior member of the movement who was leading the recruitment drive in Chad. 'We can't bring peace in Darfur unless we change this government.'[35] The plan, he said, had been to advance from Hamrat al Sheikh to Dongola on the Nile with a force of 1,000 men – three-quarters of them JEM's. After Dongola, said another Zaghawa commander, 'God willing, we will be on our way to Khartoum!' But JEM had once again overreached militarily, as it had in the early stages of the war, and the attackers got no further than Hamrat al Sheikh. The operation served no strategic purpose – Hamrat al Sheikh was not a garrison town. Instead, it threatened to damage efforts to mend relations with civilians of all tribes in the wake of Minawi's defeat. Hundreds of Kababish lived in North Darfur, and their relatives had helped many survive the firestorm period of 2003–04 by smuggling life-saving supplies from Kordofan. 'Kababish and Zaghawa have been living together for more than fifty years,' said a Kababish woman married in Wakheim in North Darfur.

The government tried to recruit Kababish by all means – money, force... It tried everything with Amir al Tom. He was invited to

Khartoum, but refused to Omar al Bashir. Instead he sent people to Wakheim and told them not to join the Janjawiid. The attack on Hamrat al Sheikh affected relations because civilians were attacked.[36]

The NRF attack and the rout of Minawi's forces in North Darfur – 'running, not fighting'[37] – convinced Bashir to give the army one more try. Within days, government forces and Minawi's former rebels launched an offensive against areas controlled by the non-signatories. The operation began on the north-eastern flanks of Jebel Marra and moved steadily north. Dozens of civilians were killed. But this was only a prelude. The army began moving 'huge amounts of troops and amazing amounts of ammunition' into al Fasher.[38] The US chargé d'affaires, Cameron Hume, said that more than 8,000 men had been transferred into Darfur in violation of the DPA's prohibition on troop movements. The government did not deny the charges. In a plan submitted to the UN Security Council in August, it opposed the growing demand for UN peacekeepers and proposed using 10,500 of its own troops to crush the NRF rebels. The NRF was not a party to the Abuja process, it said, and therefore had no right to control territory; fighting the NRF did not violate the DPA. With atrocious timing, the AU took a step that further damaged its neutrality: it agreed to expel the non-signatory rebels – JEM and SLA–Abdel Wahid – from the Ceasefire Commission.

The government offensive began on 28 August. Rebel-controlled villages north of al Fasher were bombed by Antonovs and then attacked by regular troops, with Janjawiid in a supporting role. The government forces, whose rank and file was composed largely of poorly trained conscripts from other impoverished regions, were not well motivated and soon lost confidence when they found themselves under attack. Corporal Arif Bahr el Din, from Gedaref, was captured by the rebels as his column advanced towards the village of Um Sidir. He said,

We were about six hundred men and more than sixty cars. There were another seventeen cars of Janjawiid. We left Mellit with the

Janjawiid in front because they are locals and know the lie of the land. After lunch, we found ourselves surrounded by the SLA. We fought for three hours. But only eighty of the 600 fought. Many ran. They never told us we were going to fight; they told us we were going to build a camp and stay to keep the peace.[39]

A second column succeeded in reaching Um Sidir, arriving on 31 August and fighting off a hastily organized SLA attack the following day. But their morale, too, was poor. Soldiers who had been told they would be 'peacekeepers' found themselves trying to keep the peace between civilians and the militia who entered Um Sidir with them and looted the market. Expecting to be welcomed as liberators, the government soldiers found themselves regarded as the enemy. 'I thought people would greet us happily, but we found they were afraid of us,' said Lieutenant Kheir al Saeed Dawa, who also was captured by the rebels. 'We found very few people in the market. They were afraid. We said: "Don't worry." But they took their things and left.' The government troops dug in, and waited for reinforcements.

They were still waiting ten days later when the rebels struck on 11 September, crushing the government force in forty minutes. The operation was organized not by JEM this time, but by the military commander of G19, Hassan 'Peugeot' Abdel Karim, who chose the afternoon to attack, ordering his men to hold their fire until the last minute. The government soldiers had the sun in their eyes and a rain-swollen wadi at their backs, and thought the cars racing towards them from three sides were the reinforcements they were expecting. The rebels estimate that a hundred soldiers died, many of them mired in the wadi. 'It was the biggest battle in the history of the SLA,' said Jar al Nabi Abdel Karim, the brother of Hassan Peugeot. 'People in forty-eight vehicles began shooting at the same time. Only one of the enemy's cars didn't run away. Everyone in it died. We captured seventy-nine of the government's eighty cars and divided them fifty-fifty with JEM.' (SLA commanders in Darfur never spoke of 'NRF'; they spoke of 'JEM'.) 'Until now we don't know where the eightieth is!'

Um Sidir was arguably the most important victory since the al Fasher airport raid of April 2003. But the relationship between the NRF/JEM and the SLA forces of North Darfur was already souring, due in part to JEM's insistence on claiming victories in the name of the NRF from its offices in Asmara. 'We are dying, and they are claiming it,' one SLA commander said bitterly. As in Minawi's days, local commanders felt themselves elbowed aside and disregarded. Jar al Nabi said,

> After the battle at Um Sidir, JEM painted 'NRF' everywhere. They said it was to avoid confusion between Minni and G19 [who were both 'SLA']. They brought paint and put NRF on everything – mountains, cars, lorries. One time when I was parking in Amarai, a guy came running with paint. I asked him: 'What do you want?' He said: 'I want to put NRF on your car!'

The tensions exploded in October after NRF/JEM and G19 attacked an army position at Kariari near the Chad border, a strategic crossing for the Darfur rebels. A 900-strong government force had arrived in Kariari earlier in the month, accompanied by a predominantly Gimr militia unit that covered its back.[40] The battle of Kariari, on 7 October, was another disaster for the government, which lost hundreds of men killed and captured.[41] But it also marked a divorce between G19 and JEM, whose leaders took most of the sixty-nine vehicles seized from the army. The few that G19 received were lost when its men clashed with Chadian rebels and Janjawiid while returning home across North Darfur. Hassan Peugeot favoured retaining the alliance with JEM, but he was outvoted and JEM's men were told they were not welcome in G19-controlled territory.

The non-signatories' challenge to the government, and the DPA, handed the rebels two major battlefield victories and showed why Khartoum had mobilized tribal militias when rebellion broke out. It was not just because they were a cheap counter-insurgency force. In the second decade of the Islamists' 'National Salvation Revolution' in Sudan, the army simply was not up to the job. Despite Sudan's new oil money, the men sent to fight were poorly

trained, poorly armed and reluctant to fight. Many preferred surrender to combat and possible death. 'I just want to go home,'
said one of the conscripts captured in Kariari. Another said:
'We don't have the courage to defeat them and we didn't have
enough ammunition. We just ran away.'[42] When the UN Special
Representative Jan Pronk remarked on the low army morale in
his weblog posting,[43] the government expelled him.

In the far south of Darfur, things did not go the rebels' way.
Beginning on 28 August, militia drawn from the Habbaniya tribe
launched a series of raids on a string of villages south of Buram.
The Habbaniya militia had attacked some of these villages five
months earlier, displacing thousands. This time it was worse.
According to an investigation by the UN, the attackers wore army
uniforms and travelled on horseback, and government complicity
was obvious.[44] Over three days of coordinated attacks, forty-five
predominantly Zaghawa villages were burned and their inhabitants driven out, congregating in IDP camps and towns such as
Buram.[45] In the village of Tirtish, one witness participated in
the burial of sixty-two people and estimated that another thirty
had been killed and a further thirty remained unaccounted for.
Dozens were killed in each of the major villages attacked. The UN
estimated the total death toll in the hundreds, with an estimated
60,000 people displaced.

Most of the villages destroyed by the militia had been settled by Zaghawa migrants in the 1970s and 1980s. Among them
was al Amud al Akhdar, where there had been plans to relocate
drought-stricken Zaghawa, at their request, in 1970. The attacks
were precisely targeted. In mixed villages, such as Legediba, Habbaniya areas were spared while Zaghawa quarters were razed. The
Habbaniya had not forgotten the rebels' destruction in Buram in
March 2004. On the eve of the DPA signing, tensions worsened as
Minawi laid claim to a large part of Dar Habbaniya on the military
map he provided to the AU's security commission. According to
him, every Zaghawa settlement in the 'green belt' south of Buram
was controlled by his fighters. After Abuja, his men raised the
SLA flag over Habbaniya offices and declared the area 'liberated'

in anticipation of a military verification mission by the AU and US. 'Liberated from what?' the Habbaniya responded. 'You are with us now!'[46]

The spark for the Habbaniya rampage was a rebel operation even further south in Darfur, close to the point where Darfur, South Sudan and Central African Republic meet. Just four days beforehand, on 24 August, a raid claimed by the NRF overran the small town of Songo – at the southern end of the green belt – and captured thirty government vehicles. This was a remarkable attack – hundreds of miles from any other rebel operations, in a remote forested area in the middle of the rainy season – and seemed to presage a new front in Darfur's war. The government feared that the Zaghawa of the 'green belt' would join the NRF rebels in preference to Minawi and its response was as rapid as it was predictable. According to the UN,[47] a recruitment meeting was held at Wad Hajjam on 25–26 August, attended by government representatives, commanders of the Habbaniya militia, and Habbaniya tribal leaders. Over the following four days, the ethnic cleansing of the Zaghawa of the 'green belt' was completed before the NRF could dispatch any forces through the waterlogged forests.

Double-dealing in Asmara

For the rebels' Eritrean sponsors, the NRF was a tool with which it hoped to gain leverage in Sudan. The Eritreans knew from experience the price of disunity: liberation postponed for nearly twenty years. Only a united front could hope to gain on the battlefield and in the negotiating chamber. President Isseyas Afewerki's strategic interest in Sudan remained unchanged from the heyday of his support for the Sudanese opposition; he wanted to see a weak Khartoum and a government in which there was strong Eritrean influence, through its support for provincially based parties. In 2005, Eritrea had tried to muscle its way into the Abuja process as a co-mediator. When it was unable to, the Eritrean entrusted with the Sudan file, Abdella Jaber, walked out of the peace talks. He tried, but failed, to take the rebel movements with him.

By 2006 there was a new twist to Eritrean policy. The country was in a state of economic collapse due to a combination of mismanaged dictatorship, trade embargo by its neighbours, and the costs of maintaining a huge standing army in anticipation of having to fight Ethiopia once again. Isseyas needed an escape route, and chose to cut a deal with Khartoum. The central part of this was an agreement to end the war in eastern Sudan, where the Beja Congress and the Rashaida Free Lions, partners in the Eastern Front, had been fighting a guerrilla war against Khartoum with military, financial and political support from Eritrea. A succession of attempts by international mediators to find a peace agreement had been thwarted, and in the middle of 2006 direct negotiations began between Khartoum and the Eastern Front in Asmara. But the front was controlled by Eritrean Security, and the real negotiations were between Khartoum and Asmara. The outcome was the Eastern Sudan Peace Agreement (ESPA), signed on 14 October 2006. It is a short text, which failed to provide any international role or guarantees – neither ceasefire monitors, peacekeepers, nor any independent assessment and evaluation mechanisms. The Eritreans simply handed the Eastern Front over to Khartoum in return for some very modest political concessions, many of which had not been implemented a year later. In return, Sudan opened its border with Eritrea for trade, allowed Eritrean companies to operate in Sudan, and paid an undisclosed sum to the Eritrean government.[48]

Why would Eritrea cut a deal so favourable to Khartoum in eastern Sudan, while at the same time supporting the NRF against the Sudanese army in the west? The answer lies in the two countries' common interest, shared with Libya, in preventing any resolution to the Darfur crisis that involved international mediation and peacekeeping. Both disliked the UN and the US, and both preferred a deal cut between their own security chiefs, who shared a shadowy camaraderie irrespective of their political masters. If this meant allowing the war to bubble for some time, so be it.

For three months, from July to September 2006, the Eritreans attempted to unite the Darfur rebel leaders it had invited to

Asmara. Khartoum's concession was to offer to talk to the NRF, reversing its previous position that 'the file of negotiation on Darfur will never be opened again, whatever the reasons are'.[49] And so, in the same week that the ESPA was signed – a week after the defeat at Kariari – President Bashir said the government was prepared to open talks with the non-signatories.

It didn't work. The Eritreans couldn't rally the fractious rebels on a single platform – but they didn't give up. Their next approach was to bring in the SPLM and Chad. Many SPLM leaders had close relations with Asmara, and said they trusted the Eritreans to take the lead on Darfur. Chadian President Idriss Deby needed all the assistance he could get to confront a growing threat from his own Darfur-based rebels, and Eritrea wooed him with an offer of a personal security detail and troops to protect his border. For six further months, Eritrea and its favoured intermediaries in Darfur – Sharif Harir among them – tried to unify the rebel groups, including by force. Harir's right-hand man was Abubaker Mohamed Kado, who entered Darfur with him in March 2007 and stayed behind when he left. A former army and PDF officer who had commanded the SFDA's forces in East Sudan, despite a previous history of abuse in Darfur and Kordofan, Kado attacked and briefly arrested a number of rebel leaders critical of the NRF – among them Jar al Nabi Abdel Karim. The rebels charged that Kado was working for Eritrean intelligence; if the SLA wasn't ready to fold itself into the NRF, then a new SLA formation controlled by Eritrea would do almost as well. But control of guerrillas operating out of Eritrean territory was one thing, and remote control of Darfurians on the other side of Sudan something totally different. At one point – March 2007 – two of the most senior Eritrean government officials were stationed in Chad, trying to pull the rebels together. But this didn't work either. Deby was quite ready to double-cross anyone in his own ruthless power game and the hold-out non-signatories stood united on one thing: the insistence that those who controlled the field should control any new negotiations. They were not going to accept being shouldered out by opportunistic neighbours with agendas of their own.

The elusive search for unity

An early setback to Eritrea's designs to control the non-signatories – and take on the central role it had been denied in Abuja – came on 20 May 2006 when JEM dissidents announced, in a letter to Salim Ahmed Salim, that 'the leadership of Mr Khalil Ibrahim Mohamed is no longer valid, and the tiny group of his relatives around him is not entitled to represent the diversity of Darfurian people'. The dissidents said Khalil and his relatives 'are desperately trying to impose their views of rejecting the DPA on the majority of the movement members' and asked for an urgent meeting to find 'a real breakthrough that encourages all groups to join the peace deal signed in Abuja'. The letter followed a 'Corrective Memorandum' a month earlier, circulated only within the movement, in which the dissidents said JEM was tribalist, undemocratic and corrupt – and demanded change. Idriss Azraq, one of the signatories to the protests, said 'JEM is not just tribal; in all important respects, it is a family business. Very crucial decisions are taken without consultation. On the issue of Islam, Khalil is to some extent fanatic. We will reach a dead end if we use tribes and religion.' After Salim failed to respond, and Khalil dismissed his critics as government agents, the dissidents gathered a hundred supporters in a 'General Congress' of their splinter group in Addis Ababa in January 2007. Insisting on keeping the name Justice and Equality Movement, they demanded separation of state and religion and said the DPA was good as far as it went. The main problem of the DPA was not the DPA, they said; it was the movements and their divisions.

While international attention focused on the problems of the SLA, JEM suffered even more critical divisions as the Kobe leadership itself split in mid-2007 along clan lines, following Khalil's dismissal of his chief of staff, Abdalla Banda. Banda's supporters accused Khalil of subsequently trying to kill Banda in order to reinforce JEM's Islamist character. 'Abdalla doesn't like Islamists at all – and Khalil is now trying to put Islamists in front,' said a Banda loyalist.[50] 'Khalil has to go. He took Kobe to fight in the south and tried to assassinate Abdalla to control the field. He met with Salah Gosh in Libya. There are rumours he is trying to make an agreement with the government.' If Khalil had cut a deal with the government, few would have been surprised. The view of most of Khartoum's political class was that JEM's war was, from the start, an exercise in getting more leverage so that Khalil and his close comrades could re-enter the ruling elite at the top.

Two months after the challenge to Khalil, it was the turn of Abdel Wahid al Nur. On 28 July 2006, a group of thirty-two commanders and officials calling themselves 'the Military Council and Field Command' of the SLA/M announced Abdel Wahid's 'ousting' and his replacement by his old comrade from the pre-SLA days, Ahmad Abdel Shafi. The thirty-two asked Abdel Shafi to appoint a new leadership to run the affairs of the SLA until a general convention could be held. Abdel Shafi had been pressing Abdel Wahid to put his house in order ever since the Abuja talks ended with division in his delegation, and was increasingly frustrated by his failure to come up with new initiatives. Abdel Wahid had rejected the NRF, saying 'I have alternatives', but he did not disclose what they were and Abdel Shafi doubted that they existed. Seeing his brothers-in-arms from the SLA 'sitting in Eritrea getting bored, thinking of going their own way', Abdel Shafi proposed a series of structural innovations to jolt the movement out of its paralysis: first a seventeen-man command council, which Abdel Wahid rejected as being dominated by soldiers; then a forty-one-man leadership council with a military majority, which Abdel Wahid also rejected, saying: 'Maximum 10 per cent. These soldiers are trying to topple me!'[51] As the lethargy continued, Abdel Shafi took Abdel Wahid and his political adviser, Ahmed Mohamadein, to a zoo on the edge of Asmara, where among the sad and underfed caged animals he thought they could talk unobserved by Eritrean intelligence. Abdel Wahid accused him of staging a coup. He replied: 'You are the top of all these bodies. Where is the coup in that?' When Abdel Wahid still refused to consider any form of organization, Abdel Shafi challenged him, saying: 'There is no one in charge of finance, no receipts, no spokesman. You are everything in this movement. I am not ready to continue.'[52]

Abdel Shafi claimed the 'ouster' of Abdel Wahid took him by surprise and met with him three more times after it, still seeking a way to move forward with him. But Abdel Wahid was unmoved. 'If anyone doesn't want my leadership, he can go!' he said. And so, on 18 August, Abdel Shafi finally went, thanking Abdel Wahid for 'his achievements and his efforts' but regretting 'divisions and splits [which] have weakened the movement both politically and militarily'. In accepting the chairmanship offered by the thirty-two commanders, he stressed the importance of unity, and said his door was open to all non-signatories seeking a 'New Sudan' – a phrase that reflected his ongoing close relationship with the SPLA, which still regarded the Darfurian rebels as its wayward children, in need of fatherly advice and discipline.

Abdel Shafi had been one of Abdel Wahid's most loyal supporters, never giving public voice to his deep frustration. But his thirty-two backers included none of the key commanders in Abdel Wahid's three main areas of control – western Jebel Marra, Korma and the Ain Siro mountains – and his support began ebbing away as it became clear that he leaned towards the NRF and his challenge would not carry the Fur. 'He cannot lead even three men,' said the SLA vice-chairman, Khamis Abakir.[53] Abdel Shafi was further weakened in December when a government-supported militia under a former aide to Abdel Wahid, Abul Qassim Imam, attacked villages controlled by his men in eastern Jebel Marra.[54] The attack made clear that the DPA – nailed into its coffin by the failure to implement any of its deadlines, especially for the disarmament of militias – had changed nothing: several hundred armed men on horseback and camelback attacked the village of Deribat on the morning of 26 December, supported by a bomber and a small force of regular soldiers. They rounded up women and children and took them to a nearby stream, where they camped and began raping the women and girls, often in front of the other captives. Women who resisted were beaten. The abducted women and children were held for about a month without medical treatment, with little food, and obliged to wait on their abductors.[55]

When Abdel Shafi finally returned to Darfur in March 2007, to attend an SLA–Unity conference in North Darfur, his stock was down. As he approached the conference site at Amarai, Abdel Wahid's supporters left in protest and conference hopes died. Six months later, six of Abdel Shafi's backers announced that they and all their men were joining SLA–Unity. But SLA–Unity itself was symptomatic of the rebels' inability to unite. Although drawing its supporters largely from the same North Darfur pool as G19, it was divided from it over cooperation with Eritrea, the wisdom of links with JEM and the expansion of the war to Kordofan. As 2007 ended, the non-signatories were split, once again, by unity talks organized by the SPLA in the Southern capital of Juba. The smallest groups flocked to Juba, but the biggest, SLA–Abdel Wahid and SLA–Unity, stayed away. 'The SPLA is not interested in Darfur,' said Abdel Wahid, suggesting that the southerners' renewed interest in Darfurian affairs lay in the desire to prepare a second front in case the North–South peace collapsed into all-out conflict. 'The SPLA is dealing with us as if we are their little followers. We are not their little brothers. We are not even their sons, in fact.'

Frustrated with the paralysis of Abdel Wahid's leadership, and his refusal to engage in new peace talks before a strong international peacekeeping force imposed its authority on Darfur, the SPLA, AU and UN circumvented him and talked directly to SLA field commanders. They supported efforts by IDP leaders and Native Administrators to pressure him to join the peace talks. Ensconced in Paris and lionized by activists there, Abdel Wahid refused to budge. As criticism of him grew, he cracked down. In January 2008, he ordered the detention of a group of SLA veterans including the SLA's liaison with the International Committee of the Red Cross, Ali Haroun Adud, who was accused of 'military irregularities'. Amnesty International said the men, most of whom came from the Ain Siro area, were arrested 'because they supported the unity of different factions of the SLA'; their colleagues in the SLA said they belonged to the movement's 'peace camp' and wanted the new talks that Abdel Wahid not only refused, but refused even to discuss. The arrests sealed a growing rift between

Abdel Wahid and his hitherto loyal supporters in Ain Siro, who were increasingly critical of his refusal to go back to the negotiating table. 'We have to talk – to anyone,' one Ain Siro leader said. 'We [in Ain Siro] stayed with Abdel Wahid to keep unity. But he deals with the SLA as if he were the only one. He is far from the field. He doesn't consult. He doesn't put the right person in the right place. We have more than thirty graduates without jobs. There are no structures. We have 2,500 fighters, but every day more are gone.'[56] Senior UN officials said they believed the arrests were meant to intimidate independent-thinking commanders at the time of a visit to Darfur by the UN and AU special envoys, Jan Eliasson and Salim Ahmed Salim.

The move against the 'peace camp' divided the Fur rebels in a way that Abdel Shafi's split did not, setting one of the rebels' mountain fastnesses, Ain Siro, firmly against the chairman. The criticism of him became increasingly outspoken. One commander said that Abdel Wahid intended 'to sideline anyone suspected of talking about reform or uttering the voice of reason.' He and his loyalists were 'very annoyed by the growing influence of graduates among the rebels, especially in North Darfur', said another. A third said: 'If every day another pro-peace group is being unjustly detained by Abdel Wahid and his gangs, then there will hardly be peace to expect in the near future.'[57] The Magdum of Nyala, Ahmed Adam Rijal, who had been dismissed by Khartoum in 2005 for his principled stand on behalf of his people, flew to Paris but was spurned by Abdel Wahid, who refused even to meet him. Back in Nyala, the Magdum bitterly commented on Abdel Wahid's readiness to spend many hours with French activists and journalists who had never been to Darfur but his failure to meet with one of the most senior tribal leaders of Darfur. 'He is nothing, absolutely nothing,' said Magdum Ahmed Rijal, predicting that Abdel Wahid would lose his grip over Jebel Marra and the displaced.[58] But the mediators continued to try to win him around. A succession of hopefuls, including US officials, UN mediators and SPLA leader Riek Machar, met with Abdel Wahid. They found him ready to talk, but were frustrated that 'even with the same conversation he would change his arguments and his demands'.[59] Five years after he announced the creation of the SLA, Abdel Wahid appeared impossible and indispensable in equal measure.

The neglected soldiers

Of all those dismayed at the final outcome in Abuja, most shocked of all were Darfur's Arabs. The Sudan government had always assured the Arabs that it would take care of their interests. But on 5 May it signed an agreement that brought a member of the Zaghawa tribe – seen as a bitter enemy of Darfur's Arabs – into the palace, promised his commanders powerful positions in the army and his nominee authority over the reform and downsizing of all Arab militias. Worse was to follow: mutterings that the government might hand militia leaders over to the International Criminal Court in hope of saving its own skin. In the year following the end of the Abuja process, the first signs of serious Arab discontent were evident, and by the end of 2007, the trickle had become a flood. The most worrying development, for the government, occurred in October 2007, after Khartoum provided forty brand-new vehicles, one hundred *Thuraya* phones and a range of sophisticated weaponry to Mohamed Hamdan Dogolo 'Hemeti', leader of a substantial Janjawiid force, who promptly switched sides. Another group that emerged in 2007 called itself *al Jundi al Mazloum* – 'the neglected soldiers'. Its leaders charged that Khartoum had instructed them to do its dirty work, and then abandoned them. While specifically referring to a particular militia of uncertain allegiance, its name stood as a symbol for a slowly bubbling Arab mutiny.

Arabs constitute approximately a third of Darfur's population and the Abbala of the north are among its poorest and most neglected citizens. Many tried to stay out of the war. For example, Mahariya clans under the leadership of Mohamedein al Dud Hassaballa had spurned government entreaties that they take on the SLA. 'I am a civilian, not responsible for fighting the rebellion,' Al Dud told Security officers in al Fasher in April 2006, refusing an offer of weapons and cars to evict the rebels who had driven his people out of their centre at Damrat Ghreir three years earlier. Security responded by first cutting the salaries of and then dismissing all seventeen Mahariya working in its offices in al Fasher. When they reported this to their chief, he told them: 'Go back to your old jobs. We are a small tribe. I am not going to kill my people for nothing. And don't forget your grandmothers are [non-Arab] Kaitinga!'[60] The Fur and Tunjur sheikhs of Fata Borno, victims of Musa Hilal's rampages in mid-2003, readily volunteered 'we never suffered at the hands of Mohamedein al Dud'.[61] After losing Ghreir, Mahariya herders had relocated to Abbarai, a burned-out village west of Fata Borno. Blocked from taking their herds to the desert pastures, they began to see their beloved camels sickening with no veterinary services to save them. Unable to market their animals in Libya and faced with bandits and rebels on the roads to al Fasher, they saw livestock prices drop and incomes plunge. Because they stayed away from relief camps and so were not officially 'displaced', the Mahariya received no food aid and no jobs with international agencies. To cap it all, the costs of self-defence – weapons, ammunition and vehicles – were forcing them to sell more animals than their diminished herds could sustain. Members of the tribe, young and old, were asking, 'Who brought us into these troubles?'

Many Abbala had joined forces with the government, motivated as much by the promise of salaries and loot as by any fuddled notions of Arab supremacy. Even these groups – preeminently the Mahamid and Ereigat – were suffering: they had gained much loot and some land, but their all-important *masars* were cut, their pastoral livelihoods were in crisis and the villages on whose markets and clinics they had depended were burnt and abandoned. Fur IDP leaders were dismissive of the nomads' difficulties – 'how can the Arabs say they have problems when they now rule the land?'[62] – but Arab centres such as Misrih remained poor and deprived. One young Mahamid expressed the emerging Abbala viewpoint. 'After Abuja, the Arabs are asking: "What is our future?" We are the first generation of educated

Abbala. Many of us still want to live life as nomads, but we need development: schools, mobile clinics, hospitals. We must slowly put people in cities and build a good relationship with farmers. We are against the apartheid of Arab versus African.' As Nazir Saeed Madibu had predicted years earlier, the Abbala were becoming politically conscious, and realizing that their future lay in stability, development and good neighbourliness.

Khartoum's immediate worry after Abuja was the Arabs of South Darfur – more numerous and better connected than their Abbala cousins. The reflex of the security chiefs and party operators was to play divide-and-rule, constantly manipulating the Native Administration system and with it jurisdiction over land. Predictably this led to numerous disputes and violence among the Baggara Arabs. During 2007, Mahariya herders fought Terjem farmers, leaving hundreds dead; Habbaniya fought Salamat and Rizeigat; Fellata fought Habbaniya; Gimir, a recently Arabized tribe, clashed with Salamat and Fellata. Abbala herders cut off from their northern grazing cycles occupied southern lands, creating new tensions. It was, an NGO observer said, 'an immense cesspit in which the different Arab tribes are at each other's throats'.[63]

The strategy of some Arab leaders was to demand a higher price for government loyalty: more money and more guns. Others came off the fence on the rebel side and cut deals with SLA–Abdel Wahid, which had always prioritized good relations with Arabs, and SLA–Unity. In Jebel Marra, one of the prime movers of the Fur's outreach to the Arabs was Mujeeb al Zubeir al Rahman, a relative of Abdel Wahid who had been general secretary of the Darfur Students' Union while at Omdurman Islamic University in 1999–2000 and who used the friendships made in those days to open channels to Janjawiid. His old friends were not militia leaders, he said, but their fathers were.[64] By early 2007, Mujeeb had arranged three non-aggression treaties with Janjawiid groups and more than 500 Janjawiid (including a cousin of Musa Hilal) had left their camps and been integrated into the SLA's in Jebel Marra. Three joint markets had been opened to rebuild confidence between estranged communities, and stray and stolen animals were returned to their owners through the market committees. The return of animals taken before the agreements were signed was voluntary; after, it was obligatory. The Arabs' reason for abandoning the government was always the same: they were victims of the government, they said, left to fend for themselves after being used to fight the rebellion in 2003–04.

Arab anxieties grew when President Bashir agreed to allow a UN force into Darfur, reversing an earlier threat that Darfur would be the 'graveyard' of any foreign forces. The belief took hold among Arabs that the force was coming not to promote peace, but to target them. The threat of a UN deployment and the demonization of the Arabs in the public rhetoric from western capitals were Khartoum's strongest card in its efforts to retain the loyalty of the Arab militia.

In May 2007, Juma Dogolo, an omda of the Awlad Mansour clan of the Mahariya, Hemeti's uncle and one of the most abusive militia leaders of South Darfur, issued an ultimatum to the government: unless 500 of his men were put on the state payroll, financial compensation was given for 'soldiers' killed in action, and a nazirate granted to the Mahariya at last, he would cease protecting the Nyala area for the government and take 1,500 members of the Border Intelligence over to SLA–Abdel Wahid. Khartoum ignored the demands and instead armed Hemeti for its Haskanita offensive. Military intelligence gave him weapons, including the latest multiple rocket launchers and even anti-aircraft guns, vehicles, communications equipment, money, spare parts, fuel, uniforms and winter clothing, but continued to refuse integration and compensation for his men. Hemeti promptly deserted to the rebel side, taking this huge armoury with him. He claimed the government had failed to honour earlier commitments to pay compensation and salaries and to provide nomads with health services, schools, water and veterinary services.

Hemeti had already signed a non-aggression treaty with JEM in March 2006. Now he signed a second with SLA–Abdel Wahid and made overtures to the predominantly Mahamid forces of the

Sudanese Revolutionary Front, an Arab rebel group led by Anwar Ahmad Khater, a thirty-one-year-old computer engineer from the Awlad Eid branch of the Mahamid. First arrested while a student activist in Khartoum for protesting against the underdevelopment of his native region, Anwar Khater started an opposition movement in 2004 after being denied permission to take up a scholarship to study in the US. In the next eighteen months he was detained three times – on the third occasion, by military intelligence. Upon his release, he hijacked a government vehicle and went to Chad, where Deby's government gave him three more vehicles.[65] Back in Darfur, his message to the Arab communities he visited was: 'The government is using you.' In December 2006 Anwar was warned that the government was planning to kill him. He escaped to a mountainous area north of Zalingei, announced the SRF and was soon joined by almost 250 militiamen from Misteriha – with their weapons.

Unlike Hemeti, Anwar Khater had always rejected the policy of ethnic militias. While Hemeti's armaments were unmatched among Darfur's militia, Anwar possessed something much more important among the Arabs: the legitimacy that comes from a respected lineage along with a reputation for steadfastness. His father had been an adviser to Musa Hilal's much-loved father, Sheikh Hilal Abdalla, and he found sympathy among other Arab dissidents including Ereigat and Awlad Zeid, the largest Mahamid clan. Abdel Wahid believed him the man best able to unite the Arabs of Darfur.

By the same token, Anwar's stand struck fear into Khartoum's Security chiefs. Early in 2007, Security determined to neutralize the troublesome young Arab and, according to one of his associates, 'paid Musa Hilal to arrest Anwar and send him to Khartoum'. In the course of three months' detention in Khartoum, he was visited by Salah Gosh, who told him: 'The UN will fight you as Arabs. If you do not join us you will never survive in Darfur. The international community's war will be imposed on you.'[66] The stratagem backfired on Musa Hilal, whom many Mahamid accused of opening an intra-Mahamid war. 'Anwar went to speak to Tijaniyya leaders in Misteriha, and was captured and chained by Musa Hilal,' said his associate.

> Musa asked him: 'Are you trying to take my place?' The government paid Musa millions to take Anwar to Khartoum. This was the turning point for the Mahamid in opposing the government: there has never been a war among the Mahamid. The Arabs believe in the strong man and Musa Hilal appealed to their emotions. When he wants to impress, he crushes tin cans with his teeth. We Arabs love this kind of thing ... [But] Musa Hilal is damaging our reputation.[67]

Anwar's arrest rebounded on the government too. It confirmed what many Arabs were coming to believe: that a shared Arab identity counted for naught when Khartoum's core interest – its own political survival – was at stake. An Arab rebellion was Khartoum's greatest fear in Darfur. In December 2007, Musa Hilal again put out feelers to the SLA: he mooted the idea of flying to Juba to join an SPLA-convened meeting of Darfurian rebels there.[68] Determined to keep him on side, and perhaps under closer watch, the following month the government appointed Hilal as adviser in the ministry of federal affairs. The appointment was a snub to the international community and, along with the appointment of Ahmed Haroun as government liaison with UNAMID the same week, it was a signal to Darfur's Arabs that the government did not intend to sacrifice its friends to the ICC.[69] The obstacles to a common Arab front remain immense. Hemeti never stopped bargaining with the government over the price of loyalty, and was ready to cut a deal with Khartoum at any time, if the right rewards were on offer.[70] The Arabs are as prone to disunity as their non-Arab neighbours. But they are formidably well-armed and should their leaders put aside their internal differences, then Khartoum will face an unstoppable force.

The attack on AMIS at Haskanita

Less than a year after its formation, the NRF had faded away. Khalil's schemes had not. In the middle of 2007 JEM forces began another series of raids into south-east Darfur and Kordofan, some of them targeting oil installations and others seeking to spark a new insurrection in Kordofan. In September, JEM forces – with SLA–Unity in support – struck in Adila, north of al Da'ien, and then, on 29 August, Wad Banda in Kordofan, prompting a vigorous counterattack by the Sudan army and air force, which used Chinese-manufactured MiG fighter-bombers for the first time in Darfur.[71] The rebels were swept out of Kordofan and into their major base on Darfur's eastern borders, Haskanita. By the end of September, the army's counter-offensive was closing in on Haskanita and the scene was set for an attack that would claim the lives of eleven AU peacekeepers and bring new depths of acrimony to relations between the rebels and the AU. The attack on Haskanita on the night of 29–30 September 2007 was not only the bloodiest incident in AMIS's troubled history, but also posed fundamental challenges to the planned joint AU and UN efforts for peacemaking and peacekeeping in Darfur.

After the DPA was signed, rebel distrust of AMIS had turned into outright hostility. As a result of the expulsion of the non-signatories from the Ceasefire Commission and AMIS observer sites, AMIS had day-to-day dealings with the army and SLA–Minawi, but not with the rebels. In many places, the SLA–Minawi representative was there chiefly to collect his per diem payment. Khartoum's men – most of them military intelligence officers – ran the show. Foreign observers were sympathetic to the difficulties facing AMIS, but admitted that 'its neutrality is an issue'. A frequent visitor to AMIS in Darfur complained that,

> After the DPA fell apart, my experience has been that the government representatives have been in charge. They used to do only Ceasefire Commission work, but now they work as intelligence. They work to stop the AU working – and anyone who visits – reporting back to their command on everything the AU does. They tell us what to do when we arrive in the base and tell the AU where not to go (pretty much anywhere) and the AU follows blindly.

Haskanita was in the eye of the storm. The area had been tense ever since July, when a convoy of JEM fighters in eighty-four armed vehicles set out from Tine, attacking positions of the government and SLA–Minawi – and civilians – on the way to Haskanita, where the rebel commander announced his defection from SLA–Minawi to SLA–Unity, in partnership with JEM.[72] Between 30 August and 30 September, the government launched 'sustained bombing raids'[73] on SLA and JEM positions at Haskanita. The 'burden of the bombings on civilians' led 1,500 people, by AU count, to demonstrate outside the AMIS site on 6 September, complaining that AMIS was not doing enough to protect them. JEM commander Abdel Aziz Nur Osher, Khalil Ibrahim's half-brother, demanded the suspension of all AMIS flights to Haskanita and pressed for the eviction of the government representative at the base, accusing him of giving the coordinates of rebel positions to government pilots. Flights were suspended, but the government representative remained. Three weeks later, on the morning of 28 September, JEM and SLA forces were driven out of a position in the village of Delil Babikir south of Haskanita after what AU officers called 'an unrelenting offensive' by government forces. The next day, government planes 'subjected Haskanita village to heavy bombardment' for two hours. The AU received reports that the rebel factions had sustained 'huge' casualties both in men and equipment, and later speculated that 'the setback suffered by the rebel factions probably induced the attack on [the AU base in] Haskanita for the purpose of replenishing their depleted logistic stocks ... to enhance their withdrawal from Haskanita'.

Across the border in Chad, on the morning of 29 September, Suleiman Jamous heard 'rumours' that the rebels in Haskanita were restive, having intercepted new ground-to-air communications which they said had to come from the AMIS observer site since they controlled everywhere outside it. In the communications, the pilots' contact on the ground, who the rebels described as speaking Sudanese Arabic, reportedly said there were no rebel positions north of Haskanita but recommended bombardment of a small camp to the east before advancing towards the town itself. Jamous warned his comrades in Haskanita that any action against AMIS 'would be a very bad strategic mistake which will affect your name and reputation'. The response he received increased his concern: popular anger in Haskanita was rising fast and there was 'strong grassroots pressure' to do something.[74]

That same night, as the Ramadan fast ended, heavily armed men in some thirty vehicles attacked the AU base. One of the men trapped inside the base said 'it was rebels – a mixture of JEM and SLA fighting together. They were very drunk!'

> The MILOBS [military observer] major was shot in the bathroom in the back but was still alive. The PAE [private subcontractor][75] guys got him to the bunker where our medic was and they worked on him but he died. I think the exit wound was through the liver so it was very bloody. They had most of the casualties with them at the bunker plus the ten dead bodies and they were in a confined space with all this for about sixteen hours. The rebels ransacked and looted *everything* – the guys were left with only the clothes on their backs – our medic had to give them his protection boots off his feet! They took all the food, fuel, vehicles, ransacked the clinic. Apparently they kept returning to the bunker where the guys were. The guys were unharmed but had guns held to their heads constantly and they never were quite sure if the rebels would come back, be pissed off if they didn't have what they wanted and would just shoot them then.[76]

An AU report into the attack ten days later said 'vehicles used by the attackers bore the bold insignia of JEM'. It said the attack was 'well coordinated' and 'targeted all known gun positions, radio room, APCs [armoured personnel carriers] and areas like the mosque where [...] personnel were likely to concentrate'. The base had only one serviceable *Thuraya* telephone among 157 soldiers and was rendered incommunicado almost immediately.

> The radio room was completely destroyed by a 106 mm projectile in the first few minutes of the attack. One out of the two radio men was instantly killed and communication via the [high frequency radio] sets was severed ... The RPG [rocket-propelled

grenade] fired into the mosque ignited fire setting the mosque ablaze ... Efforts to manoeuvre the APCs into firing positions met barrages of the attackers' AA [anti-aircraft] guns (12.5 mm) used in an infantry role at close proximity ... One of the APC gunners who responded with a burst of fire was killed right inside the APC. Two others, a gunner and a driver who were accosted in their vehicle (APC), were shot and wounded on the abdomen and shoulder respectively before the APC was set ablaze. The [company commander], a lieutenant, lost contact with his [junior commanders] and men because virtually all but one Hand Held Radio was in the possession of the attackers. Moreso, he became causality [sic] from RPG shrapnel few minutes after the attack commenced. A few PF [protection force soldiers] mustered at the west end of the camp to offer resistance, but could hardly fire for fear of hitting MILOBs, CIVPOL [civilian police] and other allied staff. Having subdued the resistance of the PF the attackers employed the services of some allied staff to either identify a key officer, or aid the removal of vital materials/equipment.

Eight hours later the base was looted. The attackers made off with weapons, ammunition, communication equipment, food, beds, mattresses and seventeen vehicles. When day dawned, and the few AU men who had stood their ground began gathering their dead, 'villagers emerged from all directions to commence the looting of the camp property'.[77] UN investigators later said that 'with one or two brave exceptions, the Nigerian force put up no fight. They admitted that they rarely even cleaned their weapons and had not zeroed them since leaving Nigeria. They were at the end of their six-month tour and at the end of a long, hot, Ramadan day. Some who were killed were in the shower block.'[78] Humanitarian officials said the UN, which had 10,000 troops in South Sudan, tried to send a rescue team to Haskanita in the hours following the attack, but was refused flight permission by Khartoum.[79] The AU's relief force arrived only at dawn.

The rebels in Haskanita denied any hand in the attack, which they blamed on the government forces that were closing in on

Haskanita. But AMIS concluded that the attack was organized by Khalil Ibrahim's faction of JEM, using SLA–Unity operatives commanded by Mohamed Osman, the former Minawi commander who had tortured Malik Abdel Rahman Mohamadein in Muzbat in 2004. Khalil denied involvement, supported, paradoxically, by SLA–Unity claims to have refused to enter into an alliance with him after JEM's leadership split. Suleiman Jamous said both JEM factions requested 'cooperation' with SLA–Unity after the split. He said SLA–Unity refused Khalil in favour of the rival faction led by Bahr Idriss Abu Garda and Abdalla Banda (who was seen in Haskanita village on the morning of the tragedy).[80] After this snub, a few days before the attack on AMIS, Khalil and his men left Haskanita.

An AU investigator concluded that the massacre in Haskanita might have been avoided 'if the JEM combatants did not move from Chad into Sudan on a yet to be ascertained mission'. Peace, his report said, 'will hardly be achieved if perpetrators of dastardly acts against civilians and peacekeepers [are] not brought to book … There is the need to bring such people to face the law.' But under pressure from senior UN officials, who feared disrupting a new round of peace talks scheduled for the end of October, and who did not want to make new enemies before UNAMID's deployment in Darfur, the AU agreed not make its findings public – and not to seek justice for its dead.

Getting the UN to Darfur

Amid the complexity of Darfur's war, the international community had one overriding aim: bringing in UN troops. This priority determined Abuja's deadline and drove the American compact with Minawi. It also pushed Vice-president Ali Osman into a gamble too far. True to his word, a month after the DPA was signed, Ali Osman introduced the UN troops proposal to a meeting of Sudan's national security leaders. Most of the professional military officers were in favour, but Bashir and Nafie suspected that Ali Osman was conspiring against them, planning to use his high standing in the US to marginalize or even remove them.[81]

On the basis of Ali Osman's promises in Paris and Brussels in March, the US and UN had taken for granted Khartoum's assent to a handover from AMIS to the UN. But as the months passed, it became clear that Ali Osman did not have the final word. American rhetoric hardened and on 31 August the UN Security Council passed Resolution 1706, which mandated a UN force of more than 20,000 troops, and 'invited' Khartoum's consent. This was pure bluff. There was no serious option of dispatching UN troops in the face of non-cooperation from the Sudan government, far less outright opposition. The troop numbers and deployment plan for Resolution 1706 were based on the security provisions of the DPA, which assumed a working peace agreement. It involved, for example, more than 3,000 civilian police personnel – and there is no precedent anywhere in the world for civilian policing without government consent. 'Non-consensual deployment' could be achieved only by invasion. Fearing that such plans might exist in the Pentagon or CIA headquarters, Khartoum's security chiefs intensified their destabilization of the expected launch pad for any invasion: eastern Chad.

On 3 September, Bashir called the UN's bluff. He walked into a cabinet meeting – hastily called without his first vice-president, Salva Kiir, or his senior assistant, Minni Minawi, present – and told his cabinet colleagues that Sudan was rejecting the UN demand. The matter was not up for discussion – or argument. Bashir proposed that AMIS be terminated when its mandate expired at the end of the month, leaving Darfur without any international peacekeepers at all, and said that he had ordered the armed forces to restore security in Darfur. In fact, as Bashir himself knew all too well – not to mention the residents and rebel forces of the Um Sidir area – the army was already attempting to impose the government's writ.

The UN did not have the stomach or any serious plan for non-consensual deployment and backed down at once. International pressure won the minor victory of an extension of AMIS and in November, at a 'high-level meeting' in Addis Ababa, Kofi Annan helped engineer – with Chinese and American support – the idea of a 'hybrid' force that was under UN command but retained African Union management on a day-to-day basis. This was less of a compromise than it might have appeared: from the earliest discussion of a UN force, its 'predominantly African' character had been agreed. Darfur's UN force was never going to be drawn primarily from NATO countries, as many Darfurians had hoped; most of its troops would be the existing Nigerian, Senegalese, Rwandan and South African troops, 'rehatted' as a UN force. The difference was better logistics and support and management systems. The Addis Ababa compromise included 'light support' and 'heavy support' packages whereby UN technicians would augment AMIS, while AMIS sent additional battalions to protect them. Khartoum dragged its feet, stalling on many aspects of the deployment and challenging many details of the proposed 'hybrid' force, the UN–African Union Mission in Darfur (UNAMID), which was finally approved by UN Security Council Resolution 1769 on 31 July 2007. The full mandated force size for UNAMID was 26,000 troops and civilian police, making it the largest UN peacekeeping force in the world – in the opinion of a western military officer, 'classic peacekeeping in an environment so wildly not a classic peace as to be ridiculous'.

Two and a half years after the idea of changing AMIS to the UN was first mooted, UNAMID was officially inaugurated on 1 January 2008. It was likely to be a year or so before its force strength reached even half its mandated size, due to the slowness in coming forward of troop contributors and equipment suppliers, the logistical challenges of operating in Darfur, and the administrative complexities of partnership between two bureaucratic, inflexible organizations. Darfurian expectations that UNAMID would protect them, get IDPs home safely and disarm the Janjawiid were hopelessly inflated. Contrary to popular perception, a Chapter VII mandate does not authorize UN troops to use force at their discretion, but only in circumstances specified by the particular Security Council resolution. The specifics of UNAMID's Chapter VII mandate were restrictive: the peacekeepers would be able to use force in self-defence and in response to immediate threats to civilians in its vicinity, but not with anything approaching the wide-ranging powers that NATO had in Kosovo. The sad reality was that UNAMID was designed to satisfy western public demand for military intervention. The vision of the mission was based on images of Darfur from the bloodbath years of 2003–04, rather than the complex conflict that had since emerged. Speaking off the record, senior UN and AU staff in Khartoum lamented that UNAMID was not tailored to Darfur's realities. At best it would be 'AMIS in new clothes'; at worst it would trip over itself and become 'the world's worst peacekeeping operation'.[82] 'It is just too large, too ungainly and too poorly led,' commented one UN official. Development experts also worried about its environmental impact, especially the voracious appetite the foreign troops would have for Darfur's already scarce timber and water resources. One UN agency calculated that each peacekeeper would use forty times more water than a local man.

Once the UN military presence in Darfur became a matter of political controversy, reliant on international pressure for achieving every small step forward, UNAMID was destined to be part of the problem rather than part of a solution. Senior UN officers knew better than anyone that Khartoum's campaign of bureaucratic obstruction would continue, creating a farrago of impediments that would render the simplest operations impossibly complicated; that, by sheer perseverance, security officers would wear down their UN and AU counterparts. As soon as IDPs and rebels saw that UNAMID was more akin to AMIS than NATO, frustrations would mount and UNAMID patrols and bases, like its predecessor's, would be vulnerable to attack. In defending itself, or in pre-empting attacks with a show of force, UNAMID would become a party to the conflict.

It was not only local forces that posed threats to UNAMID, which Khartoum considered an American creation; no sooner had Resolution 1706 been adopted than Ayman al Zawahiri, deputy to Osama bin Laden in al Qa'eda, denounced it as an another instrument of American imperial occupation of Muslim lands.[83] A year later, bin Laden himself released a videotape in which he called for 'jihad against the crusader invaders ... infidel apostates'.[84] And shortly after midnight on 1 January 2008, in UNAMID's very first moments of existence, gunmen shot dead a USAID staff member, John Granville, and his driver as they left a New Year's Eve party in Khartoum. A week later, government soldiers fired on a clearly identified UNAMID convoy, seriously injuring the driver and destroying a fuel tanker. Khartoum admitted responsibility for the attack, but said UNAMID had failed to report the convoy's movement. In the weeks following the murder of John Granville, senior UN officials had one overriding concern: the safety of their own soldiers and civilian staff. In Khartoum – normally a very safe city – higher-ranking officials were required to move around town with personal bodyguards. Boding even worse was the prospect of any attacks on UNAMID or UN agencies in the field. Should that happen, western governments would focus on the protection of the UN troops and not on Darfur's problems. Darfur's peacekeeping mission would become a test of resolve between the UN Security Council and whatever force was taking on UNAMID, with Darfur itself merely the theatre for this confrontation. Ever since the attack on the AU in Haskanita, even before the transition to UNAMID, the priority for all countries promising to contribute troops to UNAMID had been self-protection. Timur Goksel, one of the UN's most experienced peacekeeping specialists, commented on the ways in which a defensive approach to peacekeeping would not only impede the mission but might also increase the dangers it faced.

> If the African Union understands that a compassionate approach
> that involves going down to grassroots, building confidence
> with the relevant public will also mean the best possible way of
> gathering intelligence and taking preventive measures based on
> that intelligence, UNAMID has a chance. Otherwise it will be yet
> another mission with soldiers in their armored cars or behind/
> inside their fortresses helplessly watching and reporting.[85]

The primary rule of peacekeeping is: first make peace. UNAMID was set up in violation of this.[86] Contemplating the wreckage of international policy six months after Abuja and two months after Bashir torpedoed Resolution 1706, the UN and AU resolved to begin a new peace process. Like so many international initiatives on Darfur, it was a good idea and even a necessary one; but it had feet of clay, in part because of the involvement of the discredited AU. It took months to appoint the joint UN and AU envoys – Jan Eliasson and Salim Ahmed Salim, both of whom were part-timers – and put together a team and a plan of action. By May 2007, when the two envoys announced a three-stage plan of action – first, getting support from the governments of the region (including Chad, Eritrea and Libya), then creating a unified negotiating position and strategy among the movements, and finally managing negotiations – events had decisively moved on. The acquiescence of Eritrea and Libya to the UN- and AU-led process was only for the cameras – each stood ready to sabotage it at any time. Left to their own devices, the rebels were more divided than ever, their fragmentation encouraged by the offer of seats at the negotiations for any group that could demonstrate a political agenda and a presence on the ground. Most significant of all, the Sudan government had no interest in making the slightest concession to the rebels. For Khartoum, the prize of peace was international recognition, and it had given up expecting anything except hostility from western capitals.

Overruling the advice of seasoned diplomats and Sudan watchers, Eliasson and Salim convened the Darfur negotiations in the Libyan town of Sirte on 27 October 2007. Everything went as predicted: wrong. The most important rebel groups, including SLA–Abdel Wahid, JEM and SLA–Unity, refused to show up. The latter two had asked for more time to prepare. Abdel Wahid had shunned all emissaries sent to persuade him to attend, insisted on recognition as sole leader of a now-mythical 'SLA' and demanded a restoration of security in Darfur before he agreed to talk about the way forward. The mediators were reduced to chasing around after individuals with meagre or non-existent power bases and cajoling them to come to Sirte, simply to avoid humiliation. They didn't succeed, and the efforts of smaller rebel fragments to make themselves visible contributed to an upsurge in violence in Darfur. In Sirte itself, more than sixty 'experts' were employed, outnumbering the rebel delegates by two to one. Most had never set foot in Darfur. The Libyan leader Muammar Gaddafi made an angry speech in which he compared the Darfur crisis to 'a quarrel over a camel' which should never have involved the international community. Minawi refused to attend as a member of the Khartoum delegation and instead insisted that his representatives would go solely as 'facilitators'. Nafie Ali Nafie, representing the government, sat without speaking for most of the proceedings. In the few words he spoke, he made it clear that the government considered the DPA inviolable, apart from details of implementation. Unless the rebels agreed to this, he insisted, there would be no agreement.

The reason for the rush was that the new Secretary-General of the UN, Ban Ki Moon, wanted quick results. He was under American pressure and, wholly unfamiliar with the nuances and challenges of complex peacemaking, seemed to believe that running a mediation was no more than an exercise in business management. Rather than assigning a low-profile team to do solid preparatory work out of the limelight, calling the principals only when a deal was emerging, Ban Ki Moon insisted on repeating the worst errors of Abuja – this time as farce. A host of reasons – from the complications of UNAMID's deployment and the crisis in the North–South peace accord to presidential elections in the United States in 2008 – meant that there was no prospect of a peace agreement in the foreseeable future.

The politics of exhaustion

By 2008, Omar Hassan Ahmad al Bashir had been Sudan's president for nineteen years, longer than any of his predecessors. He was an often puzzling figure: a simple soldier at heart, yet intensely proud; prone to fiery outbursts in public speeches, yet a good listener in private and open to discussion, even with westerners. Above all, Bashir was a master of survival. His government had been ostracized and sanctioned for hosting Osama bin Laden and other international jihadists, but had held on to power. He had faced armed invasions by his neighbours, a cruise missile attack on his capital, and a US policy of regime change by proxy, and he had survived. Burdened with an unmanageable international debt, his government had never been solvent and yet had funded its army and security services. The gravest threats to his regime had been internal. For a decade, Bashir was over-shadowed by Hassan al Turabi, who ran a state within a state, promoted a radical vision of political Islam, and then sought to remove him. Following that, he was sidelined by Ali Osman Taha and his project of reinventing the regime as a friend of America. But he had survived. Bashir was sparing in his direct political interventions, saving them for moments when the regime faced its direst crises. One such instance was in September 2006, when he personally rejected the UN Security Council's demand for a UN force in Darfur as an affront to Sudan's sovereignty and his own dignity as its president.

Bashir had seen a succession of Sudanese politicians exhaust themselves, each of them defeated by the intractability of the country's problems. He had seen the international community throw everything it could at Sudan, save its own combat troops, and dash their aspirations to pieces on Sudan's realities. He considered that time was on his side and decided to wait it out in Darfur, confident that the rebels would bicker and fight among themselves while the UN consumed its energies with an impossibly complex peace mission. He suspected that the Americans, supported by the British and the French, might try to use the UN in Darfur, the European troops in Chad or even the rebels to get rid of his regime. Expert in the politics of prevarication, he planned to outlast domestic rebels, internal rivals and western adversaries. Darfur would remain a crisis, but a manageable crisis far from the centre of power. The shifts in the loyalties of Arab tribes were a major worry, but Bashir lost no time in addressing the problem with a one-two punch of threat and promise, firepower and favours. If the cost of loyalty threatened to become financially painful, it would at least be politically manageable.

Bashir would continue to play the armed politics of Chad as though that country were an extension of his own – expecting sooner or later to instal a more pliable regime there and, in the meantime, determined to tie down in interminable, painful fights both Idriss Deby and the European soldiers who were in reality Deby's first line of defence and, as such, targets themselves.

Contemplating the threats he faced, internal and external, Sudan's president could comfort himself with the thought that he had seen off tougher challenges to his survival and was secure for the time being. For the people of Darfur, there was no such solace. The trauma of the war, massacres and displacement was matched only by hopelessness about the future. 'Dar Masalit was destroyed four times: 1997, 1998, 1999 and 2003,' Ibrahim Yahya, a Masalit politician in JEM, said in 2004. 'The Fur can forget. Not the Masalit and Zaghawa. The Masalit and Zaghawa will never forget this. Even future generations will take revenge.'[87] Three years later, with no end in sight to the suffering of his community, Yahya saw no alternative but to cut a deal with the government and go back to Khartoum.

During the years of firestorm, 2003–04, the government's armed forces and militias terrorized Darfurians, caused the deaths of some 200,000 non-combatants, and left millions homeless. The legacy was a torn and fractured society in which the little trust that remained between neighbours was strained to its limits by the cynical double dealing of Khartoum, the self-serving policies of Eritrea, Chad and Libya, and the abuses of armed men on all sides. An international response sought quick and simple fixes time and again, not learning from its mistakes, and failed time and again. Solving complex and intractable conflicts demands skill, expertise, timing and luck – an alignment of the political planets that comes rarely and passes swiftly. That alignment was possible to discern, perhaps, in 2005 and 2006, but clumsiness, haste and a failure of international leadership let it slip away. By 2008, as the demands of preventing a return to war in South Sudan returned to the centre of Sudan's political stage, Darfur's political prospects seemed to have slipped irretrievably.

As Darfur descended into lawlessness, bled dry by a criminalized war economy, and as the UNAMID project looked more and more like a waste of hope, Darfurians faced a bleak future. For many, the past was already a different country – and one they feared they might never recover.

'We did not know the word Janjawiid when we were young,' Sheikh Heri Rahma of Muzbat said in 2005, two years short of his eightieth birthday.

> The Arabs came here looking for pasture, and when the grass was finished they went back. They used up our grass, but they took good care of the gardens and the people. There were no robberies, no thieves, no revolution. No one thought of domination; everyone was safe. We were afraid only of lions and hyenas. Now there is nothing but trouble, all over Sudan. There is no government, no control. Look around you. What do you see? No women, only armed men. We no longer recognize it, this land of ours.

Chronology

*c.*1630   Foundation of the Fur sultanate

1787 Dar Fur conquers Kordofan

1821 Egyptian conquest of the Sudanese Nile

1874 Overthrow of the Fur sultanate

1884 Mahdists take control of Dar Fur

1898 Defeat of the Mahdists and restoration of the Fur sultanate

1913 Drought and *julu* famine

1916 Overthrow of Sultan Ali Dinar and incorporation of Darfur
      into Sudan

1922 Incorporation of Dar Masalit into Sudan

1920s Creation of 'Native Administration' system

1956 Independence of Sudan

1960 Railway reaches Nyala

1966 Chadian opposition front FROLINAT (forerunner of the
      CDR) founded in Nyala

1969 Jaafar Nimeiri takes power in Sudan

1970 Ansar and Muslim Brothers flee Sudan

1971 Native Administration abolished

1973 Libya starts smuggling weapons to Chadian opposition
      through Darfur, beginning of Islamic Legion activities in
      Chad

1976 Ansar–Muslim Brothers invasion of Sudan from Libya

1980 A regional government and elected governor provided for
      Darfur

1983 Hissène Habré takes power in Chad

1984 Drought leading to famine in Darfur

April 1985 Overthrow of Nimeiri and opening of Darfur–Libya
      border

1987 Acheikh Ibn Omar sets up Chadian armed camps in Darfur

1987–89 First Arab–Fur war, first organization of ethnic Arab
      militias

June 1989 Omar al Bashir takes power in Khartoum

December 1990 Idriss Deby takes power in Chad

December 1991 SPLA incursion into Darfur

1994 Darfur divided into three states, Native Administration reintroduced

March 1995 Eight 'amirs' appointed for the Arabs in West Darfur

1995–99 Arab–Masalit conflict

1999 Split in ruling Congress Party

May 2000 Publication of the *The Black Book* detailing marginalization of Darfur

2001 Organization of armed opposition in Darfur

2002 Conferences at Nyertete and Kass to try to mediate the conflict

December 2002 Vice-president Ali Osman warns Darfur not to follow the path of the South

2003

February SLA announces its existence and publishes manifesto

March JEM announces its existence

April Rebels attack al Fasher airbase

May Rebel attacks on Kutum, Mellit, Tina

June Musa Hilal released from house arrest and militia mobilization begins in earnest

July Government counter-offensive in North Darfur, major massacres up to September

August First relief operations begin

September Government–SLA ceasefire talks in Abeche, Chad

December Second major government offensive begins, in North and West Darfur, major massacres up to March 2004

2004

January Two senior rebel commanders killed

March UN Coordinator Mukesh Kapila calls the crisis 'genocide'

April Government–rebel talks in N'Djamena agree on a ceasefire and AU monitoring mission

May First AU monitors (African Union Mission in Sudan) arrive

June US Congress describes Darfur as 'genocide'

July UN Security Council gives Khartoum 30 days to disarm the Janjawiid and facilitate humanitarian assistance

August Government and rebels meet in Abuja, Nigeria, for the first round of peace talks

September US Secretary of State Colin Powell declares Darfur
        to be 'genocide' and the UN Security Council sets up an
        International Commission of Inquiry on Darfur

October AMIS mandate increased to include modest civilian
        protection

2005

January Comprehensive Peace Agreement signed between
        Khartoum and SPLM

        ICID delivers its report

        End of major hostilities between Sudan government and
        rebels

March UN Security Council refers Darfur to the International
        Criminal Court

July Government of National Unity formed including SPLM

        John Garang dies in a helicopter crash

        Sudan government, SLA and JEM sign a 'Declaration of
        Principles' at the Abuja peace talks

September SLA commanders challenge Minawi over his refusal to
        participate in peace talks

November SLA–Minawi holds Convention in Haskanita that
        divides the movement

        Final round of Abuja peace talks convenes

December US government begins a push to handover AMIS to a
        UN force

        Civil war erupts in eastern Chad as rebels attack Adre

2006

January African Union rejects President Bashir to head the AU

March Government and rebels reject ceasefire

        Hostilities increase on the ground

        AU agrees to hand over AMIS to UN in the event of a peace
        agreement

        19 SLA commanders reject Abdel Wahid al Nur's leadership

April Intense negotiations as Abuja deadline approaches

        Chadian rebels attack N'Djamena and are repulsed with the
        assistance of JEM

May Darfur Peace Agreement signed by Khartoum and Minawi
        but rejected by Abdel Wahid and JEM

June Non-signatory rebels create the National Redemption Front in Asmara

Splinter groups from the rebels sign a 'Declaration of Commitment' and join the government

July SLA leaders led by Ahmed Abdel Shafi seek to oust Abdel Wahid

August Minawi becomes Senior Assistant to the President

Fighting intensifies as AU expels the non-signatory rebels from the Ceasefire Commission

UN Security Council demands that Sudan accept a UN force

September Sudan rejects UN force

Government offensives repulsed in Darfur

November Sudan agrees to a 'hybrid' UN–AU force for Darfur

December SLA commanders in the field push for unity

2007

April ICC issues indictments against Ahmed Haroun (government minister) and Ali Kushayb (militia leader)

May UN and AU adopt a new plan for peace negotiations

US announces targeted economic sanctions against Sudan

June Abdel Wahid rejects participation in new peace talks

July Negotiations are finalized on the size and mandate of the hybrid UN–AU Mission in Darfur

August Rebel offensives in eastern Darfur and Kordofan

September Government pushes back rebels from Kordofan

Rebel attack on the AU base at Haskanita

October New peace talks convene in Sirte, Libya; no progress is made

Major Janjawiid militia desert the government

2008

January UNAMID takes over from AMIS

Gunmen kill a USAID staff member in Khartoum

The Sudan government makes Ahmed Haroun liaison with UNAMID and Musa Hilal adviser in the Ministry of Federal Affairs

Darfur-based Chad rebels begin a major push to overthrow Idriss Deby

Glossary

Abbala	camel herders
amir	'Prince': Arab tribal leader under 1995 local government system
AMIS	African Union Mission in Sudan
Ansar	followers of the Mahdi
AU	African Union
Baggara	cattle herders
CDR	Conseil Démocratique Révolutionnaire, Chadian opposition front
CPA	Comprehensive Peace Agreement, signed with SPLM January 2005
damra	Arab settlement within a *dar* or *hakura* belonging to another group
dar	tribal homeland
DLF	Darfur Liberation Front, forerunner of SLA
DPA	Darfur Peace Agreement, signed May 2006
FROLINAT	Front for the Liberation of Chad
fursha	middle-ranking administrative chief in Dar Masalit
Fursan	horsemen, used for Arab militia
hakura	land grant under the Fur sultanate
ICC	International Criminal Court
ICID	International Commission of Inquiry on Darfur
Islamic Legion	Libyan-established international brigade for Sahelian countries and Sudan
JEM	Justice and Equality Movement
masar	livestock migration route
Murahaliin	Baggara militia
nazir	paramount chief, usually of an Arab tribe
NCP	National Congress Party
NDA	National Democratic Alliance, umbrella opposition group
NIF	National Islamic Front

NRF	National Redemption Front (headed by JEM)
omda	middle-ranking administrative chief
PCP	Popular Congress Party
PDF	Popular Defence Forces, government paramilitaries
Qoreish	tribe of the Prophet Mohamed
shartai	senior chief in the Fur hierarchy
sheikh	lowest-ranking tribal leader
SLA	Sudan Liberation Army
SPLA	Sudan People's Liberation Army
UNAMID	UN–African Union Mission in Darfur
UNMIS	UN Mission in Sudan
wadi	seasonal watercourse

Dramatis personae

The government:

Lieutenant General Omar Hassan al Bashir: President of Sudan since 1989, commander of the Sudan armed forces and leader of the National Congress Party. Ja'ali.

Ali Osman Mohamed Taha: First Vice-president and the architect, with John Garang, of the North–South Comprehensive Peace Agreement. Shaygiyya.

Lieutenant General Nafie Ali Nafie: Assistant President, former Minister of Federal Government and former Minister of Interior for External Intelligence. A regime hardliner.

Majzoub al Khalifa Ahmad: head of the government delegation to the Abuja peace talks. Killed in a car crash in July 2007.

Lieutenant General Mohamed Ahmad al Dabi: head of Darfur Security Arrangements Implementation Commission. Former head of military intelligence and external security, and President Bashir's personal representative in Western Darfur in 1999.

Lieutenant General Ismat al Zain: head of Western Military Command and head of the government security arrangements negotiating team at the Abuja peace talks.

Major General Salah Abdalla Abu Digin 'Gosh': head of the National Intelligence Security Service, liaison with the CIA and a key member of Sudan's inner security circle.

Colonel Ahmed Mohamed Haroun: Minister of State for Humanitarian Affairs and liaison with UNAMID. Indicted by the ICC for crimes against humanity committed in Darfur in 2003–04 in his capacity as Minister of State for the Interior and head of the Darfur Security Desk.

General Ibrahim Suleiman, governor of North Darfur 2001–03 and former army chief of staff. Berti.

Major General Abdalla Safi al Nur: Minister at the Council of Ministers and former governor of North Darfur. Ereigat Arab from Kutum.

Tayeb Ibrahim 'Sikha': governor of Darfur 1990–92 and responsible for crushing the SPLA incursion.

Arab leaders

Musa Hilal: leader of the Um Jalul clan of the Mahamid Arabs. In his own words 'Mujahid, Sheikh and Amir of the Swift and Fearsome Forces' based, under Sudan army control, in Mistiriha in North Darfur. Son of Sheikh Hilal Abdalla.

Ali Mohamed Ali Abdel Rahman 'Kushayb': indicted by the ICC as commander of the militia forces of Wadi Saleh, liaison with the Sudan government and a participant in murders, rapes and torture in 2003–04.

Mohamed Hamdan Dogolo 'Hemeti': leader of a Mahariya Arab militia in the Nyala area of South Darfur who mutinied in October 2007 and rejoined the government in February 2008.

Mohamedein al Dud Hassaballa: leader of the Mahariya of North Darfur.

Saeed Madibu: Nazir of the Baggara Rizeigat of South Darfur and steadfastly neutral in the conflict.

Ali al Ghali: Nazir of the Habbaniya Arabs of South Darfur.

Al Hadi Issa Dabaka: Nazir of the Beni Halba Arabs of South Darfur; raised a militia to fight the SPLA in 1991 but tried to remain neutral in 2003–04. Died in 2007.

Northern Sudanese political leaders

Hassan al Turabi: Sudanese Islamist leader, head of the Popular Congress Party and *éminence grise* behind the regime 1989–99. Removed from power after disagreeing with President Bashir and subsequently a vigorous opponent of the government.

Ali al Haj Mohamed: leading Islamist from Darfur, Minister of Federal Affairs responsible for the administrative reform that divided Darfur into three states in 1994; later a leader of the Islamist opposition from abroad. Bornu.

Sadiq al Mahdi: leader of the Umma Party, Prime Minister 1986–89.

The Rebels: Sudan Liberation Army

Abdel Wahid Mohamed al Nur: Chairman of the SLA and, after its division, leader of the Fur wing based in Jebel Marra. Unchallenged spokesman for the Fur displaced despite rejecting the Darfur Peace Agreement and being self-exiled ever since in Paris.

Abdalla Abakir: first military commander of the SLA, killed by helicopter gunship attack in January 2004. Zaghawa/Ohuru.

Khamis Abdalla Abakir: Masalit Vice Chairman of the SLA, never clearly identified with any faction after the rebel movement divided. One of the first self-defence leaders in Dar Masalit.

Jar al Nabi Abdel Karim Younis: SLA commander in North Darfur who led the Group of 19, or G19, break from SLA–Abdel Wahid in March 2006. Zaghawa/Kaitinga.

Ahmed Abdel Shafi: co-founder of SLM. Leader of a breakaway Fur faction announced in July 2006 to demand structure and accountability in the rebel movement. Coordinator of the original SLA.

Juma Mohamed Hagar: Minni Minawi's loyal military chief. Zaghawa/Dawa.

Suleiman Jamous: humanitarian coordinator of the SLA in North Darfur, arrested by Minni Minawi in May 2006 for opposing the Darfur Peace Agreement and joined SLA–Unity. Bideyat.

Suleiman Marajan: Meidob SLA commander arrested by Minni Minawi after attending the sixth round of the Abuja peace talks.

Minni Arkoi Minawi: Senior Assistant to the President of Sudan. Abdel Wahid's Zaghawa challenger for the chairmanship of the SLA and the only rebel leader to sign the Darfur Peace Agreement. Ila Digen.

The Rebels: the Justice and Equality Movement

Bahr Idriss Abu Garda: JEM Secretary General and former National Islamic Front official. Broke with Khalil Ibrahim in August 2007 in a clan-based split within the movement. Zaghawa Kobe.

Abdalla Banda: former businessman and JEM's military commander until he joined Bahr Idriss in breaking with Khalil Ibrahim in 2007. Zaghawa Kobe.

Jibreel Ibrahim: adviser to Khalil Ibrahim, his brother, and head of JEM's wealth-sharing delegation at the Abuja peace talks.

Khalil Ibrahim: JEM Chairman and former senior regional official in the NIF. Refused to sign the Darfur Peace Agreement. Zaghawa Kobe.

Abdel Aziz Nur Osher: JEM Deputy Political Leader and Commander of the Eastern Front. Khalil Ibrahim's half-brother. Zaghawa Kobe.

Abubaker Hamid Nur: JEM general coordinator and former NIF official. Zaghawa Kobe.

Ahmad Tugod Lissan: JEM chief negotiator at the Abuja talks. Zaghawa Kobe.

Taj al Din Bashir Nyam: JEM humanitarian coordinator and deputy chief negotiator at the Darfur peace talks in Abuja. Zaghawa Kobe.

Ibrahim Yahya: JEM Speaker of Parliament and Chairman of the Executive Committee until he joined a pro-government faction after JEM rejected the Darfur Peace Agreement. Masalit.

The rebels: others

Ahmad Diraige: veteran Darfurian leader and governor 1981–83, head of the opposition Sudan Federal Democratic Alliance. Fur.

Sharif Harir: academic and opposition leader based in Eritrea. Foreign affairs spokesman of SLA–Unity and former deputy head of the SFDA. Zaghawa.

Sudan People's Liberation Army

John Garang: Chairman and Commander-in-Chief of the SPLA until his death in 2005.

Daud Bolad: former Islamist from Darfur who joined the SPLA and died leading an ill-fated military expedition into Darfur in 1991. Fur.

Yasir Arman: most prominent Northern Sudanese within the SPLA, responsible for the Darfur file.

Abdel Aziz Adam al Hilu: SPLA commander, of mixed Masalit–Nuba parentage, military commander for the 1991 SPLA mission and subsequently in charge of military training for Darfurians in the SPLA.

Adam Mohamed Musa 'Bazooka': Chadian Masalit soldier who joined the SPLA and died fighting in Darfur in January 2004.

Chad

Idriss Deby: President of Chad since 1991, formerly military commander. Zaghawa.

Hissène Habré: President of Chad 1979–81 and 1983–91, strongly anti-Arab, fought against Libya. Goraan.

Acheikh Ibn Omar Saeed: Chadian Arab, Commander in the Libyan Islamic Legion and head of the Conseil Démocratique Révolutionnaire, involved in the first Arab–Fur war of 1987–89.

Notes

1 *The people of Darfur*

1· See O'Fahey and Abu Salim (1983).

2 This section draws heavily upon the excellent study of Dor in Abdul-Jalil (1984).

3 The phenomenon of richer farmers in the Jebel Marra investing their wealth in cattle, changing their lifestyle and cultural traits, and 'becoming Baggara [Arabs]' was noted in the 1960s. See Haaland (1969).

4 Eleven livestock routes were demarcated in 1936 but only three reach the desert itself. See Young et al. (2005), p. 55.

5 Interview with Mohamed Omar Diko in Itiri, March 2007. The fighting began after a member of the Arab Um Jalul clan forcibly disarmed Diko.

6 Meeting with Darfurian Arab leaders at the house of Abdalla Safi al Nur, Khartoum, November 2007.

7 The proverb is cited by Musa Abdul-Jalil.

8 See Kapteijns (1985).

9 Interview with Omda Taj el Din Abdalla Jibreel, Misrih, November 2007.

10 Daly (2007), p. 108.

11 Kapteijns (1985), p. 78.

12 Sir Harold finished his career as the last British governor of Palestine, overwhelmed and bewildered by modern political forces that were so different from his beloved Sudanese rural aristocracies.

13˙ The Beni Hussein and Zayadiya Arabs both obtained nazirates.

14 Sudan National Archive, Civsec (1) 64-2-11, 'Economic Development, Darfur Province', 1945.

15 Daly (1991), pp. 106–8, 123, 260–1, 347.

16 Doornbos (1988).

17 Interviewed in Legediba, May 1986.

2 *The Sudan government*

1 See e.g. Babiker (1984) and Garang (1992).

2 Interviewed in N'Djamena, January 2005.

3 Interviewed in Khartoum, January 2005.

4 Ushari and Baldo (1987).

5 Amnesty International (1989); African Rights (1995); Christian Aid (2001).

6 Undated message from Musa Hilal to 'our government, our people and the leaders of the state', around April 2004.

7 De Waal and Abdelsalam (2004).

8 De Waal (2004).

3 The Janjawiid

1 From Alex de Waal's diary, 6 November 1985.

2 BBC interview with Mukesh Kapila, UN Humanitarian Coordinator for Sudan, March 2004.

3 Emily Wax, 'In Sudan, "a Big Sheik" Roams Free', *Washington Post*, 18 July 2004.

4 Philip Sherwell, 'Tribal Leader Accused Over Darfur Says He was Acting for Government', *Daily Telegraph*, 22 August 2004.

5 Wax, 'In Sudan'.

6 Interview with Mohamed Basher in Abuja, September 2005.

7 Interviewed by Human Rights Watch in Khartoum, September 2004.

8 Human Rights Watch (2005) identified Lt Col. Saeed as commander of the 2nd Border Intelligence Brigade based in Misteriha. It said he took his orders from the minister of state for the interior, Ahmed Mohamed Haroun, for whom the ICC issued an arrest warrant in May 2007 in connection with alleged war crimes committed in Darfur.

9 Confidential information to the authors, April 2004.

10 Western diplomatic sources, 2007.

11 Interview with Hassan Ahmad Mohamed in Amarai, March 2007.

12 Power (2004).

13 Young et al. (2005), p. 127.

14 Interview with Omda Khidir Ali Abdel Rahman Hussein Abu Kawda in Amarai, March 2007.

15 Details from the Sudan National Archive, Khartoum, file Civsec (1) 66-12-107, 'Rizeigat', 1917–41.

16 This putative *dar* exists in documents in the possession of Mahariya sheikhs. A summary of the claim was provided to the authors by Mahmoud Adam, Kutum, November 2007.

17 Several of these are not part of the Rizeigat lineage but came under its political patronage. The Ereigat are a small group long associated with the Rizeigat in Darfur and the Awlad Rashid are a large Arab tribe, mostly living in Chad, which had until recently just a few stray lineages in Darfur.

18 Al-Bashir (1978), p. 38.

19 Ibid.

20 de Waal and el Amin (1986), pp. 33, 38–9.

21 Interview with former Aamo resident, Khartoum, January 2005.

22 Interview with Mohamed Matar Mukhtar in Amarai, March 2007.

23 Kulaka is a reference to the marcher ants that were attracted to the tree by the honey Sheikh Hilal smeared on his prisoners.

24 Musa Hilal denied this story to the authors, with a smile.

25 Abdel Kassim Ferseldin, 'Devils in Disguise', unpublished essay (2004).

26 Telephone interview, 17 January 2008. The authenticity of Qoreish 1 has never been questioned, but the authors have been unable to locate a copy.

27 Abdullahi al Tom, 'The Arab Congregation and the Ideology

of Genocide in Darfur, Sudan', 24 July 2007, <http://aeltom.com/index.php?option=com_content&task=view&id=30&Itemid=38&limit=1&limitstart=6>.

28 Some Western commentators on Darfur seem unable to escape making specious parallels with Nazism. Cf. Genocide Watch which calls the Arab Gathering 'a shadowy Nazi type brotherhood deeply embedded in the Bashir regime', Genocide Watch, 'Genocide Emergency: Darfur, Sudan, Update: 1 April 2006', <http://www.genocidewatch.org/Sudan GENOCIDEEMERGENCYDARFUR update1April2006.htm>.

29 Ruiz (1987).

30 Harir (1994).

31 Telephone interview, 9 March 2005.

32 'MPs Charge Conspiracy in Darfur', *Sudan Times*, 15 January 1989.

33 Burr and Collins (1999), p. 236.

34 See Harir (1994), for details.

35 E-mail from Tijani Sese, 12 November 2007.

36 'The leader says "There is a determination in Sudan to bury reactionarism and sectarianism"', *JANA Bulletin*, 28 October 1990.

37 See Kapteijns (1985).

38 Meeting with Alex de Waal, December 1985.

39 Alex de Waal, diary, December 1985.

40 Ali Hassan Taj el Din's grandfather was sultan from 1905–10. He died fighting the French at the head of a joint Masalit–Arab army.

41 Discussions with Arab leaders, Geneina, September 2005, reported by Yousif Takana, January 2008.

42 Interviewed in Abuja, December 2004.

43 The Council of West Darfur State, Law Organizing Native Administration, 1999, Part 1 Section 3. Though passed in 1999, the logic and intent were clear from March 1995. A similar provision was made for the most senior Fur chief, the *Dimangawi* of Zalingei.

44 Interviewed in Khartoum, November 2007.

45 Telephone interview, 22 December 2007.

46 Interviewed in Khartoum, February 2005.

47 Telephone interview, 17 January 2008.

48 Interviewed in Khartoum, November 2007.

49 Telephone interview, 17 January 2008.

50 Telephone interview, 17 January 2008.

51 These particular phrases were used by Yousif Takana in a telephone interview, 17 January 2008.

52 Data from the 1997 Arab–Masalit reconciliation conferences. See Young et al. (2005), p. 165.

53 Interview with Yousif Takana, Khartoum, November 2007.

54 Variants of this version were provided by Arab leaders in Khartoum, interviewed in November 2007 and Abdalla Adam Khater,

Hassan al Imam, al Sanosi Musa and Yousif Takana, December 2007 and January 2008.

55 Interviews with Arab leaders, Khartoum, November 2007.

56 Telephone interview, 17 January 2008.

57 The Masalit Community in Exile, 'Not-Ready-For-Prime-Time Genocide', 1999.

58 Telephone interview, March 2008.

59 Interviewed in Abuja, December 2004.

60 Telephone interview, March 2008.

61 Data obtained from Yousif Takana, December 2007.

62 Interviews in Abuja and N'Djamena, 2004–05.

63 Interview with Daud Taher Hariga in N'Djamena, December 2004.

64 Interview with Tom Suleiman Kosa, then leader of the activists, in N'Djamena, January 2005.

65 Interview with Ibrahim Yahya in Abuja, December 2004.

66 Interviews in Khartoum and Darfur, November 2007.

67 Interview with Mansour Nayer Juma in Bahai displaced camp, January 2005.

68 Interviews, Khartoum and Darfur, November 2007.

69 Interview with Mubarak Abakir Musa in Bahai displaced camp, January 2005.

70 Interviewed in Abuja, December 2004.

71 Interview with Hassan Ahmad in Amarai, March 2007.

72 *Um Kwakiyya* is the name popularly given to Darfur's quarter-century of chaos and bloodshed after the downfall of the sultanate in 1874.

73 Interview with SLA Commander Tayyib Bashar in Abuja, January 2005.

74 Interview with Shartai Suleiman Hassaballa Suleiman in Amarai, March 2007.

75 Interview with SLA commander Mohamed Harin in Abuja, December 2004.

76 Interview with Ibrahim Yahya in Abjua, December 2004.

77 Interview with Awadalla Nahar in Oure Cassoni camp in Bahai, January 2005.

78 Telephone interviews, 15 and 17 January 2008.

79 Interview with al Sanosi Musa, December 2007.

80 Interview with Shartai Suleiman Hassaballa.

81 Interviewed in Nyala, November 2007. His name has been withheld at his request.

82 For details of this campaign, see the 'Memorandum submitted by the Darfur Relief and Documentation Centre to the UK Parliament', 11 January 2005.

4 *The rebels*

1 Interview in Dar Masalit, March–April 2004.

2 Interviewed in Dar Masalit, April 2004.

3 The Masalit Community in Exile, 'Not-Ready-For-Prime-Time Genocide', December 1998.

4 Interviewed in Dar Masalit, March and April 2004.

5 Interviewed in Abuja, December 2004.

6 Interview with Ahmad Abdel Shafi in Abuja, December 2004.

7 Interview with Omda Bakhit Dabo Hashem in Bahai refugee camp, January 2005.

8 Sudan Human Rights Organization, 'Sudan Government Fails to Insure Stability and Peace in DarFur', 1 March 2003.

9 Daly (2007), p. 77.

10 In 2000, Sadiq renounced the armed struggle, returned to Khartoum, and took up civic politics.

11 Interview with Ahmad Nur in Gorbora, January 2005.

12 Interview with Adam Ali Shogar in Abuja, December 2004.

13 Interview with Minni Minawi in Abuja, October 2005. Almost every person interviewed gave different details of the Bir Taweel attack, but most put the number of dead in the scores and the date as April–May.

14 Interview with commander Kamal Imam Gasy, Muzbat, January 2005.

15 Interviews in Abuja and N'Djamena, December 2004 and January 2005.

16 Some SLA officials say this attack was the first claimed in the name of the DLF, but the claim does not appear to have reached the outside world – most likely because the rebels were not yet equipped with the satellite telephones with which they would, by early 2003, be calling human rights organizations and journalists.

17 Details of the Zaghawa departure for Jebel Marra differ between Fur and Zaghawa sources, and among Zaghawa. This is the account of Daud Taher.

18 Interview with Sherif Harir in Amarai, March 2007.

19 Interviews in Abuja, December 2004.

20 Not to be confused with Mohamed Salih Baraka, an Arab nomad MP.

21 Sudan Organisation Against Torture press release, 23 August 2002.

22 Interviewed in Abuja, September 2005.

23 Interviewed in Khartoum, January 2005.

24 Interview with Abdel Wahid in Abuja, March 2006.

25 Interview with Jab al Din Hussein in Abuja, December 2004.

26 Fur Diaspora Association, 'Appeal to the International Community to Save the Fur from Genocide', 6 January 2003.

27 Interview with Saif el Din Nimir, February 2008.

28 Interview with Abdella Jaber, September 2005, Yasir Arman, November 2007.

29 Interview with Salah Mohamed Abdel Rahman 'Abu Sura' in N'Djamena, March 2007.

30 Interview with Abdel Wahid Mohamed al Nur in Abuja, September 2005.

31 Interview with Babikir Abdalla in Abuja, September 2005.

32 Interview with Ahmad Abdel Shafi in Abuja, December 2004.

33 Interview with Babikir Abdalla.

34 AFP, 'New Rebel Group Seizes West Sudan Town', 26 February 2003.

35 'SPLM Position on Developments in Darfur', 20 March 2003.

36 Interviewed in Abuja, December 2004.

37 See UN Panel of Experts report, <http:daccessdds.un.org/doc/undoc/gen/No5> of January 2006, for a later admission by a former JEM official that Eritrea supplied JEM with weapons.

38 See de Waal (2004), chapter 6.

39 There is little written on this important sideshow to the Sudanese and Congolese civil wars. See: 'Central African Rep.: Enemy's Enemy', *Africa Confidential*, 5 April 2002; Carayannis (2003); Small Arms Survey (2007). Some reports indicate that Rwandese soldiers from the former (genocidal) government fought alongside the Chadians.

40 Interviews with Ugandan intelligence officers, London, 2004, and South Sudan, 2007.

41 Interviews with SLA commanders in Darfur, January 2005.

42 Interviewed in Nairobi, April 2005.

43 According to Minawi's account, Abdalla Abakir became commander-in-chief, Jaber Izhaq head of logistics and Mohamed Ismael 'Nyeri' head of training. He himself became 'secretary general'.

44 A new recruit to the movement, Mansour Arbab, claimed the title in an interview with a Khartoum newspaper at the fourth round of the Abuja talks, which he attended as a simple delegate – the only position he ever held in the SLA.

45 Fur witnesses say Shartai Yousif was killed by Zaghawa Commander Salah Bob, while 'resisting arrest'.

46 Interview with Adam Ali Shogar in N'Djamena, January 2005.

47 E-mail from Babikir Abdalla, 2 January 2008.

48 Interview with Abdel Wahid al Nur in Abuja, September 2005.

49 Interviewed in Abuja, December 2004.

50 Interview with *Asharq al Awsat*, 3 May 2005.

51 Later fronts included the Alliance of Revolutionary Forces of Western Sudan (January 2006) and the National Redemption Front (July 2006).

52 Interview with Ibrahim Madibu in Abuja, September 2005.

53 Interviewed in Abuja, December 2004.

54 This is the view of the French historian Gerard Prunier, See Prunier (2005).

55 Interview, Khartoum, November 2007. The Justice Party's founders – a diverse group that included the mercurial Southern politician Lam Akol – subsequently fell out among themselves and two fractions of the party continued on the fringes of Sudanese politics.

56 Interview with Idriss Ibrahim Azraq in London, July 2007.

57 Interview with Abdel Wahid al Nur in Abuja, September 2005.

58 'Resolving the Issue of Religion and the State', <http://www.sudanjem.com>.

59 International Commission of Inquiry on Darfur (2005).

60 Interviewed in Abuja, March 2006.

61 Interview with Khalil Ibrahim in London, July 2005.

62 Interviewed in Khartoum, November 2007.

63 Khalil claimed JEM was involved in an attempted coup in Khartoum in October 2004. The government claimed that the attempt was meant to scuttle the North–South peace process, spring Turabi from jail and spirit him out of the country.

64 Telephone interview, February 2005.

65 Interview with Ibrahim Madibo in Abuja, March 2006.

66 Interview with Mohamed Issa Aliu in Abuja, March 2006.

67 Press release of the Sudan Union of the Marginalized Majority, 31 August 2003.

68 The International Crisis Group cited suspicions that the split was funded by the National Congress Party. International Crisis Group (2007), p. 14.

69 Interview with Idriss Ibrahim Azraq in London, July 2007.

70 Amnesty International, 'Too Many Killed for No Reason', February 2004.

71 IRIN, Chad–Sudan: 'How Credible is Darfur's Third Rebel Movement?', 13 January 2005.

72 Interview with Nourrain Minnawi Barcham in Abuja, December 2005.

73 Internal UN report, 10 November 2005.

74 John Ryle, 'Disaster in Darfur', *New York Review of Books*, 15 July 2004.

5 *A war of total destruction*

1 Scott Anderson, 'How Did Darfur Happen?', *New York Times*, 17 October 2004.

2 Interviews, Khartoum, November 2007.

3 Anderson, 'How Did Darfur Happen?'.

4 Telephone interview, 17 January 2008.

5 Memorandum submitted by the Darfur Relief and Documentation Centre to the House of Commons, November 2004.

6 Interview with Khamis Abakir.

7 Masalit Community in Exile, Press Release, 1 April 2003.

8 'Sudan's Ruling Party Says Force Will be Used To Smash Rebels', AFP, Khartoum, 27 March 2003.

9 Interview with Ismail 'Abunduluk' Adam in Ain Siro, March 2007. The account of the battle of al Fasher is based on first-hand testimonies, primarily that of Abunduluk.

10 Interviews with rebel commanders in Dar Zaghawa, January 2005.

11 Details provided by Hamad

Abdalla Jibreel, November 2007 and al Sanosi Musa, December 2007.

12 Anderson, 'How Did Darfur Happen?'.

13 Stephanie Nolen, 'Sudan Pays for Ignoring Prophet', *Globe and Mail*, 17 August 2004.

14 Interviewed in Hatfield, August 2007.

15 Interview in Misrih, Darfur, November 2007.

16 Interviews in Misrih, Darfur and Khartoum, November 2007.

17 Interview with Sheikh Hamad Abdalla Jibreel, Khartoum, November 2007.

18 Interviewed in N'Djamena, March 2007.

19 Interviews, Kutum and Fata Borno, November 2007.

20 Information provided by Abdalla Safi al Nur, January 2008.

21 Interview with Hafiz Yousif in Abuja, March 2006.

22 Interview with Omda Gamr Musa in Cherkerio, April 2004.

23 Interviews in London, November 2004.

24 Interviews with survivors in Dar Masalit and Chad, March 2004.

25 Interview with Futr Abdel Rassoul in Dar Masalit, March 2004.

26 Interview with Mohamed Basher in Abuja, September 2005.

27 Interview with Omda Khidir in Amarai, March 2007.

28 International Criminal Court, Office of the Prosecutor, 'Situation in Darfur, the Sudan, Prosecutor's Application under Article 58(7)', 27 February 2007, p. 6.

29 Interview with Khamis Yousif Haroun in London, March 2005.

30 International Criminal Court, Warrant for Arrest of Ali Kushayb, 27 April 2007.

31 Document dated 16 August 2004.

32 Confidential briefings from a range of military observers in Darfur.

33 Human Rights Watch (August 2004).

34 International Criminal Court, 'Situation in Darfur', p. 6.

35 Telephone interview, 15 January 2008.

36 Interview with Omar Angabo in Abuja, December 2004.

37 Interview with a survivor in Cherkerio, April 2004.

38 Amnesty International reported that 168 people from ten villages in Wadi Saleh were extraditionally executed on a single night in March 2004 'by a large force which included members of the Sudan army, military intelligence and Janjawiid'. It said 'they were blindfolded and taken in groups of about forty, on army trucks to an area behind a hill near Deleij village. There they were then told to lie on the ground and shot by a force of about forty-five members of the military intelligence and the Janjawiid.'

39 Interview in Bahia camp, January 2005.

40 Interview with Imam Izhaq Abdalla Adam Saber in Cherkerio, Chad, April 2004.

41 Interview with SLA Commander Mohamed Harin in Abuja, December 2004.

42 Marlowe et al. (2006).

43 BBC2, 'Sudan's Secret War', 21 July 1995.

44 Interview with a government defector in Tam, Western Upper Nile, April 2003.

45 Interview with Hassan Ahmad Mohamed.

46 Brian Steidle interview with Danny Peary, October 2007.

47 International Criminal Court, 'Situation in Darfur', p. 6.

48 Confidential interview with a displaced woman from Girgira, now resident in Khartoum, April 2007.

49 'Ethnic Cleansing in Desert of Death for Black Muslims', *Sunday Telegraph*, 25 April 2004.

50 International Commission of Inquiry on Darfur (2005).

51 Interview in Muzbat, January 2005.

52 Darfur Association of Canada (Branch of Ontario), 'Repatriation of Refugees before the Solution of Problem is a Crime', 15 March 2004.

53 Ibid., footnote 35.

54 Interviews, Khartoum, November 2007 and telephone interview with Abdalla Safi al Nur, January 2008.

55 Interview with SLA Commander Saleh Adam in Abuja, October 2004.

56 Interview with Siddiq Umbadda in Khartoum, November 2007.

57 Interview with Minni Minawi in Abuja, March 2006.

58 Interview with Suleiman Marajan in Abuja, September 2005.

59 Minawi's Zaghawa critics have gone as far as to compile a list of those for whose deaths they hold him responsible. Between rebels and civilians, it runs into more than seventy. They include Ali Abdel Rahim Shendi, an Arab commander who became an SLA hero after attacking the Abu Jabra oilfield in South Darfur and who died two months later in a 'car accident' in which he was the only SLA casualty.

60 Interview with Abdel Munim Mohamedein Ali Mohamedein in Oure Cassoni camp, March 2007.

61 Interviews with four members of the family in Oure Cassoni camp in Chad, March 2007.

62 On 9 October 2007, the African Union reported that Mohamed Osman was the commander who led an attack on its base in Haskanita that had killed ten African peacekeepers ten days earlier.

63 'A rejoinder to Julie Flient's commentary' [sic], <sudaneseonline.com>, 26 November 2005.

64 Interview with Minni Minawi in Abuja, December 2005.

65 Commenting on these events on behalf of SLA–Minawi, Ali Tirayo, a senior member of the group, said the story was 'concocted' and 'based on false

premises'. He urged the authors to recognize that 'there is action and reaction; it was an unequal situation of a heavyweight action by the government and a lightweight responding'. Telephone interview, March 2008.

66 Interview with an SLA commander who requested to remain anonymous in Hashaba, March 2007.

67 Interview with Mohamed Izhaq Jiddo in Amarai, March 2007.

68 Five sources, including four SLA commanders then under Minawi's authority, have given details of the killings separately.

69 Telephone conversation, March 2008.

70 Human Rights Watch, December 2005.

71 E-mail from SLA humanitarian coordinator Suleiman Jamous, 14 September 2005.

72 International Commission of Inquiry on Darfur (2005).

73 Interview with Yousif Takana, January 2008; see also Reuters, 'Cruelty and Killing Widespread in Sudan's Darfur', 11 April 2004.

74 The UN said this committee presented 'the most coherent governmental perspective on the conflict' of all those it met on its mission.

75 Interview with Yousif Takana, January 2008.

76 Sudan Organisation Against Torture, 'Aerial Bombardment of Villages in Southern Darfur', 22 July 2004.

77 Confidential AU report, October 2004.

78 Interviewed in Darfur, November 2007, name withheld.

79 Human Rights Watch (2005).

80 Amnesty International, (September 2004).

81 International Commission of Inquiry on Darfur (2005).

82 Human Rights Watch (May 2004).

83 Jan Egeland, UN Under-Secretary for Humanitarian Affairs, cited by the UN News Center, 18 February 2005.

84 USAID 'Fact Sheet #15, Darfur – Humanitarian Emergency', 23 July 2004.

85 See Keen (1994).

86 de Waal (1989).

87 Interviewed in el Da'ien, December 1986.

88 Nicholas D. Kristof, 'The West Stands by While Genocide Unfolds', *New York Times*, 1 June 2004.

89 Reuters, 'Annan Assures Darfur Displaced of No Forced Return', 1 July 2004.

90 Centre for Research on the Epidemiology of Disasters (2005).

91 Amnesty International (2003).

92 Interviews in Dar Masalit, March–April 2004.

93 Amnesty International (June 2004).

94 Amnesty International, 'Urgent Action', 10 May 2004.

95 'Villagers Put Their Lives on the Line to Tell of Atrocities by Sudanese Militia', *Scotsman*, 25 May 2004.

6 *Wars within wars*

1 The ICID findings echoed the earlier, much less publicized report of the African Commission on Human and People's Rights, which sent a delegation to Sudan in July 2004 and reported in September 2004. The African report disappeared into the African Union secretariat and was never referred to by the Peace and Security Council or the Summit.

2 UN Security Council Resolution 1593, 31 March 2005.

3 <http://www.icc-cpi.int/library/cases/ICC-02-05-56-Anx3_English.pdf>. The graph was derived by the following method. It comprises statistics of wilful killings of civilians or prisoners of war that have been specifically reported and appear to meet the elements of the crimes under the ICC Statute. The sources are mainly reports from NGOs and international organizations. The information focuses on military attacks on villages: incidents in IDP camps and subsequent deaths as the result of disease or malnutrition are not included. The total number of victims reported by these sources for incidents that meet these strict requirements, between November 2002 and December 2006, is between 6,000 and 9,200. The horizontal lines show a scale by hundreds. The highest peak in the graph shows a value of some 900 (August 2003). The values aggregated by months are based on the average number of victims reported per incident (mean value between the minimum and maximum figures reported for each incident). The standard of evidence is a reasonable basis on which to believe that the incident took place and it constituted a crime under the ICC Statute. The sources were subject to systematic source evaluation (by standard criteria of credibility and reliability) and verified with a sample of evidence collected by the ICC Office of the Prosecutor (e-mail from ICC OTP, 15 January 2008). In addition three further comments are in order: (1) the figure is extremely conservative and represents only a fraction of the true number of cases; (2) the figures for the period after mid-2004 are more reliable than the earlier figures because of the larger number of international witnesses – the underestimation is confined largely to the killings prior to mid-2004; (3) the time pattern of killings is consistent with all other estimates of fatalities through violence, e.g. Petersen and Tullin (2006).

4 Confidential briefing, March 2007.

5 Interview, Arab leader, Nyala, November 2007.

6 Haggar (2007).

7 Interviewed in Darfur, November 2007, name withheld.

8 Interviewed in Darfur, November 2007, name withheld.

9 Confidential UN report on meetings with community leaders in Gereida, September 2005.

10 Confidential UN report on

meetings with community leaders in al Da'ein, September 2005.

11 Quoted in a confidential UN report, June 2005.

12 UN report on Shearia Brotherhood and Peaceful Co-existence Conference, 31 May 2005 to 2 June 2005.

13 Joint Statement by the African Union Mission in the Sudan and the United Nations Mission in Sudan on the attack and destruction of Khor Abeche.

14 IRIN, 'Continuing Insecurity Hurting Civilians', 1 March 2006.

15 Interview with Mohamed Tijani in Abuja, September 2005.

16 Interview with Abdel Wahid al Nur in Abuja, March 2006.

17 Interview with Ibrahim Madibu in Abuja, March 2006.

18 Coordination Council of Arab Congress (Sudan) Political Committee, 'Report of the Above-Mentioned Committee Trip to Local Councils of Buram, Tullus, Reheid al Birdi and Idd al Fursan', 15 November 2003. See Haggar (2007).

19 Interviews with Arab leaders, Nyala, November 2007.

20 Interview with Jar al Nabi Abdel Karim in Abuja, September 2005.

21 Interview with Mohamed Issa of the Darfur Forum in Abuja, December 2005.

22 Conversations with JEM commanders in Abuja, 2005.

23 There are many different estimates for the number of tribes in Darfur, of which 177 is an expansive figure.

24 Interview with Ramadan Jaber in Abuja, October 2005.

25 Interview with Mohamed Tijani.

26 Interviewed in Abuja, December 2006.

27 Interview with Suleiman Marajan in Abuja, October 2006.

28 Interviewed in Abuja, September and October 2005.

7 *International reaction*

1 'Death in Darfur', *Africa Confidential*, 22 November 2002, documented confrontations on a much larger scale than the traditional disputes between neighbouring communities.

2 Until May 2001, the US assistance policy for Sudan was to provide emergency relief only to Southerners and to displaced people in the North. One of the early actions of Andrew Natsios as administrator of USAID was to change that policy to include all people in need of assistance.

3 Telephone interview with Roger Winter, 3 January 2008.

4 Ruiz (1987).

5 Winter (2000).

6 Hearing before the Subcommittee on Africa, of the Committee on International Relations, House of Representatives, 'Reviewing the Sudan Peace Act Report', 13 May 2003, p. 22.

7 MSF Foundation (2007).

8 US Department of State, 'On-The-Record Briefing, Andrew Natsios, Michael Ranneberger and Roger Winter, on US Policy on Sudan', 27 April 2004.

9 Telephone interview with Roger Winter, 3 January 2008.

10 The ceasefire was signed on 8 April and came into effect seventy-two hours later.

11 E-mail from Andrew Natsios, 15 January 2008.

12 'UN and US Warn that Huge Toll in Darfur Crisis is Now Inevitable', AFP, 3 June 2004.

13 USAID, 'Darfur–Humanitarian Emergency, Fact Sheet #2, FY 2005', 8 October 2004.

14 Colin Thomas-Jensen makes the same point. See his article, 'Advocating for Humanitarian Access in Darfur', OFDA Report FY2004, pp. 38–9.

15 Quoted in IRIN, 'Sudan: Government, Rebels Sign Landmark Protocols', 27 May 2004.

16 <http://www.janpronk.nl/>.

17 In the event, Pronk was absent as the Darfur peace negotiations reached their climax in the first days of May 2006, summoned to New York by Kofi Annan for a routine meeting to present his progress report and help secure the next round of funding. He appears in the photographs of the signing ceremony, having arrived in time only for the last formalities. The deadline for completing the talks had been demanded by the UN Security Council but the UN hadn't contrived for its principal man in Sudan to be there to help pull off the deal.

18 IGAD is the organization of the north-east African countries. Later the 'friends' were renamed the IGAD Partners' Forum.

19 Centre for Research on the Epidemiology of Disasters (2005); Hagan and Polloni (2006). There is a high margin of error in all estimates for mortality.

20 Ibid.

21 Article 4(h) of the Constitutive Act of the African Union.

22 Interview with General Ismat al Zain, Abuja, March 2006.

23 Comments to the Carnegie Council, 4 April 2007.

24 Interviews, Nyala, November 2007.

25 'Sudan's Camp Rwanda in Deadly Tawila', *New York Times*, 9 September 2006.

26 Danny Peary, 'Brian Steidle vs. The Devil of Darfur', <http://www.brink.com/talk/2772>, accessed 21 December 2007.

27 The UN did, however. A photograph of a Sudanese military plane painted in UN colours was reproduced in a UN report. See 'Sudan Flying Arms to Darfur, Panel Reports', *New York Times*, 18 April 2007.

28 Speaking to reporters on 19 March 2004.

29 UN News Centre, 'Humanitarian and Security Situations in Western Sudan Reach New Lows, UN Agency Says', 5 December 2003.

30 'Remember Rwanda, but Take Action in Sudan', *New York Times*, 6 April 2004.

31 Interviewed in Khartoum, November 2007.

32 Hamilton and Hazlett (2007).

33 Murphy (2007).

34 Totten and Markusen (2006).

35 International Panel of Eminent Persons, 'Rwanda: The Preventable Genocide', July 2000.

36 The report was released at the Extraordinary Session of the African Commission on Human and Peoples' Rights on the Situation in Darfur, Sudan, held in Pretoria, South Africa, on 18–19 September 2004.

37 Khartoum formally complained that it had not consented to the ACHPR inquiry and its extraordinary session on Darfur. The AU did not respond to the complaint.

38 Colin L. Powell, 'The Crisis in Darfur', written remarks before the Senate Foreign Relations Committee, Washington DC, 9 September 2004.

39 International Commission of Inquiry on Darfur (2005), p. 4. This can be read as arguing that although the *actus reus* of genocide may have taken place, the *mens rea* was defeating the rebellion and not destroying the ethnic groups suspected of supporting the rebellion.

40 Fabrice Weissman, 'Humanitarian Aid Held Hostage', <http://www.doctorswithout borders.org>, 15 November 2006.

41 Petersen and Tullin (2006), p. 17. They used the Lexis-Nexis database of English-language newspapers.

42 Murphy (2007).

43 Hamilton and Hazlett (2007). The phrase was used by Gayle Smith, formerly National Security Advisor for Africa to President Clinton.

44 Confidential e-mail, 19 October 2007.

45 Telephone interview, December 2007.

46 African Rights (1997).

47 Presentation to the Humanitarian Affairs Programme, School of International and Public Affairs, Columbia University, 22 February 2007.

48 Interviewed in Paris, November, 2007.

49 E-mail from Siddig Umbada, 17 January 2008.

50 Data compiled for this book by Sam Rosmarin.

51 Centre for Research on the Epidemiology of Disasters (2005); Petersen and Tullin (2006).

52 Based on a compilation of UN reports.

53 Reuters, 'Sudan Forces Killed 100s of Civilians in Darfur – UN', 4 December 2007.

54 Fabrice Weissman and Jean-Hervé Bradol, Médecins Sans Frontières, 'An Appeal for Darfur: Killing and Demagogy', *Libération*, 23 March 2007.

55 UN News, '"Humanitarian Situation in Darfur Deteriorating", Senior UN Official Says', 1 September 2007.

56 Confidential e-mail, 2 January 2008.

57 Briefing by Jan Egeland, 28 August 2006.

58 Interview with Kaltouma Musa Hassan in Bornyo, March 2007.

59 30 May 2006.

60 'Transcript: US Natsios, Senator Menendez Clash over Darfur', *Sudan Tribune*, 16 April 2007.

61 Craig Timberg, 'Sudan's Offensive Comes at a Key Time', *Washington Post*, 5 September 2006.

62 Eric Reeves, 'The Dying Has Begun', 28 September 2006.

63 <http://www.american rhetoric.com/speeches/george clooneyunitednations.htm>.

64 WorldPublicOpinion. org and the Chicago Council on Global Affairs, 'Publics Around the World Say UN Has Responsibility to Protect Against Genocide', 4 April 2007.

65 Interviewed in Khartoum, November 2007.

66 Ibid.

67 Cf. Michael Abramowitz, 'U.S. Promises on Darfur Don't Match Actions', *Washington Post*, 29 October 2007.

68 Some versions of this story indicate that it was Samantha Power's *A Problem from Hell*, 2002.

69 Speaking in May 2006.

70 Weissman and Bradol, 'An Appeal for Darfur'.

71 Weissman, MSF Foundation, 26 October 2007.

72 Pantuliano and O'Callaghan (2006).

73 Michael Abramowitz, 'US Promises on Darfur Don't Match Actions', *Washington Post*, 29 October 2007.

74 John Prendergast quoted in Jonathan Foreman, 'Endgame in Africa', *Men's Vogue*, 23 October 2006.

8 *The Abuja peace talks*

1 Much of this chapter is based on the authors' engagement in the Abuja peace process.

2 Interviewed in Paris, December 2007.

3 Interviews with SLM delegates to the Abuja peace talks, January–April 2006.

4 Interviews in Abuja, March 2006.

5 Speaking in Abuja, 6 May 2006.

6 E-mail from Mulugeta Gebrehiwot, 15 January 2008.

7 Similar proposals were rejected, on the same grounds, in January 2005, January 2006 and March 2007.

8 Interview with SLA Commander Mohamed Nimr, in Amarai, March 2007.

9 Stéphanie Braquehais, 'N'Djamena en campagne contre Khartoum', Radio France Internationale, 28 December 2005.

10 Reuters, 'Sudan Recruited Chad Rebels', 24 April 2006.

11 Minawi's aides report that the US threatened to take him to the International Criminal Court. The Americans insist that they were indicating only financial sanctions, travel bans and similar administrative measures.

12 The details of the seven rounds of the Abuja peace process are recounted by Toga (2007).

13 See Nathan (2007).

14 The rebels' concern with borders mystified some observers. The key issue was two customs posts near the Libyan border which had been transferred from North Darfur to Northern State.

15 Commentators like the International Crisis Group failed to mark the difference between coercive and voluntary disarmament. ICG's 'Darfur's Fragile Peace Agreement', 2006, states that disarmament is a task 'normally' left for peacekeepers. But this is the case only for voluntary disarmament, not the kind of coercive disarmament that would be needed in Darfur. On the forcible disarmament in Jonglei state, see Small Arms Survey (2006–07).

16 Interviewed in Paris, December 2007.

17 See Toga (2007), p. 231.

18 A number of 'independent' SLA commanders agreed with this estimate.

19 The British made an error. They did not specify a percentage. The government later created a handful of small new localities, carved out of existing ones, to give to the rebel nominees.

20 Interviews in Nyala, November 2007.

21 A detailed account of the final twenty-four hours is included in de Waal (2007).

22 Khalil told the mediators his only significant objection on security was that he wanted salaries for his troops.

23 'NATO Role in Darfur on Table', *Washington Post*, 10 April 2006.

24 Interviewed in Paris, December 2007.

9 *Endless chaos*

1 A sixth member has since been added, from the Eastern Front.

2 Confidential e-mail from an eyewitness to the aftermath, 22 July 2006.

3 In September 2007, Amnesty International said Minawi's men were 'implicated in summary killings of about forty-two people' in Gereida a year earlier. The UN's High Commissioner for Human Rights spoke of 'credible reports' of 'enforced disappearance, torture, and possible summary execution' of Masalit by Minawi's men in Gereida.

4 Flint (2007).

5 Confidential e-mail, 13 June 2006.

6 Interview with *Asharq al Awsat* newspaper, 18 May 2006.

7 Interviews in North Darfur, March 2007.

8 Interview with Omda Hamid Manna in Bakaore, North Darfur, March 2007.

9 Taped testimony from one of the detainees, Abdalla Ali Hasballa. The detainees were released only after six days' detention in Muzbat.

10 Craig Timberg, 'In Darfur's Death Grip', *Washington Post*, 6 September 2006.

11 Amnesty International, 'Korma: Yet More Attacks on

Civilians', 31 July 2006.

12 Interviewed in Anka, April 2007.

13 Interview with Omda Hamid Manna in Bakaore, March 2007.

14 Interview with Omda Yousif Dili in Bir Maza, March 2007.

15 Interview with Suleiman Marajan in Helif, Dar Meidob, March 2007.

16 Interviewed in Ain Siro, March 2007.

17 Confidential e-mail, 27 July 2006.

18 AU, Preparatory Consultations for DDDC, Nyala Trip Report, June 2007.

19 Interview with camp sheikh, who requested anonymity, November 2007.

20 AU, Preparatory Consultations for DDDC, Zalingei Trip Report, June 2007.

21 Interviews, Darfur, November 2007.

22 Interviews, Darfur, November 2007. The camp leaders requested that their names and the name of the camp be withheld.

23 UN Department of Economic and Social Affairs, Population Division, 'World Urbanization Prospects: The 2005 Revision Population Database', <http://esa.un.org/unup/p2kodata.asp>.

24 African Rights (1997), pp. 156–63.

25 One Darfurian social scientist has described this as urbanization without integration. Munzoul Assal, 'Urbanization and the Future of Sudan', <http://www.ssrc.org/blog/category/darfur>, posted 29 January 2008.

26 Urbanization in Darfur during the war has already rendered obsolete the UN population projections.

27 World Bank, 'Darfur: Dimensions of Challenge for Development, a Background Volume', 29 June 2007, p. 33.

28 Eric Reeves, 'Ban Ki-moon in Sudan: Vacuous Diplomacy and Specious Declarations', 7 September 2007.

29 International Criminal Court, 'Statement by Mr Luis Moreno-Ocampo, Prosecutor of the International Criminal Court, Statement to the United Nations Security Council Pursuant to UNSCR 1593 (2005)', 5 December 2007.

30 Interview with Abdel Wahid in Paris, 7 December 2007.

31 Interview with Abdella Jaber in Abuja, September 2005.

32 Interview with Khalil Ibrahim in Abuja, March 2006.

33 Various reports in the independent daily *Al Mashaaheer* newspaper.

34 E-mail from Suleiman Jamous, 31 August 2006.

35 Interview with Nourrain Minawi Barcham in Abeche, March 2007.

36 Interviewed in Wakheim, April 2007.

37 Interview with Jar al Nabi Abdel Karim in Anka, March 2007.

38 Confidential interview with a western officer, March 2006.

39 Interview with Corporal

Abbas in Ain Siro, March 2006.

40 Interview with Private Mohamed Abdalla, a prisoner of war, in Ain Siro, March 2009.

41 Lydia Polgreen, 'Sudanese Soldiers Flee War to Find a Limbo in Chad', *New York Times*, 16 October 2006.

42 Ibid., footnote 32.

43 <http://www.janpronk.nl/index264.html>, posted 14 October 2006.

44 Fifth periodic report of the United Nations High Commissioner for Human Rights, on the situation of human rights in the Sudan, 'Killings of Civilians by Militia in Buram Locality, South Darfur', United Nations High Commissioner for Human Rights and UN Mission in the Sudan, 6 October 2006.

45 IRIN, 'UN Urges Probe into Attacks on Darfur Civilians', 9 October 2006.

46 Interview in London, August 2007.

47 Fifth periodic report of the United Nations High Commissioner for Human Rights, 'Killings of Civilians'.

48 Interviews in Khartoum, March 2007.

49 'Sudan Says Ready for Talks with Darfur Non-Signatories', *Sudan Tribune*, 18 October 2006.

50 Telephone interview with Ibrahim Hashem, August 2007.

51 Interview with Ahmad Abdel Shafi in Shigeig Karo, March 2007.

52 Ibid.

53 Telephone interview, 19 January 2008.

54 The first Fur to sign a 'Declaration of Commitment' with the government, Abul Qassim Imam was rewarded, in February 2007, with appointment as governor of West Darfur. The DPA gave rebels the right to the governorship of one of Darfur's three states.

55 'UN Accuses Military, Allied Militias of Possible War Crimes', *UN News*, 21 August 2007.

56 Interviewed in Ain Siro, March 2007.

57 Interviews with SLA militants from Ain Siro, January 2008.

58 Interviewed in Nyala, November 2007.

59 E-mail from Andrew Natsios, January 2008.

60 Interview with dismissed Security officer Hassan Ahmad Mohamed in Amarai, March 2007.

61 Interviewed in Fata Borno, November 2007.

62 IDP camp leaders, interviewed in Fata Borno, November 2007.

63 Confidential e-mail, 19 December 2007.

64 Interview with Mujeeb al Zubeir al Rahman in Amarai, March 2007.

65 Interview with Anwar Khater, November 2007.

66 Interview with el Sanosi Badr in London, August 2007.

67 Ibid.

68 Miraya FM, 'SPLM Prevents Musa Hilal from Visiting Juba', 5 December 2007, <http://www.mirayafm.org/news/news/_200712052223/>.

69 Katy Glassborow, 'UN

Resolve over Darfur Appears to Crumble', Institute for War and Peace Reporting, 11 January 2008.

70 On 29 February 2008, Hemeti signed a deal with Khartoum that brought 2,500 of his men into the armed forces, including more than fifty as officers. They also received local government posts and other rewards. A few weeks earlier, Khartoum also succeeded in cutting a deal with Anwar Khater, after arresting a number of his close relatives.

71 Confidential information from AMIS.

72 AU, 'Investigation Report on the Attack on MGS Haskanita on 29/30 Sep. '07 by Armed Faction to the Darfur Conflict', confidential report, 9 October 2007.

73 This and subsequent quotes come from the AU report into the incident.

74 Telephone conversation with Suleiman Jamous, 1 October 2007.

75 Pacific Architects and Engineers, a Lockheed Martin subcontractor; see Pratap Chatterjee, 'Darfur Diplomacy: Enter the Contractors', *Corpwatch*, 21 October 2004, <http://www.corpwatch.org/article.php?id=11598>, accessed 5 January 2008.

76 Confidential e-mail, 2 October 2007.

77 AU report, 9 October 2007.

78 Confidential e-mail, 10 October 2007.

79 'Khartoum "Prevented UN Troops Evacuating Wounded Peacekeepers"', *Independent*, 2 October 2007.

80 Telephone interview with Suleiman Jamous, 4 October 2007.

81 Telephone interviews with military officers, Khartoum, July 2006.

82 Interviews in Khartoum, November 2007.

83 'Al Zawahiri Criticises Bush, Pope', *Al Jazeera News*, 1 October 2006.

84 'Bin Laden Calls for Holy War against Darfur Peacekeepers', *Sudan Tribune*, 24 October 2007.

85 Timur Goksel, 'Mosques and Coffee Shops', <http://www.ssrc.org/blog/2007/08/24/mosques-and-coffee-shops/>, 24 August 2007.

86 See Jan Pronk's fifteen guidelines for peacekeepers, presented to UN staff on his departure, <http://www.janpronk.nl/index308.html>.

87 Interviewed in Abuja, December 2004.

Bibliography

Abdul-Jalil, Musa, 'The Dynamics of Ethnic Identification in Northern Darfur, Sudan: A Situational Approach', in Bayreuth African Studies Series, *The Sudan: Ethnicity and National Cohesion*, Bayreuth, 1984.

— 'Some Political Aspects of Zaghawa Migration and Resettlement', in F. N. Ibrahim and H. Ruppert (eds), *Rural–Urban Migration and Identity Change: Case Studies from the Sudan*, Bayreuth, Geowissenschaftliche Arbeiten, 1988.

Action Contre La Faim, 'The Land Issue in Darfur: Sowing the Seeds of Peace', Paris, January 2006.

African Rights, *Facing Genocide: The Nuba of Sudan*, London, 1995.

— *Food and Power in Sudan: A Critique of Humanitarianism*, London, 1997.

Al-Bashir, Ahmed Abdel Rahman, 'Problems of Settlement of Immigrants and Refugees in Sudanese Society,' unpublished D.Phil. thesis, University of Oxford, 1978.

Amnesty International, 'Sudan: Human Rights v Violations in the Context of Civil War', London, 1989.

— 'Empty Promises? Human Rights Violations in Government-controlled Areas', 16 July 2003.

— 'Sudan: Incommunicado Detentions, Unfair Trials, Torture and Ill-Treatment – the Hidden Side of the Darfur Conflict', 8 June 2004.

— 'Darfur, Sudan: UN Security Council Must Challenge Human Rights Violations', 2 September 2004.

— 'Sudan: Who Will Answer for the Crimes?', London, 18 January 2005.

Babiker, Fatima, *The Sudanese Bourgeoisie: Vanguard of Development?*, London, Zed Books, 1984.

Burr, J. Millard and Robert O. Collins, *Africa's Thirty Years' War: Chad, Libya and the Sudan, 1963–1993*, Boulder, CO, Westview, 1999.

Carayannis, Tatiana, 'The Complex Wars of the Congo: Towards a New Analytic Approach', *Journal of Asian and African Studies*, 38, 2003, pp. 232–55.

Centre for Research on the Epidemiology of Disasters, 'Darfur: Counting the Deaths', Brussels, May 2005.

Christian Aid, 'The Scorched Earth: Oil and War in Sudan', London, March 2001.

Collins, Robert O., 'Disaster in Darfur', *African Geopolitics*, Nos 15–16, Summer–Fall, October 2004.

Daly, Martin, *Imperial Sudan: The Anglo-Egyptian Condominium, 1934–56*, Cambridge, Cambridge University Press, 1991.

— *Darfur's Sorrow: A History of Destruction and Genocide*, Cambridge, Cambridge University Press, 2007.

de Waal, Alex, *Famine that Kills: Darfur, Sudan, 1984–1985*, Oxford, Oxford University Press, 1989.

— 'The Politics of Destabilization in the Horn, 1989–2001', in Alex de Waal (ed.), *Islamism and Its Enemies in the Horn of Africa*, London, Hurst, 2004.

— 'Darfur's Deadline: The Final Days of the Abuja Peace Process', in Alex de Waal (ed.), *War in Darfur and the Search for Peace*, Cambridge, MA, Harvard University Press, 2007.

de Waal, Alex and A. H. Abdelsalam, 'Islamism, State Power and *Jihad* in Sudan', in Alex de Waal (ed.), *Islamism and Its Enemies in the Horn of Africa*, London, Hurst, 2004.

de Waal, Alex and Malik Mohammed el Amin, 'Survival in Northern Darfur 1985–1986', Nyala, Save the Children Fund, January 1986.

Doornbos, Paul, 'On Becoming Sudanese', in T. Barnett and A. Abdelkarim (eds), *Sudan: State, Capital and Transformation*, London, Croom Helm, 1988.

Flint, Julie, 'Darfur's Armed Movements', in Alex de Waal (ed.), *War in Darfur and the Search for Peace*, Cambridge, MA, Harvard University Press, 2007.

Garang, John, *The Call for Democracy in Sudan*, London, Kegan Paul, 1992.

Haaland, Gunnar, 'Economic Determinants in Ethnic Processes', in Frederik Barth (ed.), *Ethnic Groups and Boundaries*, London, Allen and Unwin, 1969.

Hagan, John and Alberto Polloni, 'Death in Darfur', *Science*, 313, 1578–9, 2006.

Haggar, Ali, 'The Origins and Organization of the Janjawiid', in Alex de Waal (ed.), *War in Darfur and the Search for Peace*, Cambridge, MA, Harvard University Press, 2007.

Hamilton, Rebecca and Chad Hazlett, '"Not on Our Watch": The Emergence of the American Movement for Darfur', in Alex de Waal (ed.), *War in Darfur and the Search for Peace*, Cambridge, MA, Harvard University Press, 2007.

Harir, Sharif, '"Arab Belt" versus "African Belt", Ethno-political Conflict in Dar Fur and the Regional Cultural Factors', in Sharif Harir and Terje Tvedt (eds), *Short-Cut to Decay: The Case of the Sudan*, Uppsala, Nordiska Afrikainstitutet, 1994.

Human Rights Watch, 'Darfur Destroyed', New York, 9 May 2004.

— 'Darfur Documents Confirm Government Policy of Militia Support', New York, 20 July 2004.

— 'Sudan: Janjaweed Camps Still Active', New York, 27 August 2004.

— 'Entrenching Impunity: Government Responsibility for International Crimes in Darfur', December 2005.

— 'Darfur 2007: Chaos by Design: Peacekeeping Challenges for AMIS and UNAMID', September 2007.

International Commission of Inquiry on Darfur (ICID), 'Report to the United Nations Secretary-General, Pursuant to Security Council Resolution 1564 of 18 September 2004', Geneva, 25 January 2005.

International Crisis Group, 'To Save Darfur', Report 105, 17 March 2006.

— 'Darfur's Fragile Peace Agreement', Policy Briefing, 10 June 2006.

— 'Darfur's New Security Reality', Report 134, 26 November 2007.

Kapteijns, Lidwien, *Mahdist Faith and Sudanic Identity: The History of the Sultanate of Masalit*, London, Kegan Paul, 1985.

Keen, David, *The Benefits of Famine: A Political Economy of Famine and Relief in Southwestern Sudan, 1983–1989*, Princeton, NJ, Princeton University Press, 1994.

MacMichael, H. A., *A History of the Arabs of the Sudan, and Some Acount of the People Who Preceded Them and the Tribes Inhabiting Darfur*, Cambridge, Cambridge University Press, 1922.

Marlowe, Jen, Aisha Bain and Adam Shapiro, *Darfur Diaries: Stories of Survival*, New York, Nation Books, 2006.

MSF Foundation, 'A Critique of MSF–France Operations in Darfur', Paris, January 2007.

Murphy, Deborah, 'Narrating Darfur: Darfur in the U.S. Press, March–September 2004', in Alex de Waal (ed.), *War in Darfur and the Search for Peace*, Cambridge, MA, Harvard University Press, 2007.

Nathan, Laurie, 'The Making and Unmaking of the Darfur Peace Agreement', in Alex de Waal (ed.), *War in Darfur and the Search for Peace*, Cambridge, MA, Harvard University Press, 2007.

O'Fahey, Rex S. and M. I. Abu Salim, *Land in Dar Fur: Charters and Documents from the Dar Fur Sultanate*, Cambridge, Cambridge University Press, 1983.

Pantuliano, Sara and Sorcha O'Callaghan, 'The "Protection Crisis": A review of Field-based Strategies for Humanitarian Protection in Darfur', London, Overseas Development Institute Humanitarian Policy Group, December 2006.

Petersen, Andreas Höfer and Lise-Lotte Tullin, *Darfur's Scorched Earth: Patterns in Death and Destruction Reported by the People of Darfur, January 2001–September 2005*, Copenhagen, Bloodhound, 2006.

Power, Samantha, 'Dying in Darfur', *New Yorker*, 30 August 2004.

Prunier, Gerard, *Darfur: The Ambiguous Genocide*, London, Hurst, 2005.

Ruiz, Hiram, 'When Refugees Won't Go Home: The Dilemma of Chadians in Sudan', Washington DC, US Committee for Refugees, 1987.

Ryle, John, 'Disaster in Darfur', *New York Review of Books*, 12 August 2004.

Small Arms Survey, 'Anatomy of Civilian Disarmament in Jonglei State', November 2006–February 2007.

— 'A Widening War around Sudan: The Proliferation of Armed Groups in the Central African Republic', Sudan Issue Brief, 5 January 2007.

Toga, Dawit, 'The African Union Mediation and the Abuja Peace Talks', in Alex de Waal (ed.), *War in Darfur and the Search for Peace*, Cambridge, MA, Harvard University Press, 2007.

Totten, Samuel and Eric Markusen (eds), *Genocide in Darfur: Investigating the Atrocities in the Sudan*, New York, Routledge, 2006.

Ushari Mahmud and Suleyman Baldo, 'El Diein Massacre and Slavery in the Sudan', Khartoum, 1987.

Winter, Roger, 'The Nuba People: Confronting Cultural Liquidation', in Jay Spaulding and Stephanie Beswick (eds), *White Nile, Black Blood: War, Leadership and Ethnicity from Khartoum to Kampala*, Trenton, NJ, Red Sea Press, 2000.

Young, Helen, Abdul Monim Osman, Yacob Aklilu, Rebecca Dale, Babiker Badri and Abdul Jabbar Abdullah Fuddle, *Darfur – Livelihoods under Siege*, Medford, MA, Feinstein International Famine Center, June 2005.

Index

Index

313